I0817064

Pitching Democracy

Joe R. and Teresa Lozano Long Series in
Latin American and Latino Art and Culture

Pitching Democracy

APRIL YODER

Baseball and Politics in the Dominican Republic

University of Texas Press
Austin

Printed in the United States of America
First edition, 2023

Requests for permission to reproduce material from this work should be sent to:

Permissions
University of Texas Press
P.O. Box 7819
Austin, TX 78713-7819
utpress.utexas.edu/rp-form

♾ The paper used in this book meets the minimum requirements of ANSI/NISO Z39.48-1992 (R1997) (Permanence of Paper).

Library of Congress Cataloging-in-Publication Data

Names: Yoder, April, author.
Title: Pitching democracy : baseball and politics in the Dominican Republic / April Yoder.
Description: First edition. | Austin : University of Texas Press, 2023. | Includes bibliographical references and index.
Identifiers:
LCCN 2022023746
ISBN 978-1-4773-2676-3 (cloth)
ISBN 978-1-4773-2677-0 (PDF)
ISBN 978-1-4773-2678-7 (ePub)
Subjects: LCSH: Baseball—Political aspects—Dominican Republic. | Baseball—Dominican Republic—History. | Baseball—Economic aspects—Dominican Republic. | Dominican Republic—Politics and government.
Classification: LCC GV863.29.D65 Y64 2023 | DDC 796.357097293—dc23/eng/20220625
LC record available at https://lccn.loc.gov/2022023746

doi:10.7560/326763

For Xoila Salomé

Contents

Acknowledgments ix

Introduction: Baseball, Democracy, and Latin America in the Cold War 1

ONE *Mens sana in corpore sano*: Baseball and Trujillista Politics 15

TWO Politics at the Plate: The Threat of Communism and the Showcase for Democracy 35

THREE Criticizing Baseball, Debating Democracy 62

FOUR *Así se hace patria*: Baseball and the Bloodless Revolution 87

FIVE Sliding into Third: The Cibao Summer League and Baseball as Development 110

SIX Making the Majors: The Baseball Industry and Dominican Democracy 127

Conclusion 149

Notes 153

Bibliography 191

Index 205

Acknowledgments

In many ways this book and my process of writing it are a testament to the power of teachers. Coaches, scouts, promoters, trainers, sportswriters, cartoonists, and journalists shaped the narratives and understandings around baseball and democracy in the Dominican Republic through their interactions with ballplayers and parents and through their reflections on games, tournaments, and policies. They taught Dominicans not only how to play the game but also how to think about it, regulate it, and make it their own. My thanks go to the teachers who left their words and images in letters, newspapers, and policies, as well as those, including Ralph Avila, Epy Guerrero, and Elvio Jiménez, who shared their experiences and insights with me directly. Jesús Alou, José Augusto Imbert, Ozzie Virgil, and Juan Henderson were especially generous with their time and insights, meeting with me multiple times or responding to questions by email and phone.

Teachers and mentors also deserve the credit for my role in this narrative. In high school, Diane Cartwright sparked my love of writing and was patient enough to make me better. Fernando Trcka inspired my curiosity about Latin America. Charlie Guthrie turned that curiosity to knowledge and an appreciation for history. Liz Oglesby was a mentor, friend, and role model during my MA while Bill Beezley led me to baseball as a topic of research. Robin Derby helped me develop the topic further by sharing her expertise in Dominican history and, later, her connection to Dominican scholar and friend Lusitania Martínez. Courses with John Tutino, Adam Rothman, and Erick Langer transformed my thinking about economics, power, and culture while David Painter helped me apply these ideas to the Cold War and US-Latin American relations. Allison Games patiently guided me as I figured out my place in sports history and learned to balance baseball and politics in my narrative. My advisor Bryan McCann ably guided me in making these ideas my own and putting them on a page and, with others who wrote so many letters, helped me gain some financial security while I wrote this. None of this would have been possible without them.

Friends and colleagues were teachers as well as companions. At Georgetown, Larisa Veloz was my rock, escape, and study buddy. Fernando Pérez Montesinos, Javier Puente, Nate Packard, Eric Gettig, Oliver Horn, Graham Pitts, and Jonathan Graham all helped me sharpen my ideas about baseball, politics, and the Cold War, in social as well as academic settings. Kathryn Gallien has been my academic accomplice and tie to my Tucson happy place for decades. She, along with other friends from Arizona and Georgetown helped add many joyful memories to a sometimes-grueling experience.

In the Dominican Republic, Don Leonard and Peggy Fukunaga were marvelous research buddies and introduced me to Melba Collado, who with Paola Duarte and Cecilia Valdez make me feel at home. Raj Chetty was a friendly face in the archives and companion for talking baseball. Héctor López made these conversations more interesting and connected us with the community leaders and coaches like Ruddy Ramírez, Daniel Portorreal, and coaches at ImpACTA Kids who showed me, and our students from CIEE's summer program, how Dominicans own baseball. Oscar Féliz's ability to find hidden boxes at the Archivo General de la Nación made my research possible. Beth Manley has been a role model for balancing work and fun in research and research and teaching at work. A Dominican Studies conference she organized with April Mayes reinvigorated my enthusiasm for research and provided helpful feedback on the prospectus for this book. In addition to being great friends and mentors, Beth, Brenda Elsey, and Antonio Sotomayor all organized projects that gave me structure to complete parts of chapters. Rob Ruck's work inspired me through the project while his comments on the manuscript helped me make it more accessible to my target audience: students and baseball fans so I may be a teacher, too.

Colleagues from the University of New Haven helped me extend the research from the dissertation and write a book. Brett McCormick and Paulette Pepin provided this support as chair while Ed Todd offered insights about connections with other work and generously read all the chapters as I completed them.

Kerry Webb at the University of Texas Press merits thanks, too, for her patience and encouraging feedback on the manuscript. Christina Vargas offered excellent assistance managing files and permissions, while John Brenner's copyediting saved me from embarrassing errors and made the writing clearer and more accessible in general. Of course, any errors or mistakes are my own.

Parents are our first teachers and siblings our classmates in our earliest lessons. Thanks to mine for supporting me through this often strange endeavor, and to my partner Arnoldo and our daughter Xoila for keeping me connected to what truly matters.

Pitching Democracy

Introduction

Baseball, Democracy, and Latin America in the Cold War

The carnival-parade dragons decorated in the national colors of Venezuela, Puerto Rico, Mexico, and the Dominican Republic meandered through the outfield gates of Estadio Quisqueya as the hosting Dominican team took the field on a beautiful early February night in Santo Domingo. A commercial came on the screen in center field, the classic dun-dun-dun-dun organ music drawing my attention from the Dominican players warming up for their first game of the 2012 Caribbean Series by playing catch with their children. A black-and-white video of Dominican closing pitcher Francisco Cordero, who would play in his final big-league game later that year, appeared on the center-field screen, with him saying "Yo sé," Spanish for "I know." A handful of other Dominican players flashed on the screen with the same line, "Yo sé," and then Jorge (George) Bell, the epithet "Dominican Big League Glory" accompanying his name,[1] repeated the same. The dun-dun-dun-dun sped up for the windup and a baseball bat flashed on the black screen, quickly replaced by white smoke as the *thnock* of bat-to-ball contact sounded. I choked up, already moved by what I expected would be a nationalist expression of support for the players gathered to represent the Dominican Republic on their home field. The music changed to a rock beat. Osvaldo "Ozzie" Virgil, the first Dominican to play in the US major leagues, repeated the line "Yo sé." My heart fluttered.

Players continued to flash on the screen, each repeating the refrain "Yo sé," with many directing their comments to their hometowns. Cordero, who led Dominican pitchers in career saves, reappeared to add a personal touch: "About saves, I'm the one who knows. About governing, I know who knows." Big-league pitcher Arodis Vizcaíno flashed on the screen next, making the letter "L" with his right hand. For any Dominican in the crowd, the "L" revealed the political nature of the commercial. Still green on current Dominican political symbols, I expected a baseball-related message would soon be revealed. Ricardo "Rico" Carty, whose smile won the hearts of Braves fans in the 1960s and 1970s, flashed on the screen and repeated, "Yo sé." The outline of a familiar back came on the screen and Juan Marichal, the first Dominican in the Major League Baseball Hall of Fame, turned to face the camera. He repeated, "I know who knows about this," and made the "L" with the right hand that won him a reputation for "The Best Right Arm in Baseball." I sat in awe, impressed by the convergence of Dominican baseball past, present, and future before the first pitch of this celebration of Latin American baseball in the historic Estadio Quisqueya.

And then the stock image of presidential candidate Danilo Medina came onto the screen in full color. A narrator summarized the commercial's point: "The best is with Danilo. Yo sé. Sector Externo [External Sector, or independent political movements] with Danilo." As my anger at having my heartstrings played by a campaign commercial subsided, I reminded myself of the many instances of the ruling Partido de la Liberación Dominicana (PLD, or Dominican Liberation Party) projecting its candidate inside the stadium. From my seat on the first-base side, I saw four PLD billboards; three pictured Danilo Medina. Two also featured his running mate, Margarita Cedeño, who, in addition to campaigning for vice president, was finishing her third term as First Lady. Two images of Hipólito Mejía, the candidate for the Partido Revolucionario Dominicano (PRD, Dominican Revolutionary Party), also dotted the stadium walls, but the propaganda in the stadium left no question about which candidate had the most financial support and had hired the best PR firm to run his campaign.

Medina's Caribbean Series commercial was but one example of what some Dominican journalists call *pelótica*, the merging of baseball, or *pelota*, with politics, or *política*. Although journalists and broadcasters often use *pelótica* to poke fun at pandering politicians or ballplayers who use their fame to enter politics, the convergence of baseball and politics was critical to Dominicans' struggle for democracy against the dictatorship of Rafael Leonidas Trujillo Molina (1930–1961) and to the country's rise in the global baseball industry. In fact, Dominican democracy and global baseball as they exist today resulted from the intertwining of the struggle for democracy, the institution of a national professional baseball league affiliated with organized baseball, and the rise of Dominicans in the US major leagues.[2] Fusing baseball and democracy allowed Dominicans to preserve their "commonsensical understanding" that democracy was a tool to create a just, equitable society.[3] Even as global political and economic realities pushed many of their Latin American peers to concede this ideal in exchange for elections and promises of economic development, Dominicans continued to insist that democracy protect them from capitalism's excesses. In the process, Dominicans created a national baseball industry reflecting their beliefs that economic development should benefit citizens. This national baseball industry attracted US investment and ultimately secured the Dominican Republic as a center in the global baseball industry.

In the pages to follow, I examine the understandings of democracy that Dominicans projected onto the national pastime and its associated institutions as they worked to create a democratic society. A canvas onto which Dominicans projected their democratic aspirations, baseball helps uncover popular participation in shaping Dominican democracy and development as citizens of varying backgrounds and interests negotiated the future with one another, the national government, and outside government and sport officials.[4] "Pitching" in the title refers to the baseball action and to the idea that the president and other leaders pitched policies to the public for approval. Juan Bosch employed this metaphor in a speech he gave at a youth baseball game during the celebrations leading up to his inauguration in 1963. As a youth, he took a devastating loss on the mound, but he was more confident leading the Dominican Republic: "Now I will pitch from the Capitolio and I know that I am going to win because I have the people as my catcher."[5] Throughout the struggle for democracy beginning in roughly 1961, after Trujillo was brought to justice, Dominicans pitched their visions for democratic society to one another and their leaders.

Regional and global events shaped these visions. Dominican baseball's affiliation with US baseball made the sport a "transnational contact zone," a point of contact between the national and international interests, understandings, and ideologies held by Dominican citizens, government leaders, and international actors including the US State Department and US baseball.[6] Early in their struggle for democracy, Dominicans hailed the opportunity for individual prosperity and nationalist pride offered by the US model of professional baseball. Their opinions on the Cuban Revolution depended on their political leanings and varied and shifted over time, reflecting divisions in the Latin American region on the Cuban question.[7] While some were weary of Cuba's relationship with the Soviet Union and Castro's commitment to making the Cuban Revolution socialist, most held off on condemning the regime explicitly until Castro declared himself a lifelong Marxist-Leninist in December 1961. Many Dominicans admired Cuba's defense of sovereignty against US-sponsored invaders at the Bay of Pigs in April 1961 and recoiled only after Cuba's betrayal of American solidarity by allowing Soviet missiles in the hemisphere in October 1962. As anticommunism hardened after the Missile Crisis and prevented Dominicans from creating the democratic society they imagined, however, they increasingly embraced elements of the Cuban model and sought their own Third Way. Politically, this Third Way meant more direct participation in national politics and consideration in economic policy; in sports, it meant government investment in human development through support for amateur sport.[8]

Baseball proved an effective symbol for Dominican democratic aspirations because it was accessible to diverse Dominicans and was popular and desirable. Like the Cuban *independistas* who used baseball to rally against Spanish colonialism, Dominicans embraced baseball in the early twentieth century as an expression of their nationalism and to integrate the nation.[9] Over time, baseball became a way to project the nation and its potential and strength abroad. This conflation of baseball and nation had gendered implications in excluding women from the playing field, similar to what Thomas Carter showed for Cuba and Brenda Elsey and Joshua Nadel have shown in Latin American countries where *fútbol* is the national pastime.[10] Still, Dominican ballparks were scenes where the Dominican family, an imagined patriarchal nation articulated under Trujillo, came together for national debates over the democratic future.[11] Though confined to gendered roles in caretaking and cheerleading at the ballpark, women, too, participated in the political and sporting debates at the ballpark and surrounding the national pastime.

Newspapers, sports and political cartoons, government and league policies, and letters to political and sports officials reflected and shaped these debates. Dominican ballplayers and teams expanded their participation and reputation for success in the pan-American baseball circuit across the twentieth century. In the process, baseball and politics became intertwined, so much so that by the 1960s Dominican media recognized them as the country's two greatest pastimes. Popular engagement previously confined to the ballpark turned toward politics when Dominicans saw the wishes they expressed in the country's democratic elections spoiled by a military coup. *Caricaturas*, or political and sports cartoons, provided a connection between popular, everyday life and the more erudite and political aspects of these debates.[12] Although they reflect the personal positions of the men who drew them, *caricaturas* serve as valuable sources for gauging popular sentiment because they present a "visual artifact of a reality that the strokes of the artist uncover in unsuspected perspectives."[13] The artists reflected their views of complex reality back to their diverse popular audiences.

By centering popular understandings of democracy and development expressed through baseball, I emphasize Dominican ownership over the political and economic consequences of their struggle for democracy and over the baseball industry. Given their connection to the public and intricate ties to national narratives and identities, sports industries, like other cultural industries, require leaders to consider popular perceptions and desires as well as economic benefits.[14] In the 1950s and 1960s, Dominicans increasingly identified baseball as a path to individual well-being and financial security and pushed the government to invest in the professional and amateur leagues. By the mid-1970s, they also saw the potential for national development as managers, players, officials, and scouts created new leagues and formalized practices that helped the national pastime become a national industry. When US baseball leaders recognized the need for globalization in the 1980s and 1990s, the Dominican national industry rose as an important center in the global baseball industry. Rather than cede control to US-based officials, Dominican trainers, coaches, scouts, players, and officials created the institutions and processes that define the player-development process for major-league teams today.[15] These local insiders continue to shape the industry nationally and globally in their efforts to meet the needs of Dominican players, coaches, cleaners, cooks, and trainers as well as Major League Baseball (MLB) officials. The public stake in the baseball industry and the politics that support it give these local insiders a degree of leverage to exercise this influence within and, sometimes, against a large multinational corporation. Public emotions such as the unity behind the game, pride in the achievements of Dominican ballplayers, and desire to see more Dominicans in the US big leagues account at least in part for the Dominican Republic's outsized influence in the global baseball industry.

A Note on Terminology and the Structure of Baseball

Major League Baseball is such a prevalent organization today that it's easy to forget the National League and American League merged under one legal entity only in 2000 and interleague play outside the World Series began only in 1997. Yet the baseball decisions and debates that I detail here took place long before MLB existed and, along with other pressures brought by globalization, informed that legal merger. To remain historically accurate, I use the proper name Major League Baseball or MLB only when I discuss the entity that has existed since 2000. Instead, I use the adjective "major-league" or the league name to discuss major-league teams and players. I use "US baseball" to refer to all affiliated professional teams, major and minor, in the mainland United States. Since the late 1940s, US baseball has maintained Winter Agreements with various Latin American leagues, including the Puerto Rican league now named for Roberto Clemente. The Caribbean Baseball Confederation (Confederación de Beisbol Profesional del Caribe) represents its member Latin American leagues in these negotiations. The Latin American leagues thus formed part of what many called "organized baseball," yet I mostly avoid this term for fear that many US readers equate it with what I refer to as US baseball. Instead, I refer to the relevant Latin American league(s) or Caribbean Confederation.

When I refer to minor-league teams, I mean US teams affiliated with major-league teams as part of what many call their farm system. All major-league teams oversee several minor-league teams where players develop their skills in the hope of being called up to play in the major leagues. The affiliated minor leagues are divided into levels, with the Dominican Summer League forming the lowest, followed by the rookie league(s) or short-season, low single-A, advanced-A, double-A, and triple-A. Players in all these leagues are professional ballplayers:

a ballplayer becomes a professional when they sign a contract with a professional team. For the sake of clarity, I confine my discussion of US baseball to ballplayers and teams affiliated with the major leagues. Although independent, unaffiliated leagues exist in the United States, I do not consider them in this analysis.

Baseball and Politics in the Dominican Republic

The story of baseball and politics in the Dominican Republic reveals the power of the Cold War anticommunist narrative in shaping the economies and politics of developing countries and the world. Baseball became a beacon of hope for Dominican democracy in the 1960s and has remained so. Yet since the 1970s and 1980s, Dominican aspirations for baseball have shifted from social improvement to individual survival or, for the lucky few, personal prosperity. Their aspirations for democracy have also shifted, though perhaps more in terms of who fills expectations than in the expectations themselves. Beginning during the Great Depression and taking hold after World War II, Dominicans, like most others in the Western world, imagined democracy as a model for society that promoted equality of rights and economic opportunity practiced through a political system of voting for representatives. Government leaders and citizens understood democracy as the means to protect citizens from the excesses of capitalism. Economic pressures in the 1970s and 1980s, along with rising authoritarianism, shifted responsibility for social welfare to the market and, for Dominican ballplayers and prospective ballplayers, to major-league teams and Major League Baseball.

Through the political and economic turmoil and debates of the Cold War and after, Dominicans acted as owners of the democratic society they wanted to create, their national pastime, and their corner of the global baseball industry. They engaged in the ideological debate by which Odd Arne Westad characterized the Cold War but saw both the US freedom and Soviet justice narratives as essential to democracy.[16] Their promotion of both professional and amateur baseball and their support for new versions of professional baseball, even those tied to US baseball, demonstrate how Dominicans combined elements of both the freedom and justice narratives to fit their needs. And they were well aware of the material economic and social implications of their choices. These social conflicts defined the Cold War in the Global South and highlight the significance of local understandings of the balance of freedom and equality in democratic society.[17] Because Dominicans projected their aspirations onto the national pastime, baseball provided a lens for viewing shifts in understandings of democracy and how these understandings shaped the baseball industry over time.

The Trujillo regime seized on Felipe Alou's debut with the San Francisco Giants in 1958, the incorporation of the Dominican Winter League in 1955, and this league's affiliation with US baseball to frame professional baseball as a gift of Trujillo and, by extension, the state to the Dominican people. A 1960 editorial in *El Caribe* equated these gifts and the national progress they provided with democracy, specifically a "democracy that has an honest consciousness of what Trujillo is, of what he represents, of what he has given, of all that he can save us from."[18] Despite these attempts to define Trujillo as democratic, the regime's failure to reproduce the spectacles of the winter tournaments with US reinforcements for the 1960–1961 season exposed the inadequacy of its personalism and patronage. In response, many Dominicans refused to attend the games and thereby freed baseball from the dictator's control. Ballplayers replaced Trujillo as symbols of Dominican potential in a democratic system because of their economic advancement, positive representation of the country abroad, and participation in winter tournaments. Baseball, not Trujillo, would help remake the country as a democratic society with economic opportunity. Months after the 1960–1961 winter season, Trujillo was brought to justice.

The image of a baseball season unencumbered by the dictator's whims sustained Dominican hopes for a democratic society defined by rights and economic opportunity even as they sacrificed winter baseball seasons to secure the 1962 elections. The participation of three Dominicans in the 1962 World Series revealed the nation's enthusiasm for democracy. An exhibition series with a group of Cuban exiles traveling from the United States reiterated the hope for an American hemisphere built on democracy. Still, demonstrations against Castro's Cuba interrupted the series and foreshadowed a shift away from democratic ideals to anticommunism. As the election approached, editorials warned of the dual threats of *trujillismo* (Trujilloism) and communism. By the time Juan Bosch, leader of the social democratic PRD, took office in February 1963, anticommunism dominated. Bosch's political opponents turned anticommunism against him in response to the new constitution's challenges to the political influence of the Catholic Church and industrial class. The accusations escalated as Bosch's standing in the United States appeared tarnished, especially after *El Caribe* published his letter asking US baseball team presidents to allow Dominican big-leaguers to participate in the 1963–1964 Winter Tournament. A military-led coup supported by the industrial class deposed Bosch on September 25, 1963, and repealed the new constitution, marking anticommunism's overthrow of the democratic ideals to which Dominicans had aspired after bringing Trujillo to justice.

Dominicans welcomed the return of the Winter Tournament in 1963–1964 as a step toward normalcy after politics had undermined or prevented the previous three tournaments. The de facto civilian government known as the Triumvirate quickly passed industrial incentives and limited the right to strike, hoping to prevent civil unrest. Yet Dominican frustrations with the military's violation of their democratic voice and with the Triumvirate's policies manifested against ballplayers and the Dominican Winter League. Early in the tournament, Dominicans criticized baseball heroes Julián Javier and Juan Marichal for their apparent disrespect toward a US umpire and their team managers. Their critics, encouraged by the sports press, emphasized what they saw as a lack of commitment from Javier and Marichal to their winter teams deriving from feelings of entitlement because of their US success. Similar sentiments underlay criticisms of ballplayers from Licey and the Aguilas, the runners-up and champions of the Winter Tournament, after they threatened to sit out an inter-American exhibition series against their Venezuelan League peers. The targeting of US reinforcements and Dominican big-leaguers likely resulted, at least in part, from suspicions that the US Embassy had played a role in the coup or had done too little to prevent it. Dominicans also directed their ire toward league officials, who were suspected of interfering with game results to prolong the tournament and boost revenues. Criticisms against baseball provided a release for the public's frustration with the lack of policies to soften economic exploitation and the Triumvirate's slow progress toward organizing elections. With the persistence of these problems and no elections in sight after the 1964–1965 Winter Tournament, Dominicans turned to a popular rebellion, known as the April War, to demand a return to democracy in 1965.

The end of the April War brought elections, but the US-OAS occupation of their country led Dominicans to compromise their democratic ideals for stability by electing the former Trujillo puppet and US-supported candidate Joaquín Balaguer. During his twelve years in office, known as the *doce años,* Balaguer included baseball as part of a political and economic Third Way. During his first term, Balaguer emphasized reconciliation with the United States through professional baseball, but relative security in the country—at least in part because of repression—allowed him to comply with popular demands that the government invest in the people, notably through amateur sport. Amateur sport expanded Dominican connections in Latin America, including with Cuba, and boosted Balaguer's reputation in the region at a moment when countries in the so-called Third World were calling for a new international economic order to lessen their dependence on the superpowers.[19] The Third Way legitimated Balaguer's development program to Dominicans by demonstrating the social benefits of industrialization and maintained his anticommunist credentials with the United States. Dominicans continued to request government resources and investments for their sports and communities, often adopting Balaguer's rhetoric to curry favor. Even as Dominicans gained more flexibility in civil rights, however, this model of patronage adapted in part from Trujillo increasingly confined their political participation to voting and requests for patronage that followed accepted scripts aligned with Balaguer's version of economic and social development. Still, the stability necessary to appease investors and US concerns about communism rested on the legitimacy of elections and Balaguer himself. Upholding the appearance of democracy forced the government to comply with popular demands, as exemplified by the renewed emphasis on amateur sport suggested by the government's support for hosting the 1969 Amateur Baseball World Series and 1974 Central American and Caribbean Games and creating a Secretary of Sports Office through the 1974 Sports Law.

While much of the public clamored for amateur baseball, professional ballplayers and promoters created two new summer leagues that aligned the national pastime with Balaguer's program for development and industrialization. Falling attendance and increased complaints about US teams' influence over Winter League rosters echoed concerns about the Triumvirate and mirrored Dominican frustrations with the Balaguer government's continued support for industry over workers. The Dominican Republic Summer League gained popular attention because of its goal to prepare young ballplayers to sign with US teams or, for those who had already been signed and released, to restart their careers by signing with a different team. The Cibao Summer League promoted itself as the vanguard of a new national industry that would protect workers and baseball fans from the excesses of capitalism that had alienated fans from the Winter League. This industry objective won the Cibao League financial support from the government because the promises to favor Dominican ballplayers legitimated Balaguer's emphasis on public investment in industry. Rather than framing investment in baseball as a sign of Balaguer's interest in the well-being of Dominican citizens, the Cibao League and the government emphasized baseball's potential contributions to economic development. Led by local scouts such as Epy Guerrero, Ralph Avila, and Jesús Alou, this industry reinforced the Dominican Republic's competitive advantages over other Latin American countries in player development.

The country's first democratic transition in 1978 marked the pinnacle of social democracy in the country and its subsequent downfall. Both Antonio Guzmán (1978–1982) and Salvador Jorge Blanco (1982–1986) took office amid growing financial trouble and trade imbalances yet worked to bring democracy and development together again. In baseball, they continued support for the Cibao Summer League and baseball as bases of a national industry that would bring jobs, pride, and opportunity to Dominican citizens. Dominican baseball fans cheered Winter League expansion in 1983 as an overdue check on the oligarchic manipulations they had suffered for decades. Even as Jorge Blanco invested in this budding national industry, however, tightening state resources forced him into negotiations with the International Monetary Fund (IMF) to curb public spending. Despite early government gestures to regulate baseball academies and support training leagues, the burden of protecting Dominican baseball hopefuls from the excesses of the market fell on Dominican scouts, successful ballplayers, community leaders, and other officials. By 2000, public outcry in the United States and the Dominican Republic about abuses in the player-development system, including theft and negligence by MLB-affiliated scouts, pushed the MLB Commissioner's Office to regulate the teams and, over time, the Dominican youths who hoped to enter the system. Responsibility for protecting Dominican citizens from the excesses of capitalism had shifted from the Dominican government to Major League Baseball.

Chapter Outline

I offer a roughly chronological narrative of debates over democracy and the development of the baseball industry in the Dominican Republic from the institutionalization of the professional baseball league under Trujillo in 1955 through the rise of academies under democratic governments in the 1980s and 1990s. The first chapter, "*Mens sana in corpore sano*: Baseball and Trujillista Politics," examines the national sports institutions in the 1940s and 1950s to show how Trujillo used these institutions to raise his and the country's reputation in the region. Dominican ownership over baseball, especially professional baseball, limited the dictator's ability to coopt this national pastime and ultimately allowed Dominicans to free baseball and then themselves from the dictatorship.

The second and third chapters center on the transition to democracy following the *ajusticiamiento* (bringing to justice) of Trujillo.[20] Chapter 2, "Politics at the Plate: The Threat of Communism and the Showcase for Democracy," traces the shift in Dominican understandings of democracy between the preparations for elections in October 1962 and the coup against the country's first democratically elected president less than a year later. Editorials and cartoons published in national papers reveal a shift in emphasis from democracy as a social good to anticommunism and stability, particularly after the Cuban Missile Crisis in 1962. The appearance of the first Dominicans in the World Series encouraged Dominicans' equation of baseball with democracy as they prepared for elections; they showed their preference for democracy over communism in their cheers for a team of Cuban exiles that visited for an exhibition series in November 1962. Chapter 3, "Criticizing Baseball, Debating Democracy," reveals how the popular social democratic vision from 1962 persisted after the coup and exposes the limitations of baseball as a democratic symbol. Drawing on Felipe Alou's 1963 article "Latin-American Ballplayers Need a Bill of Rights," the chapter analyzes the international components of the coup against Bosch along with the rise of anticommunism to replace democracy among elites. Demands that the government invest in amateur rather than professional sport rose during this period.

Chapters 4 and 5 trace how Balaguer used baseball to consolidate power and gain legitimacy for his development policies during the three terms known as the *doce años* from 1966 to 1978. Chapter 4, "*Así se hace patria*: Baseball and the Bloodless Revolution," demonstrates how Dominican negotiations with the Balaguer regime created a political Third Way—what Balaguer described as the Revolución sin sangre, or Bloodless Revolution. By 1966, Cuba's prohibition of professional sport in 1961 and investment in amateur sport began to pay off in terms of the small country's success in international competition. Balaguer responded to popular demands to invest in amateur sport by borrowing from the Cuban model to raise the country's profile in international sporting events, while also maintaining ties to the US model and individual opportunities of professional baseball. Combining these models created a sporting microcosm of Balaguer's Third Way. Balaguer institutionalized this sporting Third Way after coopting professional baseball in his first term (1966) and creating the Office of the Secretary of Sports, Physical Education, and Recreation in 1975. Ultimately, the Secretary of Sports and the narrative of the Third Way integrated paternalism in the Dominican government by framing Balaguer and the Secretary of Sports as paternal leaders concerned with the well-being of Dominican citizens.

This narrative of Balaguer's concern for the Dominican people carried into 1975 and the government's investment in baseball as a national industry. The rise of the Cibao Summer League and Dominican Republic Summer League in the spring of 1975 created new models of professional baseball that countered the earlier baseball narratives. The new leagues responded directly to complaints that the Winter League neglected national baseball stars in favor of US hopefuls while draining government coffers for personal profit. The new leagues promised increased employment opportunities for Dominican ballplayers, coaches, and managers, and offered those dismissed by US teams the chance to rehabilitate their careers. Chapter 5, "Sliding into Third: The Cibao Summer League and Baseball as Development," shows how Balaguer supported the Cibao Summer League because its language of industrialization legitimated his development policies. With government support bolstering the league, it became a symbol of Dominican ownership of the baseball industry and industrial innovation. Although Balaguer successfully created a legacy of Dominican development, economic pressures and successive calls for democracy led to his demise in the 1978 elections and the country's first democratic transition of power.

The final chapter, "Making the Majors: The Baseball Industry and Dominican Democracy," demonstrates the ongoing debates over the significance of democracy even after the democratic transition in 1978. Dominican leaders, industrialists, and citizens continued to look to baseball as a manifestation of what democracy would bring to their country. These debates manifested in the expansion of the Dominican Winter League in 1983–1984 as well as ongoing discussions of development centered on sport. Considering these debates and the Dominican innovations that underlay the globalization of baseball through the 1980s and 1990s, this chapter demonstrates the lasting significance of Dominicans' early conflation of baseball and democracy as well as the impact of neoliberal policies in pushing corporations like Major League Baseball to fulfill roles once expected of the government.

By focusing on Dominican ownership of a democratic future and the baseball industry that developed with it, I break with perceptions of Dominicans and other actors in the Global South as victims of or bystanders to superpower battles. Attention to debates over the future of democracy and its relationship to development demonstrate the active engagement by Dominicans of all social levels in their democratic process, political culture, and national industry. They worked within and pushed against structures that limited their options at any given time, but they created a democracy and a center in the global baseball industry. Both are flawed, but looking at the ways their development intersected can provide clues for reform.

ONE

Mens sana in corpore sano

Baseball and Trujillista Politics

In October 1955, Dominicans from the baseball cities of Ciudad Trujillo (Santo Domingo), San Pedro de Macorís, and Santiago lined up in front of the new Estadio Trujillo (renamed Estadio Quisqueya in 1961) to buy tickets for what many saw as the most important event in their lives as baseball devotees. For the first time in their nation's history, the four professional baseball clubs—Leones del Escogido (Lions of Escogido), Tigres del Licey (Licey Tigers), Estrellas Orientales (Eastern Stars), and Aguilas Cibaeñas (Cibao Eagles)—would face off in a winter season affiliated with US baseball. Beyond adding excitement with US players on Dominican fields, affiliation with organized baseball, which included the US major and minor leagues and, later, winter leagues in Puerto Rico, Cuba, Venezuela, and Panama, legitimated the Dominican Professional Base Ball League as a professional institution. The league, new stadium, and affiliation were the culmination of the sporting component of dictator Rafael Leonidas Trujillo Molina's project to modernize the Dominican economy and its citizens in line with the so-called First World, timed to coincide with the Year of the Benefactor celebrations that marked the twenty-fifth anniversary of the Trujillo regime.[1]

Although no fan of the game himself, Trujillo incorporated professional baseball into the narrative of national progress that touted him as the "Father of the New Fatherland" (Padre de la Patria Nueva) and a model for all Dominicans. Estadio Trujillo and the presence of US players on Dominican fields provided physical evidence of the dictator's largesse and his success in guiding Dominicans' ascent among their Caribbean neighbors. A near replica of the Miami Stadium opened in Florida in 1949, Estadio Trujillo boasted modern conveniences including a drainage system, water heaters for two hundred simultaneous hot showers, and enough light towers to make the stadium "the best illuminated in all of Latin America."[2] The stadium represented the dictator's successful efforts to educate and modernize the citizenry in his image of a healthy mind in a healthy body, or *mens sana in corpore sano.* Even though his brother Héctor and Joaquín Balaguer served as president in 1952 and 1960 respectively, Trujillo led the country from 1930 until he was brought to justice in 1961. As Lauren Derby has demonstrated, Trujillo embodied the nation, placing himself at its head as a father would place himself at the head of a family.[3] The paternalistic rhetoric created an illusion that Trujillo ruled in the interest of the Dominican people and rationalized violence as fatherly discipline: he used the threat of violence to maintain order and rewarded the Dominican family with gifts like roads and baseball games in what Richard Turits described as the "paradoxes of popular consent to despotic rule."[4] The institutionalization of sport under the Dirección General de Deportes (Office of the National Director of Sports) in 1943, like the incorporation of the Dominican Professional Base Ball League more than a decade later, both disciplined and rewarded Dominicans. Amateur tournaments and leagues extended the state's reach into small towns and hamlets, much as the land policies that Turits detailed had done during the first two decades of *trujillismo,* while professional baseball reached an increasingly critical middle class centered in the cities and the urban working class.

Baseball encompassed a combination of cultural, political, economic, international, and military factors that historians have considered essential to Trujillo's ability to maintain power for more than three decades. The infiltration of the military into daily life and the social mobility offered by the military, as described by Valentina Peguero, created an illusion of order and control centered on the dictator.[5] The militarization of Dominican society touched baseball, too: some of the best Dominican players, including Hall of Famer Juan Marichal, developed their skills on the amateur Air Force team Aviación (Aviation), managed by the dictator's son Ramfis. Affiliation with US professional baseball deepened Dominicans' impression that US officials supported Trujillo.[6]

Despite the regime's resources and efforts to control baseball, the dictator's hold on the sport was incomplete. Dominicans projected their own meanings onto the national pastime and participated in baseball on their terms, often compelling the dictator to support baseball and pushing the limits of his control through what Derby described as a "dramaturgy of power."[7] Glorifying the dictator by putting his name on tournaments and awards and reciting the script of the Benefactor's gifts and superlatives, baseball organizers won financial and moral support for the tournaments without losing their control over the meanings of the national pastime and the democratic society they increasingly associated with it. This chapter illustrates those negotiations between the dictator and the public, beginning with the formal incorporation of sport under the regime with the Sports Law of 1943. The success of fans and sportswriters in claiming Osvaldo "Ozzie" Virgil's playing rights for the new Dominican League suggested that Dominicans would maintain control over the national pastime despite Trujillo's investment. Although the regime gained the upper hand after Felipe Alou debuted with the San Francisco Giants in 1958, international events, which had earlier buffered Trujillo against US actions, would push him too far. By the time five more Dominican players earned their major-league debuts in 1960, the Dominican Republic suffered economic sanctions that undermined the 1960–1961 Winter Tournament and exposed the contradictions in the regime's narrative of progress. Dominicans found space to free baseball—and later themselves—from the dictator's hold.

Trujillo and the Bases of Modern Sport

The 1955–1956 Winter Tournament built on the foundations Trujillo laid more than a decade before to modernize Dominican institutions and citizens through sport as well as half a century of Dominican infatuation with professional baseball, their *deporte rey*, or king sport. While professional baseball existed in the Dominican Republic as early as 1907, when a group of men from the capital founded the Licey Tigers, the lack of a national league meant that teams competed in barnstorming series. The near bankruptcy of Dominican professional teams after experiments with a national baseball tournament in 1936 and 1937 suggested to regime members that while Dominicans reveled in the quality of play, the country lacked the institutions necessary to support professional baseball over the long term.[8] Dominican professional teams continued to barnstorm across the region and to play short tournaments on national fields, but the best Dominican professionals had to play in the US Negro Leagues or on Puerto Rican or Cuban teams to make a living.[9] The regime and Dominican fans turned instead to amateur baseball, where national teams could exemplify the benefits of Trujillo's leadership to their neighbors across the American continent.

The incorporation of sport into the Dominican narrative of national progress, or modernization, officially began with the Sports Law of 1943 and the founding of the Office of the National Director of Sports (Dirección General de Deportes) headed by the national director of sports. The Sports Law created an institutional base to organize national sport and to promote the advancement of the Dominican people through the ideology of *mens sana in corpore sano*.[10] Similar to Muscular Christianity's linking of moral and physical development in the nineteenth-century United States, *mens sana in corpore sano* posed sport as the means to transform the Dominican population. Baseball and other athletic activities guided by the dictator would transform backward peasants eking out subsistence lifestyles into the productive, modern consumers and producers who would carry the progress of the nation.[11] The Office of the National Director of Sports oversaw the training of Dominican citizens in the values of modern sport—including teamwork, self-sacrifice, respect for authority and rules, physical fitness, and good hygiene—by administering requests for sporting patronage, organizing amateur tournaments, and overseeing the construction of national sports installations. Good Dominicans followed the dictator's example: boys trained in the national pastime of baseball, girls built their physiques through calisthenics, young men trained for the military, and women kept their homes and served as team mothers. All supported their national teams and most followed baseball despite (or because of) the dictator's lack of personal interest in the *deporte rey*. Trujillo created the institutions and infrastructure that would imbibe Dominican citizens with the same modern ideals as their Benefactor.

Amateur teams nurtured Dominican enthusiasm for the national pastime with intense competition and spectacle. The National Police and each branch of the military fielded strong teams that competed against local teams sponsored by sugar mills or other local businesses. These amateur teams acted much like the semi-professional teams that preceded professionalization in other countries, hiring strong players for fluff jobs or to train in sport without the title of "professional." Juan Marichal was one such employee: he was officially hired to mow the lawn for the local branch of the United Fruit Company's executive golf course before his pitching caught the eye of Ramfís Trujillo, who drafted him into the Air Force. In the Air Force, Marichal received an above-average salary and practiced pitching for the team Aviación.[12]

The amateur system spread the oversight of the regime across the country through the Office of the National Director of Sports, which coordinated transportation for intercity tournaments, subsidized uniforms, and registered players. The best teams traveled to the capital to compete for the national championship. The best players joined National Selection tournaments with the hope that the sports director would recruit them to represent the country in one of an increasing number of international exchanges with teams from across the Caribbean or in larger tournaments such as the Amateur World Series or the Pan American Games. Success in these international exchanges and tournaments inspired calls for the return of professional baseball.

As local teams incorporated and trained better players, national selections offered a means to prove the benefits of Trujillo's policies to those at home and to project his achievements across the hemisphere. Dominican officials measured the modernization of their nation against those of their Caribbean peers, especially Puerto Rico and Cuba, from whom they borrowed in formulating sport policies and constructing professional teams.[13] The Amateur Baseball World Series (Serie Mundial de Béisbol Amateur), which Cuba had dominated since it moved from England to the Americas in 1939, provided one of the scenes for proving the country's rise among its regional peers. A second-place finish in the 1942 Series helped to carry the Sports Law through to approval, while a Dominican victory in the 1948 series confirmed its benefits. As Dominicans honored their compatriots, who had pieced together a championship after many of the nation's best players died in a plane crash remembered as the 1948 Tragedy of Río Verde, the national press declared the victory a "happy consequence of the progressive development" that Trujillo had achieved in the past years.[14] Through "the famous leader's educational policies," Dominicans had become a "Vanguard Nation before all the civilized continents" for their civility and sportsmanship.[15] Success again in 1950 confirmed for Dominicans that the nation was ready for the highest echelons of baseball modernity: professional baseball.

After the 1950 Amateur World Series victory, local sportswriters joined Dominican baseball leaders and former Negro League players Enrique Lantigua and Horacio Martínez to prepare for the return of professional baseball. They formed the Dominican Baseball Federation (Federación Dominicana de Béisbol) and tested the audience for professional baseball in March 1951 with a week-long series between independent teams representing local companies. Dominican Beer (Cerveza la Dominicana) wore the red traditionally associated with Escogido, while the Diplomats (Diplomático) representing the Barceló & Company rum house wore Licey's blue.[16] Popular enthusiasm, boosted by promotional stunts led by Pichulí Manzueta of Escogido and Licey's queen Doña Maricusa Mercado de Gautier, pushed the sports director to meet with the National Baseball Commission and the directors of the Professional Ballplayers Federation to organize the return of professional baseball. A month later, the four traditional teams had restructured their boards of directors and initiated a national tournament.

Baseball administrators like Martínez and Lantigua and their media colleagues including *El Caribe*'s Rafael E. Martorrel led the rebirth of professional baseball, but their success depended on the permission if not the direct support of the regime. While Trujillo preferred horse racing and other equestrian sports to baseball, his brother-in-law Francisco Martínez Alba and son Ramfis participated in the reorganization of professional baseball as members of Escogido's board of directors.[17] Their positions in the administration of the king sport ensured that the regime would remain close to the tournament. Officials performed their submission and gratitude to Trujillo through the tournament names, including the 1951 "Trujillo Era Tournament," 1952 "Pro-Election of General Héctor B Trujillo Molina" for the dictator's brother who presided over the nation, 1953 "Leonidas Radhamés" for the dictator's younger son, and 1954 "Benefactor" for the dictator himself. Organizers effectively balanced the need for foreign reinforcements to strengthen the teams against their own financial restrictions to meet Dominicans' demands for competitive baseball and earn the dictator's attention. By 1953 they had earned institutional, infrastructural, and financial support for professional baseball.

The regime began the process of incorporating professional baseball under its control in 1953 with changes to the regulations for professional and amateur baseball. Trujillo's vision of modernization demanded order, which led to the centralization of the *deporte rey* under his authority. Although the national sports director had only an advisory role in professional sport, his recommendations shaped the regulations for the professional league and determined who Dominican president Héctor Trujillo would name to oversee professional baseball.[18] After loosening restrictions to allow amateurs to enter professional baseball more easily, Héctor Trujillo, likely taking instruction from his brother, approved a list of industrialists, a judge, and others who had served on the ad hoc organizing committees to staff a National Commission of Professional Baseball.[19] Many of these same men later formed the core of the allegedly independent Dominican Professional Base Ball League (Liga Dominicana de Base Ball Profesional).

Despite the centralized legal framework laid for the organization of professional tournaments, some members of the Trujillo regime hesitated to offer public support to professional baseball and did so only after the dictator intervened. Debates happened in government documents away from the public eye but followed a familiar script that demonstrated the dictator's power and documented his intervention to meet public demands. The sports director argued in favor of providing $50,000 to the four professional teams ahead of the 1954 national tournament because of "the convenience that these sporting competitions have from the view of social policy and because of the interest that the masses who love this sport are constantly showing."[20] Only two weeks before, he and his superior had advised against the financial gift, arguing—rightfully, it turned out—that it would set a precedent of government support for professional baseball.[21] While no documents showed Rafael Trujillo's direct intervention to change this position, his brother the president paid for the gift to the teams through a discretionary fund that the dictator had used for similar matters. The director of sports later asked the dictator to allow him to name the championship the Benefactor's Cup in recognition of his help in securing financial assistance.[22] The name of the tournament and news of the government's financial support left no question that Trujillo was "faithfully interpreting the feelings of his people" in meeting popular demands for professional baseball.[23]

While Trujillo managed to use the financial gift to the league to support his image as the Benefactor of the Nation, official control over professional baseball remained loose until at least 1955. The regime responded to the demands of baseball officials rather than dictating terms to them. Both the National Commission of Professional Baseball and financial assistance for the 1954 season likely came as part of an ultimatum that Escogido president Francisco Martínez Alba shared with the commission. Martínez had threatened the commission in 1953 that Escogido would not participate in a tournament unless Licey's Alonzo Perry, a player originally contracted from the United States, was prohibited or other teams received support to recruit foreign players.[24] The commission acquiesced, offering $15,000 each to the Aguilas and Escogido and only $10,000 each for Licey and the Estrellas, who were better equipped with players. Even with the financial support, however, the Aguilas and Escogido withdrew from the tournament early, leading the sports director to charge them over $4,000 each to compensate the government for its $50,000 investment in the Benefactor's Cup.[25] The dictator would have to do more to ensure the development of the national pastime. Even before Licey clinched victory in 1954, planning began for Estadio Trujillo, affiliation with US baseball, and the change to winter for the 1955 professional tournament.

Trujillo, Modernity, and Professional Baseball

The failure by the teams and commission to organize a viable tournament allowed Trujillo to step in to save the *deporte rey* in 1955. With construction on Estadio Trujillo initiated in late 1954, the regime moved quickly to incorporate baseball into the 1955 Year of the Benefactor celebrations. Team leaders agreed to new professional baseball regulations to facilitate the passage of Dominican players to professional status in mid-June 1955 and agreed to form an official professional baseball league. In meetings headed by the director of sports, leaders of the four teams agreed to terms for the 1955 tournament and debated the relative benefits of affiliation with organized baseball, which was pending. Laying the bases for affiliation, Héctor Trujillo signed the incorporation of the Dominican Professional Base Ball League into law in August 1955 and heard appeals from the teams for the financial support necessary to ensure that the tournament "is the most brilliant of all, in accordance with the celebrations for the Year of the Benefactor of the Fatherland."[26] With the institutional legitimacy provided by the Dominican Professional Base Ball League (Dominican Winter League), the infrastructure provided by Estadio Trujillo, and the promise that Dominicans would one day see their compatriots play alongside US major and minor leaguers, Trujillo asserted his control over the *deporte rey* in 1955.

Incorporation approved by the government and affiliation with US baseball signaled Trujillo's great efforts to lead Dominicans to progress by legitimizing the Dominican Winter League in international baseball and placing it on par with US baseball and the Latin American members of the Caribbean Baseball Confederation (Confederación de Béisbol Profesional del Caribe). Formed in 1948, the Caribbean Confederation oversaw the Winter Agreements between the Latin American winter leagues and the US summer leagues and organized the Caribbean Series, a World Series of sorts for the national tournament champions from member countries.[27] The director of sports happily informed the president, Héctor Trujillo, that the incorporation of the league "regulated and organized [professional baseball] in a definitive manner" and avoided the "multiple inconveniences" around the organization of the tournament each year.[28] These inconveniences, which the ad hoc organizers encountered because of their lack of institutionalization under the Trujillo regime, had resulted in a bad reputation for Dominican baseball in the Caribbean. As one sportswriter explained, affiliation "eliminated completely the guerrilla tactics and piracy" that had previously characterized Dominican baseball and made it the "bad boy of the Caribbean."[29] Under the watchful eye of Trujillo, the national pastime acquired new tools to confront difficulties in the organization of the national tournament and the signing of players—including Dominican players who participated in other leagues. One cartoonist celebrated this institutional security with an image of a dominating pitcher (Liga D.) striking out Problems (Problemas) while pitching to Organized Baseball (Béisbol Organizado) (fig. 1.1). The new league and affiliation, made possible by Trujillo, ensured that professional baseball would defeat any problems that threatened the national tournament. The annual tournament became the symbol of government competence.

With the 1955 tournament, the Trujillo regime incorporated the attempts of the ad hoc organizers to create a new era of Dominican professional baseball and tied the *deporte rey* to the government. The government provided institutional legitimacy through incorporation, financial guarantees, and infrastructure such as Estadio Trujillo. By 1956, Dominicans expected this official financial and institutional support for professional baseball as part of the government's service to the population. Sportswriters hailed "the unlimited protection that in all moments the Superior Government has provided" for making tournaments possible, noting that "the provisions and concessions offered by

Figure 1.1. "The League's Curveball," Miche Medina, *El Caribe*, September 11, 1955, p. 5.

the Superior Government have guaranteed the economic security of the classics."[30] These provisions and concessions included the construction of Estadio Leonidas Rhadamés (Estadio Cibao) in Santiago in 1958 and Estadio Oriental (Estadio Tetelo Vargas) in San Pedro de Macorís in 1959 as well as teams' administration of the stadiums, decreased electricity rates, tax exonerations, and a financial gift that was raised from $40,000 in 1955 to $100,000 in subsequent years during the Trujillo era.[31] The government provided the institutional framework and the financial security necessary to ensure that Dominicans could enjoy professional baseball in their country for decades to come, at least as long as Trujillo was in power.

At the inauguration of Estadio Trujillo in 1955, Joaquín Balaguer, the secretary of education, reminded Dominicans that they owed this support for professional baseball and their own progress to Trujillo. Balaguer, a writer and poet, compared the nation to an immense stadium where a gladiator, Trujillo, had realized great feats during the past twenty-five years. He reminded them that Trujillo "has not only taught his people to improve themselves and to supersede their destiny; not only has he educated his compatriots in the moral of success, in the motto of victory, and the lesson of the fight; but he is also teaching, in anticipation, the lesson of the triumph for future generations."[32]

A New Narrative of Progress

As Balaguer spoke, Dominicans gazed at the freshly planted grass of Estadio Trujillo and the US professionals lined up alongside their compatriots. Undoubtedly, the crowd imagined that one day soon a Dominican would play in the US major leagues and become an exemplar of a modern Dominican citizen formed under Trujillo's programs for *mens sana in corpore sano*. The decision to shift the Dominican season from the summer to winter facilitated the sharing of players, providing Dominican ballplayers the opportunity to play in the US minor and major leagues without abandoning their Dominican team—at least in theory. The year before affiliation, Trujillo had protected Dominican teams' claims on local players, as in his decision to deny a visa to Garabato Sackie, who Leo Durocher of the Brooklyn Dodgers had hoped might "impress the American people with the similarity of interests and sportsmanship in our country and theirs."[33] Affiliation provided Trujillo the opportunity to impress American and Dominican citizens by incorporating ballplayers as well as baseball into the narrative that his regime brought modernity and progress to the country. However, the dependence on individual Dominicans and the connections to the United States limited the regime's control over the meanings of professional baseball. The Dominican Winter League's struggle to win the playing rights for Ozzie Virgil in 1955 tarnished the sheen of the Father of the New Fatherland tournament and weakened the regime's hold on the sport. Although Felipe Alou's major-league debut in 1958 allowed the regime to reclaim Virgil as a product of the Trujillato, Dominicans increasingly saw ballplayers, and not Trujillo, as the exemplars of national progress and potential.

Dominican sportswriters and baseball fans took the early steps against the Trujillo regime's claim on baseball by insisting that Virgil participate in the 1955–1956 Dominican Winter League tournament. Virgil, who had moved to the United States at age fourteen and signed with the New York Giants in 1953, was problematic for the regime's claim that Trujillo led the nation's youth to realize the ideal of *mens sana in corpore sano*. Virgil had developed as a ballplayer and adult in the United States, not under Trujillo, and had played the previous three winters with the Indios de Mayagüez in the Puerto Rican league. Rather than disregard Virgil and his achievements, however, the Dominican press and baseball league publicly affirmed his Dominicanness. In a special article that quoted his maternal grandmother and uncle, *El Caribe* asserted Virgil's Dominican identity, adding that he "has always said that he is Dominican."[34] The Trujillo regime made no public claims on Virgil's playing rights, but the debate over whether he would join the new Dominican League or return to the Indios de Mayagüez stood as a criticism against the regime.[35] Offering a preemptive defense, *El Caribe* reported that Virgil feared traveling to the Dominican Republic because of "false propaganda" that he would be conscripted into the Dominican military or treated poorly because of his US citizenship.[36] The public hearing over Virgil's Dominicanness and questions about where he would play in 1955 revealed holes in the dictator's reputation as the "Maximum Protector of National Sport."

His participation in the 1955–1956 season, although brief, confirmed Virgil's Dominicanness and began his rehabilitation as a symbol of Dominican potential that allowed many to imagine the possibility of a Dominican Republic without Trujillo. Before he returned to the Dominican Republic with hopes of achieving a second straight championship for Escogido in the 1956–1957 winter season, Virgil became the first Dominican to play in the US major leagues. Days after his debut on September 23, 1956, an editorial cartoon proclaimed, "Virgil arrived!"[37] The cartoon showed a young man with a Dominican shield on his uniform leaping into two rings labeled "Big Leagues" while the mascots of the four Dominican teams commented on his great achievement (fig. 1.2). Some in the sports press revealed plans for a special reception to honor Virgil's "definitive triumph in the North, the triumph of a Dominican, one that raises the name of the country very high," while others cautioned their countrymen about Virgil's "slippery" commitment to the country because of his delayed arrival the previous year.[38] This time, Virgil himself confirmed his Dominicanness and his understanding that he carried the Dominican nation with him to the big leagues. As he told *El Caribe*'s sports editor Cuchito Alvarez, "In that moment [playing for the Giants], I was the happiest man in the world because I knew that I was the first professional Dominican player to make it to the Major Leagues."[39] His achievement on the field and acknowledgment of his homeland rehabilitated Virgil as a Dominican hero despite his mixed

Figure 1.2. "Virgil Arrived!," Octavio, *La Nación*, September 26, 1956, p. 9.

nationality, though he still posed a challenge to the regime. Virgil, not Trujillo, carried the Dominican Republic to the major leagues.

When Felipe Rojas Alou, known in the United States as Felipe Alou, joined Virgil in the big leagues in 1958, Dominicans had no need to assert his Dominican identity. Alou had come through the national amateur system, starred on the University of Santo Domingo team, and represented his nation in international competition before signing with the Dominican bird-dog scout Horacio Martínez in 1955.[40] As the "first Dominican player, discovered by a Dominican" to make it to the US major leagues, Alou's ascent represented "a new milestone of the improvement of sport in this Era of Trujillo."[41] All Dominicans could celebrate Alou as one of the "men of healthy minds and bodies" who "gives more brilliance and renown in sporting competitions to the country made great by the Generalísimo Trujillo."[42] A Dominican newspaper cartoon portrayed Alou's success in nationalistic symbols associated with the nation's second-favorite sport, and one enjoyed also by the dictator: horse racing (fig. 1.3). The cartoon depicted two horses relaxing after a hard race. The first horse said, "There's nothing better than throwing back a morsel of fresh herbs after winning a race." The other then proved his greater nationalism by replying, "No, man. What's better is receiving big news, like that about Rojas Alou, who was promoted to the Giants!"[43]

Alou's achievement reshaped the narrative of progress surrounding baseball, attributing success again to Trujillo and coopting Virgil under

Figure 1.3. "Felipe to the Giants!," Octavio, *El Caribe*, June 9, 1958, p. 14.

him. The rise of Alou and Virgil from humble beginnings to international renown became integral to the narrative surrounding Dominicans in US baseball, as was the insistence that they owed their success to Trujillo. Alou, who sacrificed his parents' dream that he become a doctor because his family needed the money provided by a professional baseball contract, rose after Trujillo had provided the structure on which he built a career. He exemplified "the nation aggrandized by the Generalísimo Trujillo."[44] Similar narratives surrounded Virgil's return to the US major leagues in 1958, this time to integrate the Detroit Tigers as the team's first nonwhite player. Calling Virgil a "noble representative of Dominican value in the Big Leagues," one sportswriter stressed his fortitude and persistence despite being undervalued by managers in the Giants organization and facing boycotts by Black fans who demanded the inclusion of African American players on the Tigers team.[45] Like a good Dominican, Virgil's strong religious faith helped him persevere through these challenges as he prayed to God and the Virgin of Altagracia, the national saint, to guide his pursuit of glory. With his moral character, Virgil proved himself a worthy representative of the Dominican nation despite his ties to the United States and Puerto Rico. Sportswriters declared that together, Alou and Virgil made a "pair worthy of representing Dominican baseball in the Big Leagues. They constitute two great examples for the youth being raised in the Glorious Era [of Trujillo] in which the country lives."[46] With the rehabilitation of Virgil's Dominicanness, sportswriters transformed him from a representative of Dominican potential without Trujillo to an example for youths raised in the Trujillo era.

Freeing Baseball

The rise of Dominicans signed in the Dominican Republic to the US major leagues could not have come soon enough for the regime, though even an unquestionably Dominican crop of major leaguers could not save Trujillo's hold on baseball. International political developments undermined his position as an exemplar to the Dominican people. Fidel Castro added another outspoken rival to Trujillo, one who promised arms and support to Trujillo's opposition. By late 1959, Venezuelan president Rómulo Betancourt, who sparred regularly with Trujillo through the press, had replaced the Dominican dictator as the continent's top anticommunist, and the US embrace of his theory that dictatorships of the right fomented communist revolution directly threatened Trujillo's standing. By the time Julián Javier, Rudy Hernández, and Juan Marichal made their major-league debuts in the first half of the 1960 US baseball season, the implications of Betancourt's influence over US policy in Latin America were clear to Trujillo. In August 1960 the United States voted with eighteen other OAS countries—the representatives from Venezuela and the Dominican Republic abstained—to implement economic and diplomatic sanctions against the Dominican Republic for Trujillo's attempt to assassinate the Venezuelan leader and overthrow the government. While the new Dominican big-leaguers provided a temporary bridge with the United States, the 1960–1961 winter season proved the limits of the regime's control over baseball and the narrative of progress surrounding it. The regime asserted its democratic credentials and framed the 1960–1961 professional tournament as a nationalistic victory, but Dominican baseball fans embraced ballplayers, not the dictator, as symbols of Dominican potential and progress.

Preparations for the 1960–1961 tournament began amid excitement over the rise of three new Dominican ballplayers to the US major leagues. After being transferred in the Rule-5 draft from the Pirates to the Cardinals, Julián Javier made his big-league debut on May 28.

Dominicans undoubtedly imagined Javier's quick hands and baserunning as a bridge with St. Louis when they read an editorial titled "Sporting Progress" touting sport as a "powerful force of cohesion and solidarity that reaches beyond territorial limits."[47] Virgil and Alou had raised the Dominican Republic to big-league status, but as the first starter, or everyday player, in the major leagues, Javier ensured that US baseball fans would see a Dominican every day. At the same time that pro-Trujillo and anti-Betancourt rhetoric in the local press signaled the country's declining position in the hemisphere, the press framed their compatriots' rise in sport as "one of the beneficial results of the fruitful peace that the Dominican people enjoy in the glorious Trujillo Era."[48] Rudy Hernández's debut with the Washington Senators on July 3, 1960, and Juan Marichal's fantastic debut just over two weeks later, in which he limited the Phillies to one hit in a complete-game victory for his San Francisco Giants, combined with news of projects to integrate sports into public school activities to make Dominicans confident in the country's sporting progress.[49] With sport, Dominicans believed, "we have already ensured our future."[50]

While ballplayers assured Dominicans of their sporting progress, Betancourt and others in the OAS investigated Trujillo's violations of the organization's nonintervention ideal. The Dominican press countered by portraying the Dominican Republic as *the* exemplary democracy in the region. Racial segregation and discrimination proved easy targets in efforts to discredit the United States. After reading the editorial about the country's sporting progress, sports fans were undoubtedly surprised to read that their compatriots were victims of the "racial problem" in the US South.[51] One sportswriter described the "savagery" (*barbaridad*) that Licey pitcher Julio Antonio "Toñín" Anglada and compatriot Julián Vicente suffered in Florida because of their skin color.[52] Sportswriter and promoter Dr. Manuel Neftalí Martínez followed, reporting that Jesús Rojas Alou and Antulio Martínez Smith, both having exceptional seasons with their Class-D teams, suffered similar difficulties.[53] These Dominican heroes were refused service in some restaurants or forced to sleep in unseemly conditions in undesirable parts of town because of their skin color. Ballplayers also complained that their managers exhibited little concern for their physical well-being: Martínez Smith explained that his manager made him play after a collision on the bases left him with stitches in his leg and injuries to his hand. Even US citizens suffered these abuses, and worse.[54] Martínez

Smith summed up the implications of this treatment: "How different all this is from my country, where no prejudices of any kind exist."[55] Even while the other American countries worked to expel the nation from the democratic brotherhood, Trujillo, as the "maximum leveler of values and of the national classes," exhibited more concern for *all* citizens than his counterparts, even those in the United States, the supposed exemplar of democracy.[56]

Domestic propaganda hailing democracy under Trujillo as the popular will "according to [the people's] specific interests and the experience of their history and social atmosphere" could not protect Dominicans from the impact of the OAS sanctions. They suffered rising unemployment, decreased foreign investment, higher costs for manufactured goods, and depleted baseball rosters.[57] In early September, George Tautman, president of the [US] National Association of Professional Baseball Leagues, wrote to Dominican League president Hipólito Herrera Billini to inquire whether Dominican baseball would continue despite the break in political relations. The press and others took Tautman's question about how the league would ensure the safety of US players—a fair question after Petán Trujillo had slapped Bahamian André Rodgers the previous year and expressed anti-US sentiment in the press—as a statement that US players would not participate in the season.[58] Winter League and team officials expressed their solidarity with the "nationalist policies implemented by the Benefactor of the Nation and Father of the New Fatherland [Trujillo]" in their decision to organize the 1960–1961 Winter Tournament with only Dominican players and umpires.

With little recourse to criticize Trujillo's attempt on Betancourt's life or his authoritarianism, Dominican baseball fans and sportswriters turned to the 1960–1961 natives-only Winter Tournament. Rather than accepting the league's decision about reinforcements, as they usually did with some complaining—and as they had in June when the league announced that each team would be allowed nine foreign reinforcements—sportswriters looked for alternatives to the natives-only tournament.[59] Weeks after the announcement, they suggested that the Dominican teams look to leagues in Mexico, Colombia, and Japan to fill out their rosters. They even suggested that Cuban professionals, many of whom stayed in the United States because major-league baseball commissioner Ford Frick prohibited US players from traveling to Cuba, might reinforce Dominican teams.[60] Regardless of assurances by the league or their own nationalist aspirations to see "genuinely

Dominican professional baseball," sportswriters agreed, "We still lack sufficient ballplayers to form four good teams."[61]

Discussions over the natives-only tournament served as a critique of Trujillo's economic policies and their threat to Dominicans. The lack of Dominican ballplayers prepared to play in the professional leagues was a consequence of the numbers of imported players in previous years, a parallel to the regime's apparent preference for foreign capital and business over Dominican products, except when local industries benefited the dictator.[62] As evident by their rationale, sportswriters were against the natives-only tournament not because they wanted to see US players replace Dominicans but because they believed a more gradual approach was needed to wean the Dominican Winter League from its heavy reliance on imported players. One sportswriter explained, "If a system of gradual reduction of imported players had been adopted since the 1955 season, when we integrated with US Organized Baseball, the policy adopted by the Dominican Professional Baseball League this year would not have produced the confusion noted among national fans, and more still among the directors of our teams."[63] The earlier decision to allow teams to import up to nine players revealed that even league officials were aware of this fact. After declaring in June that the nine reinforcements rule was "the best that can be done [. . .] until, within four or five years more, some native ballplayers come forth with the capacity to occupy some of the reinforced positions," sportswriters and Dominican baseball fans saw the natives-only tournament as a threat to Dominican ballplayers and to Dominican professional baseball more generally.[64]

The unequal distribution of Dominican talent among the four teams illustrated the effects of Trujillo's personalistic policies and how the façade of nationalism in the face of the sanctions threatened the work-arounds the league had developed to protect the national pastime. Although sportswriters attributed inequities to "luck" in their reports, baseball fans knew that Ramfis Trujillo's preference for Escogido, for which his amateur team, Aviación, served as a feeder, had contributed to that team's dominance since 1955.[65] In fact, part of the controversy over Virgil's participation in the Dominican Winter League tournament in 1955 had centered on the Giants' insistence that he play with Escogido, with whom they had signed an agreement just before the season, despite the contract that Virgil had signed with the Aguilas. Although few suspected that the dictator or his family interfered with the outcome of individual games, there was widespread belief that they influenced the distribution of Dominican talent. Regime policies and personal manipulations around contracts to benefit Escogido reflected the same one-on-one relationships and ad hoc decisions that privileged some industrialists over others. By pointing to Escogido's advantage as part of their rationale against the natives-only tournament, sportswriters and fans told the Trujillo regime that it could not have it both ways: Dominicans would not allow the regime to use "nationalism" to secure another ill-gotten victory for Escogido. Dominicans would not stand for politics blatantly threatening the national game.

Despite the long debates between league officials, sportswriters, and fans, the inauguration for the 1960–1961 Winter Tournament followed the usual script, with some extra hammering for the league's nationalism in hiring only native players, umpires, and scorers. Twelve thousand fans flocked to Estadio Trujillo to witness the opening ceremonies—only three quarters the number reported in 1955. After Dominican president Joaquín Balaguer made the symbolic first pitch by handing the ball from his seat in the presidential box to Escogido catcher Rene Marté, league president Hipólito Herrera Billini spoke to the crowd, cheering the "illustrious Benefactor of the Fatherland" for making the tournament possible with his recommendation for a government gift of $100,000 and his wise leadership in creating the sporting policies that had helped more than a hundred Dominican ballplayers develop into professionals.[66] Referring to the rosters filled with native players only, Herrera Billini defended the decision to baseball fans: "We did it persuaded that this is the conduct required, in the current circumstances, by the dignity, patriotism, and loyalty to the politics and the person of our distinguished leader, the Generalísimo Trujillo."[67] The league owed Trujillo.

Dominicans expressed their discontent with baseball's subservience to politics by not attending the games. Deteriorating economic conditions caused by the sanctions and the decreased prospect of seeing future US stars resulted in Dominicans staying home from the ballpark. Announced attendance figures were notable only for their vagueness, with sportswriters dismissing falling numbers as natural. The presence of only twelve thousand fans in the inaugural game, in contrast to the sixteen thousand at the inauguration of Estadio Trujillo in 1955, revealed the truth. In sacrificing the quality of baseball in defense of his "nationalist policies," Trujillo had failed as "Maximum Protector of National Sport" and exposed his declining international reputation.

The 1960–1961 season punctured the popular image of Trujillo as the embodiment of the nation and freed baseball from the dictator's grasp. As the number of their compatriots on major- and minor-league rosters in the United States rose, Dominicans increasingly saw ballplayers as proxies for those who dreamed of the opportunity brought through democracy. They no longer needed Trujillo, and before the start of the next winter baseball season, he was dead.

TWO

Politics at the Plate

The Threat of Communism and the Showcase for Democracy

On November 7, 1962, as Cuban pitcher Pedro Ramos warmed up for the top of the fifth inning against Dominican professional ballplayers, a group of young fans took the field of Estadio Quisqueya in Santo Domingo carrying banners that proclaimed "Fidel 'K'astro ¡Asesino!" (Fidel Castro, Murderer) and "Cuba será Libre" (Cuba will be free).[1] The crowd erupted as more Dominicans, all part of the Juventud Dominicana Cristiana (Dominican Christian Youth), made their way to the pitcher's mound and handed Ramos a Cuban flag. Filled with emotion, Ramos waved his cap above his head, acknowledging the gift and thanking the youths. The crowd of over ten thousand Dominicans, many of them active in the country's own struggle for democracy, escalated their applause for the solidarity that the young Dominicans showed with the exiled Cleveland Indians hurler and his countrymen.[2]

The show of support for Ramos came during the fourth installment of what would be an eight-game exhibition series between a team of Dominican professionals and the visiting Cuban Stars. Taking place as Soviets dismantled nuclear weapons a few hundred miles away in Cuba, the series confirmed Dominicans' commitment to democracy even as their conceptions of what democracy meant shifted. Editorials, reports, and even public announcements about the country's progress toward democracy through late 1962 portrayed democratic society as being founded on widespread political participation and economic opportunity. After the threat of nuclear war became tangible, many Dominicans, like others around the world, lowered their expectations. Over time, they equated democracy with elections, the absence of communism, and stability for economic growth. This shift was not instantaneous, and the press and politicians had frequently cited communism, or what they called "strange and foreign slogans," as a threat to their democratic future even before the Cuban Missile Crisis.[3] But the crisis made the threat of nuclear war real to citizens across the Americas and allowed conservative forces to weaponize anticommunism. As society polarized, accusations of communism were used to discredit moderate reformers or slow their efforts.[4] In the Dominican Republic, the shift from an idealistic vision of democratic society defined by freedom and opportunity to one defined by anticommunism undermined the first democratically elected president in over thirty years: Juan Bosch.

Baseball brought Dominicans together in what would be a defining moment in their political history, in part by obscuring the serious divisions that threatened their democratic future. As Dominicans listened intently to radios and scoured newspapers for information about their three compatriots in the World Series through the first half of October 1962, baseball united them with their American peers in a *magnífico estímulo* of sport and democracy. Welcoming the exiled Cubans two weeks later reinforced Dominicans' commitment to democracy and professional baseball and their rejection of communism while projecting their position to the world. The real work began after Dominicans offered the successful elections as "Our example to America" in December 1962.[5] A sports week and visits by democratic leaders from across the Americas for the inauguration of Juan Bosch on February 27, 1963, kept divisions at bay for a while, but the tensions between Bosch's idealistic democracy and growing anticommunist sentiment undermined the new president's leadership and the country's nascent democracy, preventing the first Dominican winter season under a democratic government from taking place.

Magnífico estímulo

On Friday, October 5, 1962, *El Caribe* proclaimed the World Series appearances of San Francisco Giants Felipe Alou, his brother Mateo "Matty" Alou, and Juan Marichal a "magnificent inspiration (*magnífico estímulo*) to Dominican youth"[6] (fig. 2.1). The epithet appeared on

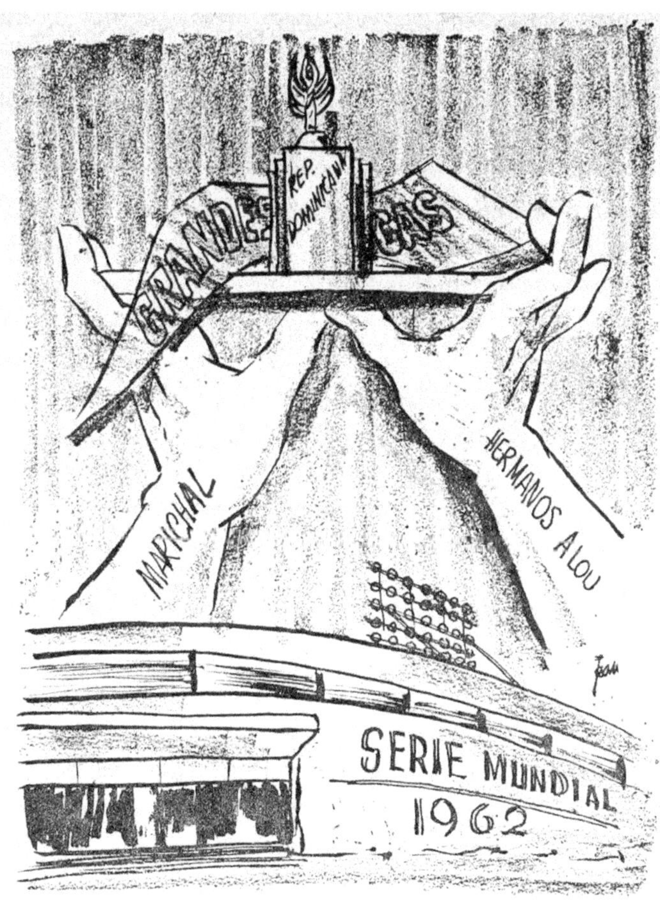

Figure 2.1. "¡Magnífico estímulo!," Jean, *El Caribe*, October 5, 1962, p. 8.

that day's editorial-page cartoon below arms tattooed with "Marichal" and "Hermanos Alou" (Alou Brothers) holding a trophy inscribed "Rep. Dominicana" over a baseball stadium. The cartoon illustrated the common refrain about ballplayers "raising our name high on foreign shores" while the dialogue connected sport and democracy with an allusion to the previous day's editorial, "Estímulo Deportivo" (Sporting Stimulus).[7] Reasoning, like in earlier columns and editorials, that sport has a "singular importance in the achievement of the health of the individual and in the same way of the general health" (of society), *La Nación*'s editors portrayed sport as a means for creating a society that "worked through constant improvement toward perfection."[8] In such a society, the editors continued, the entire public and the government joined together to develop the physical and mental capacities of all citizens. Sport provided the means for this development. All Dominicans shared the obligation of ensuring opportunities for the "constant improvement" of their compatriots, just as they shared the triumphs of their major leaguers. Seeing their ballplayers reach the pinnacle of US baseball, the World Series, at the same time that democracy appeared to be within their grasp united Dominicans in a project to build a future of economic opportunity and widespread political participation.

National ballplayers raising a trophy for their country over Candlestick Park in San Francisco or Yankee Stadium in New York, both sites for the 1962 World Series, illustrated the sporting spirit that united the Dominican Republic and the United States in the struggle for Dominican democracy. The social base for democracy invoked with the references to individual and general health in the *estímulo deportivo* editorial echoed the objectives of the Alliance for Progress, the US-led aid program ratified by the Organization of American States (OAS) in August 1961.[9] All American nations except Cuba agreed to uphold the ideals of the Alliance for Progress, which was defined as a "great cooperative effort" to ensure "maximum levels of well-being, with equal opportunities for all." Together, they would fulfill what US president John F. Kennedy described as the hemisphere's mission to "demonstrate to the entire world that man's unsatisfied aspiration for economic progress and social justice can best be achieved by free men working within a framework of democratic institutions."[10] In the eighteen months since Kennedy announced the Alliance, Dominicans had proved themselves reliable allies in the partnership for democracy and social progress. They had brought Trujillo to justice and sent his family and prominent members of the regime, including the president, Joaquín Balaguer, into exile. As they participated in demonstrations in support of democracy, organized strikes, and demanded better working conditions and wages, Dominicans at all levels of society imagined themselves working with one another, the United States, and most of America to fulfill their democratic destiny.

Elections seemed the only obstacle to Dominicans' bright spot in the hemisphere, and the Giants' one-run loss to the Yankees with Matty Alou just ninety feet from home in Game Seven of the World Series guarded Dominicans against taking victory for granted. With about two months left until December 20, the press warned that the elections were under attack from the left and the right. According to some editors and politicians, *trujillista* forces and the totalitarian left (read Castro) had formed a "diabolical union" ready to seize on the chaos caused by political unrest to crush democracy before it began.[11] In one case, bullets fired by police injured two young people who were allegedly bystanders during a protest in San Pedro de Macorís, the center of the country's sugar industry. To protect elections from these "agents of subversion," editors argued, Dominicans should curtail demands for social reforms and better wages and focus on elections.[12] An editorial published the same day that Dominicans welcomed the Alou brothers and Marichal home called on "the democratic groups, commerce, and industry" to stand up against these agitators or else "we [Dominicans] will fall in chaos and we will return to the tragic days of tyranny and terror."[13] With Castro communism "in our doors, full of fury and enthusiasm," and tied to *trujillismo*, Dominicans had to take care to protect the gains they had made toward democracy, even if it meant stopping short of creating the ideal society they had imagined.

The return of the Alou brothers, Marichal, and forty-three-year-old Licey veteran Guayubín Olivo boosted the national sporting spirit and united the population and Council of State in the project of building democracy despite reports on the violence in San Pedro. Hundreds of Dominicans received the big-leaguers at the airport and carried them on a victory tour to the center of Santo Domingo. Greeting the players at the airport, sports director Bienvenido Hazim Egel recognized the stars' work to "cultivate baseball, making the *deporte rey* a true apostolate," a mission to the nation.[14] The front page of *La Nación* the next afternoon extended the national baseball euphoria to include members of the Council of State by picturing them alongside the ballplayers at the National Palace.[15] Their association with the symbols of national progress legitimated the councilmen's claims to be working for the people and may have suggested that they acknowledged the government's obligation to expand sport. Criticisms swirled around the council's failure to implement social reforms or to effectively squash threats from the left or the right, but baseball buffered them. The council's efforts to prepare the nation for elections was joined with those of the ballplayers on US fields in the project to ensure that "the name of our country resounds in all the World."[16]

Adding to the celebrations to welcome the Dominican big-leaguers, *La Nación* reported the same day that two prominent Dominicans,

George Chottin and Dr. Juan Luis Castellanos, had demonstrated their commitment to building a democratic society by donating land to the government through the Office of the National Director of Sports. Located in the Ensanche Ozama, a working-class development on the east side of the River Ozama, the land would be used to construct fields and courts for baseball, basketball, and tennis. The new installations would extend the opportunity for underprivileged youths to practice sport and to receive the *estímulo deportivo* necessary for democracy. In donating the lands, Chottin and Castellanos, along with two companies that had donated lands earlier, exemplified how more-privileged Dominicans "have joined the national sporting spirit."[17] The sporting spirit obscured the deepening political and class divides that sparked consistent strikes and demonstrations as it projected a unified nation intent on creating a democratic society defined by opportunity.

Hours before Americans across the continent learned of the nuclear weapons in Cuba on October 22, Dominicans marked another step toward democracy: the successful completion of the first party convention. The Partido Revolucionario Dominicano (PRD, Dominican Revolutionary Party) became the first political party to select candidates for president, vice president, and the Senate, as well as for the Chamber of Deputies, which would draft a new constitution. *La Nación*'s editorial page clarified the significance of the convention with a cartoon announcing "El Line-Up del PRD" and showing presidential candidate Juan Bosch as pitcher and his running mate Buenaventura Sánchez as catcher (fig. 2.2).[18] The cartoon showed Bosch in a baseball cap and glove accenting his quintessential white suit, while Sánchez was depicted wearing a chest protector, a glove on his left hand, and a backward cap. Pictured in the accoutrements of the national pastime, the erudite Bosch and bespectacled activist Sánchez became everymen with whom even the most humble Dominicans could identify.

Baseball brought the elections and democratic process to the people, too. Speeches about putting democracy into practice and selecting candidates at party conventions may have gone over many citizens' heads, but seeing the PRD candidates in front of a banner declaring "Play Ball!" signaled to Dominicans that democracy had begun. The arrival of the Cuban Stars a week later extended the feeling of democratic solidarity across the hemisphere, even as the Cuban Missile Crisis hardened the divides among competing visions for the future.

Figure 2.2. "El Line-Up del PRD," Miche Medina, *La Nación*, October 22, 1962, p. 4.

Un No Hit, No Run

The opening game of the Cuban-Dominican series on November 1, 1962, rewarded Dominicans for carrying the sporting spirit through the party conventions and projected their commitment to democracy to the world. Although the eight-game exhibition series could not compensate for sacrificing two winter seasons to free themselves from the Trujillo dictatorship, the camaraderie and goodwill among the seventeen thousand baseball fans in Estadio Quisqueya confirmed that their faith in the national pastime was well placed. Press coverage of the game emphasized the atmosphere "free from divisive problems, from quarrels, and full of fraternity," an attitude that Felipe Alou attributed in part to Dominicans' desperation for baseball.[19] "Even the most rabid of the political reactionaries," he reasoned, "was willing to take an afternoon or two or three away from their submachine guns and hand grenades" to see a baseball game.[20] Denunciations of one candidate by another deepened political divisions as elections approached, but the series offered a salve, a "tension-relieving device" that brought Dominicans together in a show of solidarity behind the democratic project that would culminate in the December 20 elections.[21] As Soviets dismantled nuclear missiles nearby in Cuba, Dominican citizens wrapped the Cuban exiles in the sporting spirit, aligning themselves with the Council of State's promise to "identify itself with the common American ideal and to act like a democratic and sovereign institution."[22] While the American ideal shifted toward anticommunism, Dominicans acted according to their own ideal of a democratic society at the ballpark.

The timing of the announcement that a "Team of Cuban Baseball Stars Will Visit the Country to Play a Series in Front of a Dominican Selection" with warnings of the imminence of nuclear war and Cuba's threat to the continent elevated the series as proof of communism's failures.[23] Falling into their habits of drumming up excitement for the games, Dominican sportswriters stressed that both teams would field the "most brilliant baseball stars." Many of the Cuban Stars were major leaguers, and all had been selected from the historic rivals La Habana and Almendares of the Cuban professional league, which had moved to Miami.[24] The Cuban players' trip from Miami rather than Havana reminded Dominicans that Castro's prohibition of professional sport had forced ballplayers to choose between their livelihood and their homeland—and often their families, too. On his visit to Japan with the Detroit Tigers, shortstop Chico Fernández had expressed concern for his family still in Cuba while warning his compatriot Roberto Barbón, who was playing for a professional team in Japan, against returning home amid the "present crisis."[25] The Missile Crisis threatened the Cuban pastime even for those ballplayers who had chosen to stay on the island. So many ballplayers had been mobilized for military duty that the Cuban sports institute had canceled all ballgames scheduled for the week of October 25, 1962.[26] While Cubans found themselves at the center of an international conflict without baseball, Dominicans glimpsed their democratic future through the glimmer of Cuban and Dominican baseball heroes on local fields.

Figure 2.3. "Un No Hit, No Run," Miche Medina, *La Nación*, October 30, 1962, p. 4.

With Dominicans looking forward to the start of the series, the Council of State marked its first major victory against communism by arresting Máximo López Molina, the leader of the armed wing of the communist party, the Movimiento Popular Dominicano (Dominican Popular Movement), or MPD. On October 30, *La Nación*'s editorial cartoon depicted a showdown between a pitcher wearing a jersey labeled Libertad (freedom) and a hitter in a jersey for Comunismo (communism), with the catcher, Democracia (democracy), pounding his mitt in anticipation (fig. 2.3).[27] In the caption Comunismo lamented: "What a shame! The only run that could have scored was López Molina and they trapped him at third!"[28] Comunismo had threatened democracy and freedom, as investigators confirmed with maps outlining an MPD-Communist attack they found in López Molina's hideout along with a stash of weapons and books by Lenin and Marx.[29] Fortunately, the Council of State had squashed the threat. The title of the cartoon, "Un No Hit, No Run" (a no-hitter), and the pitcher's cool windup and easy smile assured Dominicans that the council protected their path to democracy. With López Molina caught, the team of Libertad and Democracia would surely defeat Comunismo in the Dominican Republic.

Dominican citizens participated in the movement for democracy and against communism that united countries across the hemisphere. Even before members of the Juventud Dominicana Cristiana unfurled the "Cuba será libre" and "Fidel 'K'astro, Asesino" banners on the field, many Dominicans likely saw their own presence at the games as a political act. To many Dominicans, Castro had betrayed his promise for a just society by prohibiting professional sport, the source of livelihood and opportunity for many Cubans. Dominicans offered "signs of care" to the Cuban ballplayers as they followed the play on the field and listened to the Cuban national anthem "with the same reverence with which they listened to [. . .] that of their liberated homeland," to demonstrate their support for the Cuban struggle against Castro.[30]

Dominican fans may have contributed financially to the struggle as well. Many of the Cuban Stars had played in similar exhibitions earlier in the winter to raise money for the Cuban Freedom Cause, a fund intended to sponsor covert operations in Cuba to oust Castro.[31] Documents from the Secretary of Sports archives and Felipe Alou's autobiographies offer evidence that the Council of State and many Dominicans saw the series as a means to fulfill their obligation to "exorcise the threat that now looms over the free peoples of the world" given Castro's violation of "democratic ideals and continental solidarity."[32] Many Dominicans agreed with one exiled Cuban historian who declared: "The fight for the liberation of Cuba [from Castro] is the fight for the consolidation of the freedom that the Dominican Republic just conquered."[33] Financial contributions to the anti-Castro cause supported their own liberation.

As Dominicans celebrated the temporary return of baseball, the political campaign escalated and the lines between communism and *trujillismo* blurred further. Rather than bill democracy as a bulwark against dictatorships of the right or left, many politicians and the press increasingly conflated democracy with anticommunism and anti-*trujillismo*.[34]

Of the five presidential candidates and the slate of prospective senators and deputies presented by eight political parties, Juan Bosch of the PRD and Viriato Fiallo of the UCN, or Unión Cívico Nacional (National Civic Union), were the most prominent.[35] While both candidates called for revolutionary change through democratic means, they differed drastically in their rhetoric and on the question of how to handle *trujillistas*.[36] The UCN joined many other parties in calling for retributive justice against Trujillo's henchmen, financial penalties against those who benefited from the dictator's favors, and exile for suspected *trujillistas* and communists.[37] Bosch, on the other hand, argued for a clean slate, a process of *borrón y cuenta nueva* (erase and start fresh). Acknowledging that many Dominicans accommodated Trujillo as a matter of survival rather than ideology, Bosch argued that there could be no *trujillismo* without Trujillo. The real threat to democracy, he argued, came from *tutumpotes*, wealthy Dominicans who abused the political system to further their personal economic interests, roughly analogous to robber barons, "fat cats," or "the 1 percent" in US history.[38] While Bosch analyzed Dominican problems through an economic and even class lens, Fiallo repeated warnings of an alliance between *trujillismo* and communism. To Fiallo, Dominican democracy required action against "extremist, sectarian, and anti-popular groups obedient to strange and foreign slogans" (read communism). Bosch, on the other hand, rallied Dominicans to build "a new democracy with social justice," one that would address the country's social and economic divides through structural change.[39]

Dominican citizens and ballplayers used fraternal gestures and material actions at the ballpark to create the democracy with social justice that Bosch imagined and Kennedy invoked in his speech to the American states. The Cuban-Dominican series and the inclusion of Dominican ballplayers in the Venezuelan and Puerto Rican winter leagues offered necessary employment as well as essential playing time for Cuban and Dominican players whose winter leagues were sacrificed to political events. As Felipe Alou reminded Dominicans, players less established in US baseball could see their careers delayed by the loss of the winter season.[40] Dominican players and their Latin American colleagues used the winter season to develop themselves with the hope of earning a promotion in the United States. Many also depended on the supplemental income they earned in the winter leagues: "Take away baseball from us in the winter," Alou explained in 1963, "and you take money away from us."[41] While Alou and compatriots like Julián Javier of the St. Louis Cardinals could support their families on their major-league salaries, Dominican players in the minor leagues, like Elvio Jiménez, the younger brother of major-league rookie Manuel Emilio, likely needed the few hundred dollars they earned in the Cuban-Dominican series.

Ballplayers also demonstrated their unity in the American struggle for democracy through their presence at the Cuban-Dominican Series. Sportswriters speculated in October that Puerto Ricans Roberto Clemente, José Pagán, and Orlando Cepeda would help compensate for the Dominican players away in Venezuela and Puerto Rico by reinforcing the Dominican side against the Cuban Stars. Although contract obligations to their Puerto Rican and US teams prevented the Puerto Ricans from suiting up, Clemente watched the opening game of the series from the Dominican bench, providing a visible reminder that the democratic fraternity extended to Puerto Rico.[42]

The Cuban and Dominican players participating in the series brought the spirit of democratic fraternity full circle by donating the proceeds from the final two games to charity. With Dominican aces Marichal and Olivo set to start the games against established major leaguers Camilo Pascual and Pedro Ramos, organizers expected the final games to fill Estadios Quisqueya and Cibao. Despite receiving a stomping in Game Six, the Dominican side led the series 4–2, washing away earlier worries that the division of the Dominican team, with leading players like the younger Alou brothers in Venezuela and Puerto Rico, would undermine their competitiveness. Middle- and upper-class women led by Emilia S. De Tavarez, Esther Sturla, and Nora S. De Hernández had worked through Hazim, the director of sports, to convince the players to give a portion of their pay from ticket sales to help "various groups in charge of realizing works of social assistance in this city [Santo Domingo]."[43] As expected, given the camaraderie that characterized the entire series, "the Cuban as much as the Dominican players proved pleased to be able to contribute to good work of this magnitude."[44] Like the men who had donated lands, the women from the social assistance campaign and the ballplayers embraced sport as a stimulus for building the "society of constant improvement" that would make the Dominican Republic a "showcase for democracy alongside Castro's dismal Cuba."[45]

Dominicans created a microcosm of democracy at the ballpark as fans crowded into Estadios Quisqueya, Cibao, and Tetelo Vargas to express democratic fraternity with one another and the Cuban exiles.

Even the result of the series, a tie at four games each, conveyed the message of goodwill surrounding the tournament and the Cubans' visit. The "good baseball, noisy relaxation and cheers" of the tournament carried Dominicans through the final grueling weeks until elections.[46] Political tensions heightened to such an extent that frontrunner Juan Bosch denounced his candidacy temporarily amid accusations that he was a communist. Anticommunism threatened to replace the ideal democracy characterized by equal opportunity even as Dominicans enacted the democratic ideal at the ballpark. Thanks at least in part to their demonstration of goodwill and the sporting stimulus at the ballpark, Dominicans resisted. On December 20, more than one million citizens went to the polls and cast their votes "without fights, riots or disorder."[47] Baseball had united Dominicans to offer "a demonstration of democratic goodwill in action," which *El Caribe*'s editorial page hailed as "¡Nuestro Ejemplo a América!" (Our Example to America).[48] Dominicans chose democracy—and more than 59 percent of them chose Juan Bosch and his democracy with social justice.[49]

Quien se crea libre de pecado: Bosch and the Opposition

Days before his inauguration brought dozens of leaders from across the Americas and Europe to the Dominican Republic, president-elect Juan Bosch stood on the mound at Estadio Quisqueya and recounted pitching eight scoreless innings as a youth in his hometown of La Vega. His credentials as a good Dominican confirmed by this youthful glory, Bosch asked those in the stands to withhold their criticism of the ugly throw he was about to make. Decades organizing for democracy in exile had kept him from the ballpark, but Bosch assured Dominicans that, with them behind the plate calling the game, the pitches he would soon make from the National Palace would be winners.[50]

Bosch's return to the ballpark contributed to the Semana Deportiva (Sports Week) festivities, which formed part of the program to celebrate Independence Day and the inauguration of the first democratically elected president in decades, both on February 27. A variety of activities immersed Dominicans of all social classes in an atmosphere of goodwill, rewarding them for the successful elections and healing some of the wounds from the hard-fought campaign. The editors at *La Nación* heard in Bosch's speech from the pitcher's mound a message of unity and expressed hope that the president-elect had realized that "many *tutumpotes* gave [him] their vote because they believe in the necessity of and desire that the social and economic reforms that [his] party proposes operate in the country."[51] Dominicans of goodwill, the editors reminded Bosch, exist "in all the social classes and in all the economic levels." To achieve the "transcendental work" of his government and ensure that everyone would win, Bosch just had to follow the advice offered by the editorial's title: "Let them help, Professor!"

The hopefulness and unity that *La Nación*'s editors expressed as Bosch prepared to take the mound for the Dominican Republic belied the divisions among Dominicans and their visions for the country's democratic future. While united in their desire to reach the "place in the sun among the advanced nations of the Americas," which Bosch promised them in his inaugural address, Dominicans, like their peers across the Americas, held different views of what the balance of individual liberties and social justice, or equal opportunity, should be in a democratic society.[52] Bosch and his partisans in Congress worked to devise laws that would secure "not only political democracy but also economic democracy and social justice," while others equated democracy with electoral procedures and policies designed to ensure the stability necessary for economic growth and investment.[53] Still others, those whom Bosch called *tutumpotes*, put their personal economic growth and investment above everything else, including democratic norms and procedures. Sitting in Estadio Quisqueya, where months ago they had embraced the Cuban Stars in democratic fraternity, most Dominicans agreed that the place in the sun included professional baseball and the return of the Tigres del Licey, Leones del Escogido, Aguilas Cibaeñas, and Estrellas Orientales. The unity behind baseball, however, created a mirage that obscured the serious conflicts and manipulations undermining Dominican democracy.

Baseball buffered Dominicans from the polarizing forces of the Cold War to carry out the elections in December. Yet by the time Bosch took office in February 1963, some Dominicans were willing to compromise their democratic ideals for the illusion of stability promised by anticommunism.[54] Others, including those who accused Bosch of being a communist during the campaign, likely favored this route even before the Cuban Missile Crisis and the Cuban-Dominican series made the dangers of communism tangible. Despite the lack of a real communist threat in the Dominican Republic by 1963, fears of communism had grown to the extent that Bosch's opposition—especially the so-called *tutumpotes*—successfully weaponized communism to undermine his leadership. The baseball metaphors and images used to project Dominicans' shared desire for democracy and social justice began to reveal the gradual conflation of anticommunism with democracy. By diminishing public confidence in the president, raising the specter of communism, and possibly obstructing the 1963–1964 winter baseball season, a group of Dominicans moved by economic interest and possibly by genuine fears of communism limited Bosch's presidency to seven months.

After celebrating the country's example to the Americas with the election, political coverage in the Dominican press returned to a civic-education tone in the month leading to the inauguration. Columnists and opinion writers offered advice to citizens, leaders of the political opposition, PRD leaders, and the president-elect about their roles in a democracy. Contributors to the op-ed pages emphasized the stakes of the PRD's and Bosch's success: Bosch's failure would destroy Dominican faith in democracy and thereby lead to the rise of communism.[55] Their warnings against communism allowed editors, columnists, and other contributors to establish their conformity to the democratic project and conveyed their advice and even criticism of Bosch and the PRD government as democratic discourse. Beneath the surface, however, their intentions were less pure. At least one industrialist based in the capital told historian Frank Moya Pons that members of the business class organized with the express purpose of ousting Bosch. The affiliation of newspaper owners, including Germán Ornes of *El Caribe,* with this group suggests that articles and cartoons published on the op-ed pages had layers of meaning intended to undermine Bosch.[56] According to Cuban intellectual Eliades Acosta Matos, these articles and images formed part of a media war, possibly coordinated with the CIA, intended to oust Bosch.[57] Even if Acosta Matos's thesis was exaggerated, the articles' use of faint praise, the guise of offering advice to Bosch and PRD leaders, and raising the specter of communism warrant consideration of these destructive alternative interpretations.

Although the congratulatory tone in the "Let them help, Professor" editorial might legitimate the advice that Bosch "let [the tutumpotes] help," it also exemplified how editorials and images used faint praise and manipulated Bosch's terms to undermine confidence in the PRD government. On the surface, the editorial suggested that Bosch had embraced Dominicans of goodwill from "all the social classes and in all the economic levels." However, the editorial misappropriated the term *tutumpotes* by applying it to any member of the business or industrial classes. By suggesting that some *tutumpotes* had voted for Bosch because of their goodwill and commitment to reform, the editors at *La Nación* directly contradicted Bosch's use of the term. Bosch applied the term to the same opponents of democracy that earlier editorials had identified as "accomplices of trujillista barbarities" but now "call themselves revolutionaries" to advance their personal interests.[58] Rather than bolstering unity, then, the editorial recalled what one columnist had described as "bile and bitterness" in Bosch's hard rhetoric and criticisms of *tutumpotes.*[59] In doing so, the editorial intimated that the president-elect, not those willing to sacrifice democracy for personal interests, threatened Dominicans' democratic future. Pointing to this earlier rhetoric and the PRD's stated objective to raise the standard of living for the working and middle classes left Bosch and the government he oversaw open to accusations of dividing the country and, in some cases, of having secret communist ties.

Baseball provided a cover of unity to messages in editorials and cartoons that undermined public confidence in Bosch and the PRD. During the first month of Bosch's presidency, editors and columnists urged patience with the new government. After a series of radio announcements and letters denounced Bosch and his party, a cartoonist at *La Nación* pictured the president at home plate with a bat, while players with uniforms labeled "UCN" and "Opposition" hurled warm-up tosses in the background, suggesting that the opposition was active and ready to challenge the new president (fig. 2.4). The label "San Juan Bosch" (Saint Juan Bosch) and the title of the cartoon, "La Oración" (The Prayer), reiterated the biblical reference in the dialogue in which Bosch exclaimed, "Let he who is without sin throw the first ball!"[60] In the context of the editorials about healthy opposition and democratic governance in the first three weeks of Bosch's presidency, many Dominicans likely received a fairly straightforward message from the editorial: the new president would make mistakes, yes, but he was the person that Dominicans chose to go to bat for them. Others likely picked up on the tongue-in-cheek reference to Bosch's saintliness and interpreted it as a dismissal of the opposition, a democratic sin of which Bosch had been accused. This message boosted accusations of Bosch's demagoguery and egoism. Amid articles urging patience with the new government and others warning of com-

La Oración

BOSCH: Quien se crea libre de pecado, que tire la primera bola!

Figure 2.4. "La Oración," *La Nación*, March 21, 1963, p. 4.

munist plots, even those Dominicans who read the cartoon as assurance that the president was going to bat for them likely felt insecure in the country's democratic future.

Reminders of the challenges facing the new president served as a check on Dominicans' optimism and perhaps on their expectations as well. Even seemingly mundane political reports reminded Dominicans of the challenges Bosch faced. A front-page article from Henry Raymount of the United Press International (UPI) published the weekend after the inauguration began as a routine report on the new president's plan to reduce "luxurious salaries" for public officials before offering a subtle evaluation of Bosch's ability to handle the threats to Dominican democracy.[61] In addition to "grave economic, fiscal, and political problems," the country faced the "incessant propaganda from neighboring Castroist Cuba" encouraging local leftists to rebel. The article stressed Bosch's independence in the face of US influence, including his "reticence" regarding the Alliance for Progress because of its slow implementation, and his attitude toward communism. Bosch's unwillingness to embrace the Alliance for Progress as a panacea contrasted with a UPI report published on *El Caribe*'s front page the next day, which quoted former Colombian president Alberto Lleras Camargo's opinion that the Alliance for Progress was the "only way to combat communism."[62] Despite the challenges he faced, Bosch appeared to be taking a challenging course by rejecting US support. His unique attitude toward communism, which contrasted with that of other leaders from the democratic left such as José Figueres of Costa Rica and Rómulo Betancourt of Venezuela, concerned US leaders. Although Raymount suggested Bosch's colleagues believed that "he will realize a more effective anticommunist campaign than many others that denounce the regime of Fidel Castro," his prediction that Bosch would depart from US policy if he felt it necessary left the new president vulnerable to accusations that this attitude undermined the Dominican Republic's economic security.

Within weeks of Bosch's inauguration, commentators confronted the new president's policies toward communism directly and repeated accusations that Bosch had allowed communists to infiltrate the government. On March 13, Mario Bobea Billini used his column in *El Caribe* to ask Bosch to align himself more clearly with the anticommunism of his colleagues from Costa Rica and Venezuela. Although Bosch's plans to develop infrastructure with US and Swiss backing clarified his capitalist credentials, Bobea Billini explained, his appeasement [*apaciguamiento*] of local communists had paralyzed local investment.[63] The same day, *El Caribe* made front-page news of Bosch's definition of communism as "death, war, destruction, and the loss of all our property" during a speech directed at Dominican troops. Bobea Billini had likely written his March 13 column before Bosch addressed the armed forces, but he picked up the narrative in his next column, printed two days later. Bobea Billini offered faint praise of Bosch's statement and conceded that it had eased tensions. However, the advice he offered to the president elevated the perceived threat of communism by repeating rumors that Bosch had appointed "known Marxist acolytes and theorizers" to high government posts as though they were facts. With his request that Bosch act more decisively to protect Dominicans from communists in student organizations at the Universidad Autónoma de Santo Domingo (UASD), a local high school, and even in the government, Bobea Billini undermined public confidence in Bosch's ability to protect Dominican democracy from communist organizers.[64]

Accusations of partisanship against Bosch and the PRD and fears over communism converged during the project to write a new constitution. The PRD's decisive victory in the December 20 elections, and especially winning 49 of the 74 seats in the Cámara de Diputados (Chamber of Deputies), whose members served in the Constitutional Assembly, raised fears that the PRD would abuse its power. After one UCN member publicly resigned from the assembly over frustrations with the PRD majority only one week after the inauguration, Viriato Fiallo, the defeated presidential candidate, expressed his unease over the "current situation in the country."[65] His fears escalated over the next week, after what he described as a "mob [*turba*] reminiscent of those used by the liquidated dictatorship" attacked a political radio program.[66] Fiallo's comparison drew a straight line between the PRD and the Trujillo dictatorship. Accusations by UCN deputies in the Constitutional Assembly that PRD deputies were "steamrolling" the opposition to pass their own policies boosted Fiallo's claim.[67] Given the "dictatorial character by which [the UCN] ideas are drowned," the deputies argued, the assembly would not produce the revolutionary constitution to which they all aspired. By amplifying these accusations, reports on the assembly effectively countered the image of the PRD as heroes of the people that had been so prevalent during the campaign.

This accusation reported on March 13 directly contradicted the hopefulness an *El Caribe* editorial and cartoon had conveyed three days earlier regarding the constitutional project. Titled "Signo Reconfortante" (Comforting Sign), the editorial reported that deputies of both parties in the Constitutional Assembly had been reasonable and cooperative in their negotiations, "acting more like Dominicans than like party-men."[68] A cartoon two days later, or one day before Fiallo's accusation against the PRD, depicted this "good example" as a man in a steamroller waving to a small car representing the minority ahead of him.[69] Although the steamroller stopped in this case, the cartoon clarified the opportunity for abuse and primed readers for the accusations levied by the UCN deputies that the constitution would be a steamroller over Dominican freedom. The contradictory messages so close together and the continuity of symbols exemplified the subtle warnings masked as faint praise that Acosta Matos associated with the media war against Bosch.

Despite accusations of PRD abuses, the Constitutional Assembly completed the constitution of 1963. As the assembly made final revisions to the draft through April, *El Caribe*'s editors and even owner Germán Emilio Ornes referenced the Trujilliato in their criticisms of constitutional articles. On April 21, *El Caribe*'s front page announced that the assembly had completed its work and submitted a final draft for President Bosch's approval. That day's editorial, "The New Constitution," confirmed the democratic origins of the constitution and the selection of the assembly while offering dog whistles at earlier criticisms of amendments they had called dictatorial. The cartoon published next to the cautious celebration of the new constitution depicted these criticisms and referenced a long editorial published the day before that had verged on ridiculous. The editors denounced the addition of a paragraph "against the intervention of foreign people, government, or military forces in the country's political matters" to Article 95, which defined the nation as a representative democracy where sovereignty resided with the people. According to the editors, the amendment, like others, was of "irrefutable authoritarian character [and] could be used to legalize situations that are normally considered contrary to the rights of human dignity."[70] Without quoting the new paragraph, the editors went to great lengths to explain that prohibiting foreign intervention might impede Dominicans' rights to seek outside help should they need to overthrow a dictator. As evidence of the necessity of foreign assistance, they pointed to the help that American allies and the international press had offered in the struggle against Trujillo, though they never acknowledged that collaboration against the regime was against the constitution of the time. Apparently, they expected a democratic constitution to offer a legal path for an outside nation to intervene in and even help to overthrow a government founded according to its principles.

Even though they were ridiculous, the criticisms served their purpose of undermining popular support for Bosch, the PRD government, and the democratic possibilities enshrined in the constitution of 1963. Doubts over the abilities of Bosch and the PRD majority to lead them to the place in the sun increased as Dominicans read of the possibly communist consequences of laws such as the Confiscations Law passed in September 1963 and the obstacles to the preparations for the 1963–1964 winter baseball season.

Communism, Coups, and Winter Baseball

As the US baseball season closed and Dominican pitcher Juan Marichal completed his twenty-eight-win season, debates about the constitution continued. The debates reflected the growing divergence between Bosch and the opposition over the meanings of democracy. While for Bosch democracy centered on social protection for individual freedoms and opportunity, those in the opposition continued to argue for the centrality of economic growth and strong anticommunist policies to secure it. Earlier criticisms of Bosch's refusal to take a strong stance against communism continued in September and escalated to the level of a general strike. Debates over the Confiscations Law, which proposed a model for redistributing land under agrarian reform, and the increasing impatience of industrialists regarding Bosch's reluctance to pass a law for industrial incentives seemed to offer further evidence of his communist sympathies and economic ineptitude. The press assisted the industrialists in making this case with reports that Dominicans had lost faith in their government, and possibly in democracy itself, because the president had not solved their problems in his six months in office. As the accusations against Bosch became more explicit and threatening, reports suggesting that Dominican big-leaguers had not been granted permission to participate in the Winter Tournament possibly proved the last straw. Whether the opposition attacked baseball directly or the PRD government overlooked permissions, Bosch's inability to provide Dominicans with professional baseball cast doubt over his ability to lead a democratic revolution.

Through the first half of September, debates over laws developed in line with the constitution of 1963 stoked fears of communism and Bosch's refusal to prohibit it. The Confiscations Law drafted in early September outlined how the government could confiscate land from large holdings (*latifundias*) acquired through questionable means during the Trujillato. As expected for a program developed in line with the Alliance for Progress, the law included details about compensation for confiscated land. Still, *El Caribe*'s editors and contributors equated confiscations with a threat to private property. In a particularly vehement denunciation, the paper's editors called the law a "repugnant political weapon" that would leave no one safe once it began. They provoked paranoia by equating PRD policies with those in Cuba, where Castro's government "began confiscating the goods acquired unjustly by Batista's collaborators and ended up completely denying the right to private property."[71] For businessmen like those represented in *El Caribe*'s pages, private property was an essential right protected by democratic governments. Democracy, to them, meant protection for private property and support for industrialization, ultimately raising the standard of living for all citizens.

Given Bosch's support among the popular classes and rural Dominicans, the intended beneficiaries of agrarian reform, *El Caribe*'s editors turned to baseball to portray their position as public opinion. The cartoon published the following day illustrated the public's rejection of the Confiscations Law. In the cartoon, a man representing the *diputados* (deputies, or representatives) took cover as a furious bat labeled "Opinión Pública" (Public Opinion) swatted a baseball labeled "Ley Confiscaciones" (Confiscations Law) back to him (fig. 2.5).[72] An analogy to the *diputados* pitching the law to the public and having it rejected, the cartoon suggested consensus behind the previous day's conclusion that "this [Confiscations Law] was not democracy."[73]

Despite stark differences in opinion across Dominican society, baseball projected a common voice for what democracy meant and the government's role in protecting it. *El Caribe*'s editors believed in the democratic revolution and even appropriated its rhetoric in critiques of the constitution or the government. In contrast to Bosch's insistence that economic policies must benefit "the great masses," the business class placed primacy on the government's obligation to provide "a framework of economic progress *for all the classes* that make up Dominican society."[74] Where the editors saw threats to private property, Bosch and the PRD saw a plan to redress the personalism and favors of the Trujillo era by reforming the structures that continued to concentrate wealth in the hands of a few. This more constructive vision of democracy would allow those Dominicans with less opportunity to rise on their own. Business leaders saw this belief as evidence that Bosch was an "impractical dreamer and dangerously leftist liberal, if not worse."[75] *El Caribe*'s cartoon made criticisms against Bosch and the PRD appear as democratic discourse while also undermining public confidence in the democratic government.

Figure 2.5. "Confiscations Law," *El Caribe*, September 6, 1963, p. 10.

As the major-league season wrapped up in the United States, Dominicans eagerly awaited news of the 1963–1964 Winter Tournament. The achievements of Dominicans in the United States heightened their excitement as Marichal became the third Latin American pitcher to win twenty games and Jesús, the youngest of the Alou brothers, became the eighth Dominican big-leaguer. Not all news was good news, however. On the same day that the cartoon against the Confiscations Law appeared, Dominicans saw the first sign of danger for the 1963–1964 season. *El Caribe* reported that the Estrellas Orientales and Licey owed $1,415.60 and $500, respectively, to the National Association in the United States.

Unless they paid the balance said to be owed for the rights to imported players and office expenses from the 1960–1961 season, the teams would not be allowed to import Dominican or foreign players associated with US baseball.[76] Curiously, the 1960–1961 season had been the natives-only tournament organized under Trujillo, and the article offered no explanation for why Dominican teams had to pay such a price for a Dominican-only season. Reports the next day that the Estrellas had signed five reinforcements and that Licey had signed St. Louis Cardinals coach Vern Benson to manage the team suggested business as usual, but the earlier news put the winter season into question.[77]

Knowing the significance of winter baseball to Dominicans' democratic future, Bosch took matters into his own hands to ensure that Dominican big-leaguers would participate in the 1963–1964 Winter Tournament. On September 10, as *El Caribe*'s editors continued their denunciations of the Confiscations Law ahead of a public debate, the paper summarized a letter from Bosch to the presidents of four major-league teams requesting their permission for twelve of the best Dominican players, including Marichal, Javier, and the three Alou brothers, to participate in the Winter Tournament. The article made no explicit connections to the earlier report about the Estrellas and Licey's debt to the National Association; nor did it suggest why Bosch felt it necessary to step in. Bosch likely saw the letter as an opportunity to demonstrate his support for the national pastime and his understanding that "it is indispensable that the Dominican people see their best ballplayers participating in this tournament."[78] The letter assured Dominicans that they could count on the president to interpret their desires and pursue their interests, but it also likely raised the question of why the leader of a sovereign democracy would have to negotiate with US business owners to ensure that Dominican ballplayers could compete on their home fields.

Beyond the public eye, the questions over the participation of Dominican big-leaguers likely resulted from foot-dragging on the part of Winter League teams and officials, many of whom belonged to the business class opposed to Bosch. Despite Bosch's instructions in July that the minister of finance send funds to the Winter League, *El Caribe* reported on September 24, the day before Bosch was ousted, that US baseball commissioner Ford Frick had not yet received the dues. Meanwhile, the Aguilas liaison with the Pittsburgh Pirates, who handled the Santiago-based team's relationship with US baseball, claimed that the fee had been deposited.[79] Without the fees, no major-league players, regardless of their nationality, would be allowed to suit up for Dominican teams.[80] Although league and team officials appeared to work with Bosch in July, by September their actions were more tentative. Perhaps they distrusted Bosch's pledges of support, or maybe they knew of plans for Bosch's ouster and delayed payment to the National Association to protect against losses should a popular uproar after a coup require the cancellation of another baseball season. The desperation many likely perceived in Bosch's appeals to US team presidents and the persisting questions over whether they would see national stars in the tournament undermined Dominicans' faith that Bosch could oversee the return of the *deporte rey*, let alone lead the democratic revolution they expected.

The foot-dragging by Winter League officials coincided with an escalation in confrontations with Bosch. Two days after *El Caribe* reported on the letters to the US team presidents, another letter, this one addressed to Bosch, deflated popular hope for a democratic future.[81] The men and women who signed the letter blamed Bosch's permissiveness toward communists for the lack of jobs and slow economic progress since elections. "[The Communist Party's] presence in our Fatherland," the letter warned, had already limited employment, dissuaded capital investments, and contributed to the loss of international credit. Unless Bosch acted quickly to push communist sympathizers underground, the letter writers would "take our own, efficient, and definitive actions."[82] The names of women on the letter likely heightened the immediacy of the request by suggesting that Bosch's refusal to expel communists, whom the press had equated with disruption and violence, endangered Dominican families.[83]

Less than two weeks later, the Dominican military imprisoned Bosch in the National Palace and forced him to resign. The National Police ransacked the headquarters of the PRD and so-called leftist groups the morning after the coup, detained protesters, and announced the upcoming arrest and deportation of a handful of other Dominicans suspected of having communist or Cuban ties the next morning.[84] They took these precautions to prevent an uprising against the violation of the public will, but *El Caribe* and other newspapers had forestalled unrest. In the days before the coup, they had declared Dominicans "only defeated" and ambivalent toward democracy because of their lack of economic progress since the elections. The national camaraderie in anticipation of democracy that carried Dominicans through the Cuban-Dominican Series and the Semana Deportiva endured for less than seven months.[85]

Conclusion

As Dominicans worked to ensure a democratic future in the country, baseball united them in a common purpose. They celebrated their compatriots' success and the opportunities professional baseball provided as they followed the 1962 World Series and cheered their baseball heroes when they arrived in Santo Domingo. Baseball provided Dominicans with language and symbols for expressing their hopes for democracy, measuring their potential, and demonstrating their preference for the US model of democracy over Cuba's communism. Professional baseball in particular provided the means for individual economic progress and offered a stimulus for democratic society.

The coup against Juan Bosch and the PRD government revealed baseball's limitations to unite the country and the propensity for the sport's meanings to be manipulated. Dominicans united with one another and their American peers to achieve the "maximum levels of well-being, with equal opportunities for all" in a democratic revolution bolstered by the Alliance for Progress.[86] But, as the editors at *El Caribe* demonstrated and the members of the Consejo de Hombres de Negocios told Frank Moya Pons, baseball obscured serious, even fatal, disagreements over the relative weight the government should provide to civil liberties versus economic protections. Especially after the Cuban Missile Crisis brought the nuclear threat to the Americas, Dominicans increasingly opted for anticommunism over building a democratic future.

Professional baseball exemplified the tensions between these competing expectations for democracy domestically as well as internationally. In the Dominican Republic, Winter League organizers used their influence over professional baseball to prevent Bosch from organizing the first Dominican Winter League tournament formed in a democracy. Their influence over the national pastime proved a powerful weapon but paled in comparison to baseball officials in the United States. As Dominicans read of preparations for the Winter Tournament under the new Triumvirate government implanted by the coup, sportswriters reported on Felipe Alou's discontent with major-league baseball, including a threat that he might retire at age thirty. Alou's discontent centered on the fines baseball commissioner Ford Frick had charged to all participants in the Cuban-Dominican Series in November 1962. Alou's call for a liaison to give Latin American players a stronger voice in US baseball revealed the gaps between the meanings that Dominican citizens or players and US officials assigned to baseball and democracy as well as the potentially fatal outcomes of these misunderstandings. Alou's activism and the promises of baseball sustained Dominicans in their democratic ideal and inspired them to once again sacrifice a baseball season to build the democracy with social justice they had sought when they freed baseball from Trujillo.

THREE

Criticizing Baseball, Debating Democracy

On the morning of Wednesday, October 23, 1963, the front-page headline "Olivo Guides Team Licey to Triumph" greeted Dominicans as they sipped their morning coffee or picked up a newspaper on their way to work. The night before, Licey's veteran southpaw Diómedes "Guayubín" Olivo had dominated the Estrellas Orientales hitters and even batted in the winning runs as he led the Tigers to a 2–0 victory in the 1963–1964 Dominican Winter League opener. Sportswriters invested the game with biblical proportions, as in a sports-page cartoon likening Guayubín's two-RBI hit against his younger brother Federico "Chichí" to the fatal blow that Cain gave his brother Abel (fig. 3.1).[1]

Though Dominican sportswriters often used biblical or other allusions in their descriptions of baseball games, the biblical terms they applied to the 1963–1964 Dominican Winter League season opener went beyond hyperbole. One month before Guayubín batted down his little brother, Dominicans living under the first democratically elected president in three decades had looked to the new winter season as a return to normality and an end to the turmoil that had undermined the Winter Tournaments since 1960. OAS sanctions against Trujillo prevented US players from participating in the tournament in 1960–1961, curfews and unrest caused the premature end of the 1961–1962 season, and the 1962–1963 season had been canceled over fears of disorder. Even before the military ousted Juan Bosch on September 25, 1963, politics had

Figure 3.1. "History Repeats with Guayubín and Chichí: Cain Killed His Brother Abel," Miche Medina, *El Caribe*, October 24, 1963, p. 6.

threatened the 1963–1964 season. Yet, despite regular demonstrations at the Autonomous University of Santo Domingo (UASD, Universidad Autónoma de Santo Domingo) and demands for the return to constitutionality, the Triumvirate, a de facto civilian government that took over from the military shortly after the coup, passed the first test of Dominican political leadership by securing the return of baseball in time for the October 22 opener.

Baseball continued to serve Dominicans as an expression of their democratic aspirations, even after the military stifled their voices by deposing the democratically elected president. The coup had exposed baseball's limitations as a beacon of unity and progress, laying bare the many different meanings their compatriots, along with their peers from across the Americas, had projected onto the national pastime. The biblical significance that *El Caribe*'s writers projected onto the season openers compensated for the ambivalence many Dominicans likely felt toward the professional tournament. Baseball returned, yes, but not under the democracy they had expected when they welcomed the Cuban exiles before the December 1962 elections. While the civilian

Triumvirate used baseball to build its legitimacy and consolidate control by projecting normality and order, Dominicans continued to debate what democracy should be in their country and to expose fractures in the American democratic and baseball fraternity they had celebrated in the Cuban series in 1962.

This chapter will examine the gap in the meanings of baseball and democracy held by members of the Triumvirate and its supporters, who accepted democracy as anticommunism, and other Dominicans who maintained the social democratic ideal. Confrontations between these understandings took place around professional baseball and ultimately manifested as criticism against the Dominican Winter League, Dominican ballplayers, and the US major leagues. While baseball helped to sustain the democratic ideal even after the coup, the confrontations around the national pastime also revealed the deep divisions in Dominican understandings of democracy.

Baseball, Normality, and the Triumvirate

The Triumvirate government quickly set out to legitimate itself and to establish a sense of normality, using baseball to boost the de facto government internationally and at home. The Triumvirate proved its competence by securing permission for Dominican players to play in the Winter League and arranging competitions with the Venezuelan and Puerto Rican leagues, even though Venezuela and the United States had severed diplomatic relations with the Dominican Republic after the coup. As in 1961–1962, editorials dismissed demands for a return to constitutionality by cautioning that instability might lead to a civil war and dictatorship of the extreme right or extreme left.[2] The return of baseball and the performance of Dominican big-leaguers like Juan Marichal provided Dominicans with a positive outlet, and they resigned themselves to the Triumvirate government with the understanding that it was only temporary.

The cast of characters from *El Caribe*'s "Cartoon of the Day" (La Caricatura de Hoy) marched triumphantly to their position on the sports pages only two weeks after the coup (fig. 3.2). In the cartoon, the mascots of each team (with an elephant standing in for the Estrellas), the Fucú, or curse, depicted as a rotund bald man who guarded the basement, and the Crow, who delivered the punchline, announced the return of baseball: "Greetings, Fans! Here we are again, ready for the fight!"[3] The

Figure 3.2. "Greetings, Fans!," Miche Medina, *El Caribe*, October 9, 1963, p. 15.

cartoon projected normality to Dominican readers and the confidence that team partisanship would replace the debate over the violation of constitutionalism perpetrated by the military and the new government.

The return of Dominican ballplayers and the trash talk and flaming of rivalries in the sports pages heightened the feelings of normality and national pride. After securing his reputation among the best Latin American pitchers of all time with a 25–8 record in 1963, Juan Marichal carried a no-hitter into the seventh inning against the Estrellas Orientales in his return to the Winter League. Marichal struck out nine in a complete-game shutout that led one columnist to proclaim him worthy of the title of "honorary doctor."[4] Questions over the success of the 1963–1964 tournament faded as Escogido took first place in the standings with their eternal rival Licey following close behind. A cartoon taunting Licey fans invoked Marichal's mastery as the capital-based teams prepared for their first matchup (fig. 3.3). Escogido's lion mascot was depicted flashing Marichal's photo to Licey's tiger, telling him, "Look, Rat Hunter, you know this guy, the one pictured here, eh? That's your daddy. . . . The one who will give you a pow-wow [spanking]

Figure 3.3. "Marichal's Spanking," Miche Medina, *El Caribe*, October 28, 1963, p. 14.

tomorrow!"[5] The tiger could only gulp and ask the lion to stop scaring him. With the season under way, the comfortable banter and feats of the national pastime diverted attention from the Triumvirate's illegitimacy.

Baseball united Dominicans once again as ballplayers returned the warmth with which fans showered them and demonstrated why athletes were considered "examples for the youth who wish to be healthy in mind and body."[6] Marichal exemplified this camaraderie, appearing in relief on four days' rest to surprise the 14,377 gathered at Estadio Quisqueya for Juan Marichal Night.[7] Well-known sports promoter Pedro Justiano explained that his group, the Fraternity of Sportswriters of the Press and Radio, had organized the event because of the popular demand to express support for Marichal. Marichal exemplified the humility and gratitude that fans and sportswriters expected from national ballplayers with his surprise appearance and by receiving the gifts presented by Justiano "with the excitement of a poor boy receiving his first toy."[8] Like Marichal, who "spoke with his pitches in the simple but effective language of the Dominican people," ballplayers continued to represent Dominican potential abroad and provide a *magnífico estímulo* for those who sought a place in the sun at home.

The successful start for the winter season eased many of the reservations that Dominicans held over the Triumvirate's ability to govern. Sportswriters stressed the Triumvirate government's actions to arrange the baseball season during the weeks between the coup and season opener. In his column "Sports Update" (El Deporte al Día) a few days before Olivo's first pitch, *El Caribe*'s Rafael Martorell credited the "good understanding of the men who direct the destiny of the country" and the work of league officials for organizing the Winter Tournament.[9] Members of the Triumvirate had demonstrated their familiarity with the Dominican people by offering their "best economic cooperation" to provide an extraordinary winter season. The Triumvirate's economic support not only ensured that Dominicans would see the fierce battles they expected among the four traditional teams but also secured plans for an International Series featuring exchanges between Dominican and Venezuelan teams. The political stability projected by the Triumvirate and its economic assistance would make the 1963–1964 season a "great sporting reality."[10]

Reports of the Triumvirate's efforts to organize the Winter Tournament contrasted with the pleas Bosch had made to US team presidents in early September. The circumstances of the article in which Bosch explained the government's need to organize a baseball tournament with native big-leaguers suggested the Dominican executive's desperation: such a request seemed below the station of a national leader.[11] The Triumvirate, by contrast, had secured the participation of the national big-leaguers with no public pleas, and this despite the United States breaking diplomatic relations. Although Bosch had secured funding for the 1963–1964 season and even arranged the interleague games with Venezuelan and Puerto Rican teams, his efforts were forgotten by early October. The "good understanding of the men who direct the destiny of the country," not Bosch, made the tournament extraordinary.

The Triumvirate's legitimacy required that Bosch's PRD government be completely discredited and portrayed as inept. In addition to hyping the Triumvirate's efforts to return professional baseball to the island, the National Palace press director published regular denunciations against the Bosch regime. Dominicans who followed the story of Guayubín Olivo's opening-day dominance of the Estrellas encountered a full-page announcement "to public opinion," paid for by the National Palace press director, as they turned to *El Caribe*'s sports section.[12] The article mocked those who opposed the coup and backed its hostility with supposed evidence of Bosch's interactions with Cuban communists and discussions of communist literature in the late 1950s. These interactions between Bosch and alleged communists, which included contacts with Fidel Castro before the Cuban Revolution, led the author to conclude, "The Armed Forces of the Dominican Republic did well to take the grave decision of expelling from Power a leader that allowed, with his dogmatic permissiveness, communist penetration in the country."[13] Rather than criticize the armed forces for violating their constitutionally mandated subordination to civilian rule, the article invented communist ties and praised the military as "the safeguard of the Fatherland, of its Institutions, that would disappear if the Nation fell into the hands of a communist dictatorship."[14] This article and others like it turned questions about the Triumvirate's legitimacy on their head. The military had indeed ended an elected, constitutional government by ousting Bosch. But the PRD government, not the de facto government that now ruled, was called a threat to Dominican interests and institutions.

Baseball also helped resolve contradictions in the Triumvirate's claims by showcasing support for the regime from other democratic nations even as they withheld formal recognition. The US and Venezuelan governments implicitly endorsed the Triumvirate, if not the coup, by granting permission for their citizens to play baseball in the Dominican Republic and allowing Dominican players to travel to their countries. Baseball agreements offered a way around politics, a means to separate public diplomacy—the effort to win citizens' hearts and minds for their version of democracy—from political realities.[15] The Venezuelan Winter League had allegedly pressured its own government to concede travel permissions by threatening to boycott exchanges with other national circuits. The Venezuelan league reasoned that the International Series was "merely sporting competition that has nothing to do with politics."[16] By pushing forward with the baseball exchanges that originated under the PRD government, however, these private entities legitimated the Triumvirate. The argument that the exchanges had nothing to do with politics provided a convenient excuse for their actions. Dominican sportswriters who credited the "men who direct the destiny of the country" for making the Winter Tournament extraordinary with "international repercussions" revealed the lie.[17] Even as the Venezuelan and US governments refused recognition in a show of democratic principles—and their adherence to the Betancourt Doctrine that prohibited relations with any government imposed by military coup—business interests in the nations endorsed and legitimated the Triumvirate through baseball.

The 1963–1964 Winter Tournament was not the first time that US baseball officials pushed or anticipated US international policy with the Dominican Republic. A similar situation had occurred during the 1961–1962 season, when baseball officials granted permission for US players to participate in the Winter Tournament despite the political and social turmoil following Trujillo's death. The situation in 1961–1962 was more dangerous than in 1960–1961, when the players had been refused permission, but the later tournament, which had to be abandoned because of social unrest, happened under a democratizing regime backed by the United States. US baseball and government officials likely viewed the lack of formal relations in 1961–1962 as unimportant. For the US government, the reasoning held in 1963–1964. While secretary of state Dean Rusk maintained that the 1963 coup had "seriously set back [the] cause [of] democracy throughout [the] hemisphere," after the assassination of President Kennedy in November, US officials wavered on their democratic principles.[18] The United States recognized the Triumvirate and reinstated military and economic aid on December 14, 1963, sending notice to Betancourt in Venezuela the day after his replacement was elected. Venezuela never recognized the Triumvirate, but for US officials, the threat of communism was too great.[19] They did not trust Dominicans to secure their country without US support and oversight, particularly after a small group of guerrillas from the 14th of June Revolutionary Movement (1J4, Movimiento Revolucionario 14 de Junio) led by Manuel Tavarez Justo, husband of the martyred Mirabal sister Minerva, set up camp in the mountains.

Fractures in American Fraternity and Limits in Baseball Diplomacy

The Triumvirate's ability to secure the start of the 1963–1964 baseball season where the Bosch administration had failed resulted from the members' alliance with national business leaders, the Dominican military, and the Kennedy and Johnson administrations in their goals for economic growth and anticommunist stability. This shift from the idealism of 1962 to the more pragmatic emphasis on democratic procedure and economic expansion came in part as a response to doubts among some US and Dominican officials about Dominicans' capacity for democracy. The experiences of Dominican ballplayers in the United States and the attitudes of US officials toward Bosch and Dominicans suggested that these doubts could be attributed partly to racism, or what historians LeeAnna Keith and Thomas Zeiler have described as an imperial mind-set.[20] This mind-set, based in patriarchal and racist assumptions that Dominicans were unable to govern themselves, limited US and Dominican-elite aspirations for Dominican democracy to procedure. Felipe Alou identified markers of the imperial mind-set in baseball relations in his 1963 article in *Sport*, "Latin-American Ballplayers Need a Bill of Rights," while US officials demonstrated it in their accounts of Dominican life.[21]

The first signs of fissures in the American fraternity emerged even before Bosch was inaugurated. In early February 1963, Dominican big-leaguers, including Felipe Alou, Guayubín Olivo, Julián Javier, and Juan Marichal, learned that US baseball commissioner Ford Frick had imposed $250 fines on each of them for participating in the 1962 exhibition series with the Cuban Stars. All the players were angered by the fines, but Alou was the most vocal. Calling the fine an outrage (*arbitrariedad*), Alou told Dominican baseball fans that he would not pay it, explaining, "We, as Dominicans, have the right to play in our country."[22] After Alou signed his contract with the Giants, which offered him a raise of $8,000 to bring his salary to $25,000 for the season, he continued to speak against the fine. An Associated Press report communicated Alou's refusal to pay to fans in the United States and the Dominican Republic along with Frick's assurances that Alou would pay.[23] Frick explained his reasoning to sports fans: the games were unauthorized because the Cuban-Dominican series was sponsored by a private promoter rather than the affiliated Dominican Winter League. Perhaps to quell the nationalism of Alou's argument that Dominicans had the right to play in their own country, Frick added that the Cuban players had received heavier fines. Alou continued to stand against the fines even after he arrived in Arizona for spring training, paid his fine, and suited up for practice.

The issue, as Alou explained, was not only the money but also what he interpreted as Frick's assumed authority over baseball and ballplayers in the Dominican Republic. Frick violated Dominican sovereignty and the rights of Dominican players to earn a living. As he told readers of *Sport*: "Mr. Ford Frick is the Commissioner of baseball—even in my country, although he has never set foot in my country."[24] The relationship between the Dominican Winter League and US baseball, and the participation of dozens of Dominican professional ballplayers on teams in the United States, gave Frick greater influence over professional baseball in the Dominican Republic than even the acting president. Alou told US readers that the government in the Dominican Republic "asked" him to play, adding that for him and other Dominicans, the authority of council president Rafael Bonnelly overrode that of the US baseball official. Although Frick prohibited the big-leaguers from participating, Bonnelly's explanation that "I am the president of the Dominican Republic and I say that it is all right to play" convinced the players.[25]

Alou explained that in addition to violating Dominican sovereignty, the fines evidenced Frick's failure to understand the stakes of the series and his refusal to accept that the Dominican and Cuban players knew better than he. Dominican ballplayers felt an obligation to their fans. Word of Frick's prohibition against the series came the day before it was scheduled to begin. With the players gathered, the threat of violence looming amid political demonstrations and strikes, and fans excited to see their national heroes on their home fields, Alou explained, "We could have been threatened with $1,000,000 fines by Frick and there still would not have been any way for us to have avoided playing—unless we were willing to risk bodily harm."[26] Alou used hyperbole in describing the reasoning that "a few hours at the ballpark would divert the minds of the Dominican people from thoughts of revolution, riot, and mayhem," but *Sports Illustrated*'s Robert Cantwell confirmed that Dominicans who attended the series saw baseball transform political tensions into "noisy relaxation and cheers."[27] The fines revealed the truth behind Alou's accusations that Frick "never understood Latins and their problems [and] had no concept of the political consequences of the three-game [*sic*] series."[28]

Alou went a step further to diagnose the root of Frick's overreach, which he graciously described as a "misunderstanding" of the "Latin temperament." Today, media and scholars correctly identify the stereotypes that Latin American players "don't care," "don't hustle," are lazy, or have "no guts" as racism.[29] As Alou explained, however, managers, the press, and even other players believed that Latin American players "don't care" because they were sometimes cheerful in the locker room after a loss and fraternized, often in Spanish, with Latin American players from opposing teams. As an example of the damage caused by this belief, Alou pointed to Giants manager Alvin Dark's threat before the start of the 1963 season to expel all Latin Americans except for Juan Marichal if the Giants did not win the pennant. Despite the strong offensive contributions by Latin American players to the Giants' 1962 season—including Alou's .316 average, 99 runs batted in, and 25 home runs as well as Orlando Cepeda's .306 average with 114 runs batted in and 35 home runs—Dark's threat demonstrated his tendency to overlook their role in the team's pennant-winning 1962 season.[30] Dark's comments backed Alou's warning to baseball hopefuls that they would have to out-hustle other players if they wanted to play professional baseball: "If you do not hustle more than everybody else, it will be said, 'You do not care. You do not have a winning attitude.'"[31]

Assumptions about Dominicans' lack of competence and initiative also affected US officials' perceptions of Dominican leaders and their goals. In his memoir of his time as ambassador in the Dominican Republic (March 1962–September 1963), John Bartlow Martin employed racist and sexist language to characterize Dominican men, calling them "vain and proud and sometimes absurd . . . only spoiled brats grown up."[32] Reserving particular disdain for Bosch, he described the Dominican president as a loner and "emotionally unstable, given to wild emotional swings."[33] Even Bosch's work ethic and dedication to his job earned criticism, which US officials also expressed against Triumvirate leader Donald Reid Cabral (after December 1963) by blaming his strenuous schedule on "poor personal organization" rather than the serious problems plaguing the country. Similar to Martin's view of Bosch, US ambassador William Tapley Bennett described Reid Cabral's apparent erratic and impulsive nature as "characteristic of Dominicans."[34] These assumptions about Dominican inability led to US interventions, as revealed by Martin's warning to President Kennedy in 1961: "If we do not intervene [in Dominican affairs] politically as well as economically now, we may some day be forced to intervene militarily."[35] Stereotypes that Dominicans did not care, that "the vast mass neither knew it was suffering [under Trujillo] nor cared if it was freed," reinforced this mind-set resembling the "white man's burden" that had justified US interventions and the European Scramble for Africa in the late nineteenth and early twentieth centuries.[36] This attitude revealed that US officials never viewed Dominicans, even those like Reid Cabral whose interests aligned with theirs, as capable partners. Martin was explicit: "The trouble was that the Dominicans didn't seem very capable of ruling. People were always saying, 'They must help themselves, we can't do it for them.' But could they? And if not, what then?"[37]

These stereotypes ignored the material consequences of poverty to frame the causes of underdevelopment, like the struggles of Latin American ballplayers, as personal or national failings rather than a result of structural inequality and circumstance. Martin's report on an exchange with a man from Neyba, a state in the southwest of the country, exemplified his attitude that Dominicans "don't hustle" or "are lazy." Seeing the alligators roaming the nearby Lago Enriquillo, Martin asked the man why he and his family did not sell the hides for profit. When the man replied that the alligators in the Lago Enriquillo were fiercer than elsewhere, Martin dismissed his explanation as a mere excuse. The assumption that the man lacked initiative ignored the reality that even if he managed to hunt the alligators and cure the hides, he likely lacked the resources or experience to find a market and transport the hides to buyers in the United States, where alligator leather was a fad. Similarly, Alvin Dark's perception that Latin American players "don't care" resulted in part from his view of Alou's discussions in Spanish with teammates, including his brother, as disruptive to team unity. At the same time, he overlooked the alienation caused by not being able to communicate comfortably, the struggles of learning a second language, and the disruption of speaking with a sibling in a language other than their native tongue. Rather than listening to Dominicans about what they needed to build a vibrant democracy or a winning team, US government and baseball officials plagued by racist stereotypes settled for anticommunism and the status quo.[38]

Assumptions about Dominicans' incapacity for democracy led US officials and the Triumvirate to reimagine democracy as paternalistic authoritarianism, eventually with elections, rather than a representation of the people's will. Distance from the Dominican situation made US officials dependent on informants from the Dominican business class, including Reid Cabral, despite hesitations about the Triumvirate's illegitimacy and knowledge that they represented a minority of Dominican interests.[39] While the US government recognized that Dominicans wanted democracy, the view of them as erratic and impractical led US officials, like the Dominican military and Triumvirate, to dismiss their desires. After a year of discord, Ambassador Bennett accepted the Triumvirate's paternalistic report that it "acts in favor of the people, even if against the will of that people" as progress over previous governments, which he implied had been populist and too concerned with the will of the people.[40] Bennett believed that the "fruits of progress and democracy" required work and sacrifice. In the short term at least, that meant Dominicans would have to settle for the Triumvirate and an economy that served foreign interests and national elites.

Criticizing Professional Baseball

While Dominicans relished the return of professional baseball to their island in the 1963–1964 Winter Tournament, their anger over repression against political dissidents, perceived police brutality, US imperialism, and the lack of movement toward elections soon merged with baseball. High unemployment, the assassination of guerrilla leader Manuel Tavarez in December, strikes in January, and generalized political insecurity did little to keep fans away throughout the Dominican season. However, the actions of some players, the perceived influence of the United States on politics and the national pastime, and distrust of the Winter League officials combined with domestic political tension to exhaust fans and players alike for the International Series against Venezuelan teams. The tensions evident in Guayubín's hyperbolic fratricide in Licey's opening game manifested as criticisms against ballplayers (even heroes Marichal and Javier), brawls, and player demands for greater compensation. Politics infiltrated baseball, revealing the limits of the *deporte rey*.

Even the most heroic of ballplayers disappointed fans as the season moved from the round-robin to the playoffs and the International Series. In December, big-leaguers Marichal and Javier were suspended at the request of their teams. Escogido fined Marichal $25 for using "disrespectful terms" against umpire Paul Kelly and subsequently suspended him for refusing to dress for any games in which Kelly officiated.[41] Javier's confrontation took place in the clubhouse against Aguilas manager Gene Baker, who earlier that summer had become the first African American to serve as a US major-league manager. Offended by Baker for "accusing me of indiscipline," Javier opted to stay home with his pregnant wife rather than play for a team that refused to back him against the manager.[42] Sportswriters chided both players for refusing to submit to authority and discussed possible trades or replacements as punishment for their disloyalty.[43] *El Caribe* was particularly critical of Marichal, blaming him for the team's first absence from the Final Series since the league's incorporation in 1955. In one cartoon,

Figure 3.4. "Aguilita Leads the Teams," Miche Medina, *El Caribe*, January 10, 1964, p. 16.

the Aguila, whose team dominated the regular season, walked the three other mascots on leashes (fig. 3.4). The elephant, the perpetual basement-dweller and favorite of the Fucú, lamented his bad luck, while the lion had a more direct explanation: "The blame for my disgrace, that goes to Marichal."[44] The same man who in October had represented the Dominican people "in the simple but effective language" of his pitches now disgraced the team.[45]

Politics outside of baseball contributed to the unraveling of the 1963–1964 winter season as frustrations over the lack of democracy punctured the tense calm imposed by the Triumvirate and military. The day after *El Caribe* announced Javier's decision to leave the Aguilas, and less than one week after the United States formally recognized the Triumvirate, a front-page headline read, "The Government Suspends Three Constitutional Rights."[46] The Triumvirate rationalized the suspension of the rights to due process and a speedy trial as necessary given the activity of guerrilla groups in the mountains and their alleged intention to impose communism.[47] Three days later, the guerrilla threat was squashed after the armed forces killed respected leader Manuel Tavarez and fourteen others. News that Emilio De los Santos, the head of the Triumvirate, had resigned and been replaced by acting foreign minister Donald Reid Cabral shared the front page. Even the anti-left editors at *El Caribe* suspected that the military and government had gone too far and called for an investigation into the coincidence of Tavarez's death and De los Santos's resignation. Though critical of the guerrilleros, the editors reflected popular sentiment against the Triumvirate by demanding a solution to "reestablish trust and bring the country to the longed-for democratic system."[48]

The Triumvirate hoped that baseball distracted from politics, but politics also offered an outlet for fans who grew increasingly disillusioned with the 1963–1964 baseball season. A satirical piece in *El Caribe* suggested a shift in Dominican preferences for "collective entertainment" as political debates replaced arguments over baseball in December 1963.[49] Baseball had once "fascinated kids, men, and women of all ages to such an extent that arguments originating on the fields or cities at times became a matter of life or death." Politics was even more exciting, and a threat to the very order the Triumvirate had hoped to establish with baseball. The examples of the disruptions reinforced the humorous tone of the article: women and cooks were so engrossed in political conversations that they burned dinner; husbands were so preoccupied with their debates that they ate the charred food without noticing.[50] Dominicans could laugh at the article, but they were well aware of the less-humorous examples of political intrigue, including labor unrest in the country's sugar mills, violence against Tavarez and the guerrillas, De los Santos's resignation, and the suspension of constitutional rights.

Frustrations with the Triumvirate's lack of transparency and progress toward elections turned baseball from the biblical metaphors that characterized the beginning of the season to questions about divine intervention. Marichal provided an easy scapegoat for Escogido fans after Licey overcame losses in the first two games of a best-of-five semifinal playoff, winning the next three to advance to the league championship against the Aguilas. The upset excited over-capacity crowds in Santiago's Estadio Cibao for the first three games of the final, which the Aguilas so dominated that one sports columnist predicted that they would easily take the series "if God doesn't intervene."[51] His suggestion that "up there (naturally, in Heaven) they could be interested in our baseball problems" proved prescient after the series moved to Estadio Quisqueya in Santo Domingo and the Tigers won three games to tie the

Figure 3.5. "A Shady Playoff?," Miche Medina, *El Caribe*, January 31, 1964, p. 14.

series. Well-known cartoonist Miche Medina expressed growing suspicions in his Cartoon of the Day, which showed fans cursing and warning the Tiger and Aguilita, along with an unnamed player in a catcher's mask and the Fucú, to clean up their act (*cuelen su maldito café claro*) (fig. 3.5). The crow delivered the punch line: "Good thing I bought a flashlight because this play-off is getting shady!" (*oscuro*).[52] Fans expected players to take the series as seriously as they did. Errors on the field, including uncharacteristic fumbles by Licey's rookie catcher Juan García Carmona, and bad behavior off the field betrayed fans' trust in the players and suggested that higher interests could be at play.

Fans' suspicions during the Final Series derived from their ongoing frustrations with ballplayers and the fact that Licey's come-from-behind victory prolonged the series—and the distraction that baseball provided from politics. Distraction benefited the government, which sportswriters had credited for organizing the tournament and the international matchups that followed. Enthusiasm for the series made all eight games "a sporting and economic success," but fans also resented what they perceived as failures by the players and suspected manipulations by team owners.[53] After all, an eight- or nine-game series would likely be more profitable than a five-game one. The fans' warning to the players and teams to clean up their act portrayed Licey's victory more as a failure by the Aguilas players than a feat by the Tigers. A story about Aguilas players starting a fight in a Santiago bar after the second game supported this conclusion, as did a bench-clearing brawl the night that the bar fight was reported.[54] The players' conduct betrayed the support fans had given them during the tournament.

Players' demands for a larger share of gate receipts for the finals and a guaranteed salary for the International Series combined with the reports of misconduct to confirm suspicions that native big-leaguers and foreign reinforcements lacked true commitment to the national tournament. *El Caribe* reported on the day of the brawl that Licey and Aguilas players had requested 25 percent of the gate receipts from the finals, rather than the 10 percent stipulated in their contracts. They also asked that the prize money for the first- and second-place teams in the Venezuela series be set at $50,000 rather than 12 percent of total gate receipts.[55] The letter, which the article noted had been written in English to suggest that US reinforcements were behind the request, left league officials so flabbergasted that they sent a cable to US commissioner Ford Frick for advice. Rather than an imposition from an out-of-touch imperial power, Frick's involvement signaled the need for disciplining out-of-control players, specifically those from the United States. Reports blamed North American Willie Stargell for "leading the movement that is threatening the International Series with failure," after he reiterated the requests in a second letter. That Dominican players who spent much of their time in the United States, including Roberto Peña, Pedro González, and Manuel Mota, signed the letter on behalf of their teams only exacerbated the image that the most privileged ballplayers were asking for more than their fair share.[56] Parallels between players' accusations that team executives put winning above their well-being and workers' complaints about the nation's sugar mills were lost.[57]

Rather than establish a sense of normality by reminding Dominicans of the *magnífico estímulo* provided by their national pastime and its heroes, the 1963–1964 winter season revealed the divisions in Dominican society. Fans felt betrayed by what they saw as a lack of commitment from national heroes like Marichal and Javier and a lack of gratitude and professionalism from international reinforcements like Stargell. A popular sports columnist diagnosed a "mental state" among national celebrities, explaining, "There is nothing as temperamental and hard to manage as the idols, be they in art, film, or sports," as he christened the ballplayers "Our Frankensteins."[58] Fans expressed their disgust with their feet: just over half as many of them attended the first game against a Venezuelan team in Estadio Quisqueya as had attended the series final. In Estadio Cibao, the mere one thousand fans who attended the International Series opener booed when the home-team Aguilas took the field.[59] Rather than easing tensions, the 1963–1964 season ended with fans angry with players, players upset with teams, and a generalized "climate favorable to subversion and disorder."[60]

Debating Democracy

Fans and sportswriters demonstrated their dissatisfaction with the circumstances surrounding the 1963–1964 season only by dropping attendance and in their newspaper columns, but many, especially in the capital, proved unwilling to stand for another season of the same. Dominicans remained suspicious of US intentions and backing for the de facto government. Knowing that US recognition conferred international legitimacy on the Triumvirate, Dominicans partly blamed the United States for the slow progress toward elections. After the anniversary of the coup passed and Dominicans prepared for another baseball season, their hostilities toward the United States and the business interests behind professional baseball mounted.

Julián Javier, whose distinction in 1964 as the first Dominican to win a World Series temporarily rehabilitated his image, again bore the hostilities intended for others. In late October 1964, the US Department of State sponsored a goodwill tour through Latin America by seven big-leaguers, including Javier.[61] A visit and photo op with members of the Triumvirate in the National Palace and a visit to the US Embassy signaled the official sanction for this incident of baseball diplomacy while the cheers the group received at a game between the Aguilas and Escogido showered them in goodwill.[62] The spell was broken the next morning, however, when the big-leaguers ran a clinic at a Santo Domingo high school. Students threw rocks and hurled insults, targeting Javier with accusations of being a *vendepatria* (traitor) and *yanquista* (a derogatory word for someone who is pro-US). A stark contrast to the heroes' welcome for Marichal and the Alou brothers just two years before, the attacks on Javier likely had multiple origins: his delay in joining the Aguilas Cibaeñas while he participated in the tour, his suspension the previous year, or simply because he played for the Aguilas and not a capital team. Fans likely felt betrayed to see Javier on the field supporting a US diplomatic gesture after announcing two weeks earlier that he needed a month to recover from the grueling US season before suiting up for the Aguilas.[63] No matter the reason, the treatment of Javier reflected the hardening divisions in Dominican society as well as the growing disenchantment with the country's alliance with the United States and the US Embassy's influence in national politics.

El Caribe acted quickly to frame the outburst as a symptom of "immature confusion" on the part of a "certain youth sector" rather than a legitimate protest against US influence or anger at Javier. The editors explained that the protesters, who chanted slogans "of well-known origin" (a reference to Cuba), either naively believed they acted on democratic principles or were Cuban agents posing as students.[64] The cartoon the next day further discredited the protesters by showing them throwing stones labeled "savageness" (*salvajismo*) at the big-leaguers and expressing shock at the incident: "It cannot be true!" (*Parece mentira*) (fig. 3.6). The fact that Felipe Alou remembered the event with embarrassment three years later confirmed the anti-US feelings behind the actions.[65] After the United States recognized the Triumvirate, a visit by a US delegation carrying friendship (*amistad*) to the Dominican Republic could not revive the inter-American solidarity that had characterized the Cuban-Dominican series. Baseball was no longer free from the fissures in Dominican society or in the hemisphere as the tensions of the previous baseball season turned physical.

The differing interpretations of baseball fans' reactions to the Dominican Winter League and the embarrassing "savageness" with the US baseball delegation reflected the growing contentiousness over Dominican visions for the nation's future. In contrast to the excitement for democracy surrounding the 1962 Cuban-Dominican series, the US-sponsored delegation arrived amid growing disillusionment with the United States and its support for the Triumvirate. Before the delegation's arrival, criticisms were subtle, as in one column by sportswriter Ph, who lamented the lack of positive attention given to Latin American players in the US press, despite "so many and such brilliant material of our race delivering on Big League teams."[66] After listing the neglected achievements of Latin Americans during the 1964 season, Ph turned

Figure 3.6. "Salvajismo," Frank, *El Caribe*, November 7, 1964, p. 4.

political by reprinting an excerpt from New York's Spanish-language *El Diario–La Prensa* that drew parallels between baseball and democracy. Although Ph quoted the original piece "without comment" to avoid politics, the conclusion that "once the team is elected and proclaimed the winner, we give them our full support, no matter who it is" served as an admonition against the United States for its support of the Triumvirate and the military coup that violated Dominicans' democratic will to bring it power.[67] Just as US sportswriters overlooked the great contributions of Latin American players, US support for the Triumvirate ignored Dominican contributions to the hemisphere's democratic project by electing Bosch in 1962 and continuing to call for elections and reform.

As the Winter League continued, Dominicans turned again to baseball to criticize Triumvirate policies that many saw as distancing them from the democratic ideal. Rather than boosting the national economy and workers, the Triumvirate's anticommunist policies, suspension of civil rights, and squashing of strikes deepened insecurity and inequality.

Figure 3.7. "¡A la pelota!," JOH, *¡Ahora!*, December 19, 1964, p. 26.

A cartoon in the newsmagazine *¡Ahora!* illustrated these popular sentiments. In the cartoon, a ballplayer representing the oligarchy (*oligarquía*) swung a bat labeled social policies (*política social*) at a ball representing communism (*comunismo*). Rather than smashing communism, which sped past the oligarchy, the bat thwacked the player standing behind him, who represented the people (*pueblo*) (fig. 3.7)[68] The sarcastic exclamation, "¡A la pelota!" (to baseball) reiterated suspicions that the Triumvirate used baseball to distract Dominicans from their lack of progress in creating a democratic society.

Rather than blaming players, Dominicans turned against the professional baseball league and the Triumvirate's financial support of professional sport. Political articles, like the cartoon suggesting external intervention the previous season (fig. 3.5), implied that the Triumvirate had supported the professional tournaments to distract Dominicans from the backslide in their democratic project since 1962.[69] Criticism by sportswriters such as Tirso A. Váldez, hijo, centered on the Winter League's misuse of funds and the government's prioritization of professional baseball over amateur sport. Moved in part by the Winter League teams' appeal for year-round administration of the government-owned stadiums—that is, more government benefits—Váldez called for transparency in the baseball league's use of public funds. He cited the visible attendance and palpable enthusiasm during the 1963–1964 and 1964–1965 seasons as anecdotal evidence against the teams' claims to have lost money, and he demanded they publicize detailed financial reports.[70] Beyond demanding this transparency for spending public funds, Váldez contrasted the Dominican government's "almost excessive" financial support for professional baseball with the financial independence of leagues in other countries.[71] The Dominican government, Váldez claimed, was the only one that offered financial assistance to professional sport. While recognizing that government finances allowed the Dominican Winter League to take risks and add great players like Willie Stargell to their rosters, Váldez maintained that the use of public benefits for private profits went against the interests of the nation. Rather than building the country from the bottom up, the Triumvirate boosted those at the top.

In the context of uncertainty and mistrust, Váldez's criticisms of government investment in professional baseball and his request that they invest instead in amateur sport resonated. Big-leaguers such as Felipe Alou inspired Dominican youths and represented the nation on foreign fields to benefit the nation indirectly.[72] Yet big-leaguers proved unreliable heroes who might sit out a winter season, like Marichal, or have their achievements go unrecognized in the United States.[73] Váldez's rejection of the notion that the government should use public funds to support endeavors whose primary objectives were to provide material benefits to private enterprises echoed Bosch's stance against calls for industrial incentives (chapter 2), and offered a response, if unintentional, to the Industrial Incentives Law passed just two weeks after the coup.[74] Rather than protecting team profits, Váldez argued, the government should favor amateur baseball. Such investments benefited the athletes of tomorrow, who "will know how to bring glory to the nation" in international tournaments. Democratic governments invested in people through social policies because, as Váldez argued, "this is how you make the nation" (*así se hace patría*).[75] Democracies invested in business only when such backing benefited the people.

The question of private enterprise, including professional baseball, and debates over its role in a nation aspiring to political participation and economic security divided baseball fans from the government officials who ensured the organization of professional tournaments. Váldez's call for more support for amateur sport echoed these demands and reverberated through the population, which had grown increasingly disgusted with the Triumvirate. By the time Dominican ballplayers joined their US teams for spring training in February and March, a plan for junior officers to depose the Triumvirate was a known secret (*secreto a voces*).[76] Baseball may have delayed the confrontation, but with the end of the winter season, the metaphorical fratricide on the field in 1963 manifested on the streets in April 1965.

Popular Democracy and Baseball for the People

On April 24, 1965, Santo Domingo exploded in a popular uprising to expel the Triumvirate and demand the return of a constitutional government, even against US wishes and threats to internal stability. Dominicans had given the Triumvirate a chance to build the institutions for democracy that they wanted, but the leaders delayed too much. Led by junior military officers who identified themselves as Constitutionalists, the uprising succeeded in overturning the Triumvirate and nearly succeeded in reinstalling Bosch in the National Palace to complete his constitutional term. Combatants stood on the Duarte Bridge armed with personal firearms, the few weapons handed out by the military leaders, and rocks. With these weapons, they prevented Loyalist forces armed with tanks and artillery from entering the main section of Santo Domingo for "five glorious days" from April 24 to April 28. They defended their democratic future.[77] On April 28, US military forces intervened at the request of the Loyalist military, allegedly to prevent communists from overtaking the popular uprising and, though US leaders refused to admit it publicly, to prevent Bosch's return.

As US officials led by the former ambassador John Martin arbitrated between the Constitutionalist and Loyalist forces, Dominicans' frustrations reached their compatriots abroad. On the night of August 22, 1965, Juan Marichal was on the mound for the San Francisco Giants against Sandy Koufax of the rival Los Angeles Dodgers. Competing in a tight pennant race, both pitchers were aggressive, but when Marichal came to bat in the third inning, he felt Dodgers catcher John Roseboro's return throws to the mound were coming dangerously close to his head, with one allegedly nicking his ear. The two men exchanged words, and when Roseboro stood and removed his helmet and mask, Marichal hit him over the head with his bat. The benches cleared. The intensity of the game, the rivalry, and the pennant race certainly played a role in the incident, but the rebellion and US-OAS invasion against what many saw as Dominicans' claiming their political destiny had a role, too. The Marichal-Roseboro incident manifested the political tensions in both athletes' communities. Marichal struggled with the political crisis in the Dominican Republic, while Roseboro, a native of Los Angeles, dealt with the messages of the Watts Riots that had occurred in the weeks prior to the game. The baseball diamond could hold off politics for only so long.

Conclusion

After the Triumvirate's successful organization of the 1963–1964 Winter Tournament so soon after the coup deflated hopes for democracy, Dominicans grew suspicious of even their *deporte rey*. The *magnífico estímulo* that baseball provided in the lead-up to the 1962 elections dissipated when the military muted the voices of the Dominican majority who had selected Bosch as their leader. Players' perceived greed and excessive behavior frustrated fans, who expected those in power to respect their loyalty to the game and their votes. Instead, ballplayers and Winter League team owners, like military officers and government officials, acted in their own interests while ignoring their social and professional duties.

The United States and other nations in the hemisphere—or at least the business interests they represented—contributed to Dominican frustrations and revealed the limits of democracy as imagined by US leaders. Concerns that popular unrest brought on by the coup would lead to a dictatorship of the extreme right or extreme left caused US officials to support the Triumvirate despite its delaying of elections. For US officials, as for businesses such as the Venezuelan Winter League, preventing communism was more important than building democracy, and, as Martin implied in his memoir, Dominicans were not yet ready for a true democracy. Investment and baseball exchanges during the Triumvirate lent the de facto government an aura of legitimacy that proved stronger than official diplomatic recognition. So long as democracy worked as an antidote to communism, members of the business classes supported it. But they were also willing to squash democracy, and the people's pursuit of it, to protect their business interests against social and economic reforms.

Soon after Marichal completed his eight-game suspension for the incident with Roseboro, US officials led by former ambassador Martin negotiated an end to the Dominican crisis, with provisional president Héctor García Godoy charged with preparing elections for June 1966. Despite not reinstalling Bosch, the April War told the world that Dominicans would accept a de facto government no more. They demanded constitutionalism, even if flawed. Political turmoil and violence continued under García Godoy and cast doubt on the 1966 elections, which saw former Trujillo president Joaquín Balaguer return to the head of the country. In this new type of constitutionalism, baseball would continue to perform an important role mediating between the government and the people. As they negotiated their democratic future, Dominicans would look to their Latin American brothers and sisters, including those in Cuba, as they came to accept new meanings for democracy and for baseball.

FOUR *Así se hace patria*: Baseball and the Bloodless Revolution

On the night of August 26, 1969, twenty thousand fans and security forces crowded into Estadio Quisqueya for the much-anticipated "showdown between teams representing radically antagonistic systems of government" in the final game of the seventeenth Amateur World Series.[1] Competitive balance enhanced political intrigue as both the Cuban state amateurs and US college students stepped on the field with undefeated records, meaning the final game would also decide the champion of the round-robin tournament. For many, the presence of the Cuban team on Dominican soil represented a victory in itself. The return of a Cuban flag among the others at the Las Américas airport after nine years of estrangement attested to the unifying power of sport. One sportswriter reminded readers: "Cuba cannot sit at the table of deliberation in hemispheric organizations [such as the OAS], but here they coexist with eleven continental countries."[2] After a close, contentious game that ended in a crescendo of "Cuba, Si! Yankees, No!" chants when the Cubans overcame a 1–0 deficit in the bottom of the eighth inning, Dominican sports director Horacio Veras declared the series proof "that sport unites nations and men." Receiving the trophy from Veras after the 2–1 victory, Cuban sports director Jorge García Bongó returned the fraternal expression with his declaration that "the prize obtained by Cuba 'belongs as much to the Dominican Republic and all of Latin America as to Cuba.'"[3] Although relations with Cuba remained informal until 1998, the goodwill and civility during the Amateur World Series inspired further sports exchanges between the two island nations and affirmed the power of sport to heal divisions.[4]

Reconciliation with Cuba in 1969 was a crucial step in a larger project by the Dominican government under president Joaquín Balaguer to incorporate amateur sport under the Revolución sin sangre, or Bloodless Revolution. As it had for the Triumvirate in 1963 and 1964, financial investment in and concessions for professional baseball during the first half of his four-year term (1966–1970) confirmed the Balaguer government's ability to sustain the Winter Tournament and US support. But fans had resented the Dominican Winter League and players in the 1963–1964 season and criticized government welfare for the professional league: professional baseball was not enough. Although they continued to celebrate the success of individual Dominican ballplayers in the United States, by 1965 Dominicans no longer projected their hopes for a democratic future onto professional baseball. Professional baseball and the US system associated with it offered immense opportunities to individual elite athletes. Amateur baseball, on the other hand, extended opportunities for sport across the population, as the amateur system had in Cuba, and would benefit all of society by developing Dominican citizens in the values of sport.[5] Investing in amateur sports, as sportswriter Tirso Váldez, hijo had said in 1965, is how a nation is made, "así se hace Patria."[6]

Balaguer and his government also saw reconciliation with Cuba as a key to raising the Dominican president's reputation as a regional champion of pluralism and sovereignty. Balaguer integrated foreign policy into his nation-making efforts under the Bloodless Revolution in two ways.[7] First, he made foreign policy decisions, such as permitting sporting relations with Cuba, to access the resources necessary to create the Bloodless Revolution as a national project. Relations with Cuban coaches allowed Dominican sports officials to gain knowledge and technical advice, which would help build the Dominican amateur system and thus reinforce the narrative of Balaguer's commitment to developing Dominican people. Second, reconciliation with Cuba raised Balaguer's profile in the region at a time when Latin American nations looked increasingly to one another to counteract the negative impact of US influence. These relations reinforced Balaguer's legitimacy by demonstrating his acceptance among his Latin American peers. While Reem Abou-El-Fadl says little about popular perceptions of leaders in her study of foreign policy as nation-making in Turkey and Egypt, Dominican perceptions of Latin American opinions toward Balaguer were crucial to the continuation and success of the Bloodless Revolution.[8] The Bloodless Revolution was to be a democratic revolution like those imagined in the Alliance for Progress. In a democratic nation, Balaguer had to win elections. Incorporating baseball, and then amateur sport more broadly, under the Bloodless Revolution facilitated sports relations with Cuba and strengthened relations with other Latin American nations. Sport helped legitimate Balaguer's claims that *desarrollismo*, his development platform, included the development of Dominicans as democratic citizens as well as national economic growth.

Balaguer came to power through an election plagued by such violence and intimidation that his opponent, Juan Bosch, was afraid to leave his home and was guarded by US and Dominican forces. Ballplayer Felipe Alou described Bosch's situation during the campaign as house arrest.[9] Bosch had widespread popular support, but as Alou explained, Dominicans knew that "the United States was especially determined to not leave the Dominican Republic until it accomplished what it wanted [. . .] And what the United States wanted was Joaquín Balaguer in power."[10] Balaguer was a compromise candidate: Dominicans accepted him in 1966 because he promised peace that Bosch could not deliver. By electing Balaguer, Dominicans protected the illusion of democracy from a military regime similar to those that took control in Brazil in 1964 and Argentina between the election and inauguration of Balaguer in 1966. Baseball, and later amateur sport more generally, helped Balaguer uphold the appearance of constitutionalism by winning elections and gaining conformity to, if not popular support for, the Bloodless Revolution.

This chapter details how Balaguer incorporated professional baseball and then amateur sport under the Bloodless Revolution to institutionalize what historian Elizabeth Manley described as a "new kind of paternalism" in the Dominican system.[11] The incredible success of Dominican big-leaguers in the 1966 US season and a popular exhibition series with the Pittsburgh Pirates in 1967 garnered popular support and US endorsement for Balaguer's development program during his first term. Yet even these ambassadors for economic development revealed inadequacies in the capitalist system. As violence escalated during his reelection campaign in 1968 and 1969, Balaguer conceded to Dominican demands for investment in amateur sport. Hosting the

Amateur World Series in 1969 marked a shift to emphasizing social development along with economic development and the opportunity to remake national sports with Cuban guidance. After securing reelection in 1970, Balaguer expanded these plans by agreeing to host the Central American and Caribbean Games in 1974. The national project to prepare for the games fully incorporated amateur sport under the Bloodless Revolution and, with the passage of a new sports law in December 1974, institutionalized paternalism in the Dominican sporting structure. Balaguer's combination of "despotic and democratic elements," expressed in part through sport, reveals the Bloodless Revolution as a Dominican Third Way, a path to development and democracy that relied on US and Cuban support while rejecting both the unrestrained capitalism of the US professional-sport model and the socialized state amateurism of the Cuban model.

Ambassadors for Development

With the nation still divided, his legitimacy unsettled, government coffers empty, and hostilities toward the United States high after the civil war and US-led intervention, President Balaguer embraced professional baseball to ease tensions between his government and the public and between Dominicans and the United States. Dominican ballplayers served as the country's "best ambassadors" to aid the reconciliation efforts with their record-setting achievements during the 1966 US season and their commitment to playing in the Winter League tournaments. A visit from the Pittsburgh Pirates, led by fan-favorite Roberto Clemente, provided the other half of the diplomatic mission. The spectacle of Balaguer opening the 1966 Winter Tournament and photos of him embracing 1967 World Series champion Julián Javier or greeting the Pirates in his office conveyed the government's interest in the national pastime and, by extension, in the Dominican people. The glow of Dominican professional ballplayers and the Pirates' visit shone on Balaguer. By publicly affiliating himself with professional baseball early in his first term, Balaguer demonstrated his concern for the Dominican people and affirmed US support for his development plans.

Just three months into the Balaguer regime, Dominicans saw hope for the rebirth of their nation from the ashes of civil war in the performance of Dominican ballplayers in the United States. For the first time in baseball history, three foreign players from the same country led the major leagues in hitting. Matty Alou's .342 average won the National League batting crown over the second-place .328 average shared by his brother Felipe and countryman Ricardo Carty.[12] Juan Marichal continued to put up Hall of Fame numbers, winning over twenty games for his fourth consecutive season, which led *Time* to name him owner of "The Best Right Arm in Baseball."[13] For Dominicans, these performances signaled more than their countrymen's baseball skills: Marichal's dominance on the mound and the feats of the Alou brothers and Carty at the plate signaled that reconciliation was possible. After all, Felipe Alou had found his swing with the Atlanta Braves after his public critique of US baseball in 1963, and Marichal had regained his swagger after the shame of hitting John Roseboro with a bat the previous August. After the contentious winter seasons in 1963–1964 and 1964–1965 and the absence of a 1965–1966 season due to the US-OAS occupation, Dominican ballplayers again represented the "glorious triumph" of the Dominican nation in the United States and the unifying power of baseball.[14]

Newspaper editors, sportswriters, and officials fueled the good feelings of reconciliation and unity as they welcomed the big-leaguers home in 1966. An early October editorial in *El Caribe* referred to the ballplayers as the country's best diplomats, acting "on a pure field, clean, crystalline."[15] Dominican ballplayers in the United States were true to their purpose and pure in their desires to represent their homeland: "Their language has been sport."[16] The editorial distinguished the achievements of the Alou brothers, Carty, Marichal, and Manuel Mota, whose .332 average impressed Dominican fans but came from too few at-bats to qualify for the batting title. The numbers evidenced the success of Dominican ballplayers abroad and demonstrated "why Santo Domingo is considered the Mecca of Latin Baseball today."[17] The next day's editorial cartoon illustrated the country's success (fig. 4.1).[18] In the cartoon, a man in a baseball uniform held a bat and a sign declaring a "glorious triumph" (*triunfo consagrador*) as he stood next to a suitcase labeled "Dominican ballplayers in the Big Leagues." On the hallowed ground of the baseball diamond and through the language of sport, the ballplayers showed US fans what Dominicans were really like. Images of Marichal's high kick or Matty Alou's unconventional swing replaced those of gun-toting revolutionaries and radical politicians in the US press.

Balaguer ensured his part in the ballplayers' "glorious triumph" by working with Winter League officials to ensure that the ball-playing

Figure 4.1. "Triunfo Consagrador," Almonte, *El Caribe*, October 4, 1966, p. 6.

ambassadors could direct their diplomatic efforts toward their own people during the 1966–1967 Winter Tournament. With Estadio Quisqueya in disrepair from the civil war and misuse, the government dedicated just under $23,000 (US$163,000 in 2012) for repairs, nearly $18,000 of which was diverted from a fund to repair a hospital.[19] Knowing the interest that the professional season held for Dominicans from every social and political stripe, Balaguer also went beyond the usual tax breaks and administration of the stadiums to offer financial assistance to the Winter League teams, including buying their debts with the Bank of Reserves.[20] The government offered each team a donation of $12,500 (US$88,000 in 2012) to prepare for the tournament and bought debts totaling nearly $40,000 for the Estrellas and Escogido before the 1967–1968 season.[21] When Balaguer hesitated to spend such significant sums while calling for austerity, vice president Francisco Augusto Lora reminded him of the importance of this financial support: "Independent of the legal considerations, I believe it is also in our political interest [to pay the debts] because it will facilitate the celebration of the next baseball tournament, which is always a sporting event of great interest for the Dominican public."[22] Balaguer and those involved in his regime understood that consolidating control over the Dominican population would require that they, too, speak the language of sport, or at least that they support the ambassadors who would do so on their behalf.

The next year, Julián Javier rose as the most prominent baseball ambassador by demonstrating his Dominican pride after the St. Louis Cardinals' World Series victory. His brilliant contributions to the victory impressed fans across the baseball world. As one Dominican sportswriter explained, Javier's "aggression and courage" at the plate, on the base paths, and on defense had led fans to talk about him "in English, in Spanish, in Japanese, and in all the languages in which the fall classic was reported."[23] Yet even with this international acclaim, Javier ensured that his *dominicanidad* (Dominican nationality) was visible. As Inés de Javier told *El Caribe*, she greeted her World Series champion husband "with a kiss and a Dominican flag" on his return to St. Louis from the final World Series game in Boston.[24] Carrying the Dominican flag to the pinnacle of what was still considered the US pastime, the man greeted with hurled stones and accusations of "*yanquista*" in 1964 now exemplified the healing powers of sport.

As they celebrated the return of their ambassador from St. Louis, Dominicans also anticipated the arrival of the first team of US baseball diplomats to visit their island since 1948. The Dominican Development Foundation, a nonprofit founded in 1966, welcomed the Pittsburgh Pirates for a five-game exhibition series with proceeds allegedly going to a project benefiting Dominican farmers. The series united Dominican ballplayers, the government, and citizens with the Pirates players to support economic development. Dominican ballplayers, like the Pirates, participated in the series for free, offering their support to the event officially sanctioned by the Balaguer government. Balaguer granted the concessions habitually offered to the Dominican Winter League and attended the inaugural game. As good baseball ambassadors for the United States, the Pirates also offered free clinics to young ballplayers in the country's baseball cities: Santo Domingo, Santiago, and San Pedro de Macorís. Dominicans showed their appreciation by supporting the players on both sides with their applause and by offering the Dominican Foundation for Development their pesos and enthusiasm. All tickets for the Pirates-Dominican All-Stars game in Estadio Cibao sold out even before the Pirates arrived, leading *El Caribe*'s Santiago correspondent to conclude, "Never before has such extraordinary enthusiasm been seen in this city, and it's for nothing less" than the great stars about to play there.[25] The baseball ambassadors drew fans to the stadium.

Dominicans' warm reception for the Pirates undoubtedly derived from their baseball obsession. But the visit proved an important diplomatic success for the United States. Although there was no official US involvement with the Pirates visit, the team represented the United States and US organized baseball.[26] The US and Dominican governments hoped the image of these baseball ambassadors taking the field with Dominican stars would replace the image of US soldiers invading the country to squash the popular movement in the April War. With the tourist industry still in the planning stages in 1967, the only US Americans most Dominicans had ever seen had been a handful of Peace Corps volunteers, soldiers, or the individual ballplayers who reinforced Dominican teams each winter. The series placed a group of US representatives dressed in baseball flannels rather than military fatigues on a Dominican field where everyone played by the same rules. The exhibition with the Pirates did not silence the anti-US or anti-imperialist sentiments in the country at the time, but Dominicans welcomed the US baseball ambassadors and the fraternal side of the United States that they represented.

Beyond the exchange of military uniforms for baseball uniforms, the Pirates reminded Dominicans that their struggle for a democratic society was a hemisphere-wide fight, one that reached into even the United States, the purported model of democracy. The Pirates of 1967 looked much different from the Brooklyn Dodgers and Montreal Royals players who had visited in 1948. Back then, Jackie Robinson (Dodgers) and Roy Campanella (Royals) were the only Black players in the two teams' spring-training lineups. In contrast, roughly half of the Pirates delegation was Black and/or Latino, presenting an image of racial inclusion and diversity—and most of all, of progress—for both the United States and US baseball. From the composition of players, Dominicans watching the games could imagine themselves on the field, a feeling reinforced by the fact that many of the Pirates had participated in the Dominican Winter League. In addition to Panamanian Manny Sanguillén's plans to join the Aguilas for the 1967 season and Bahamian André Rodgers's time with Escogido in 1959–1960, Bill Mazeroski had played with the Aguilas for two seasons (1955–1956, 1956–1957) and Willie Stargell and Bob Veale played in 1963–1964, when Stargell had been singled out as a troublemaker for his efforts to organize players. By reflecting Dominicans in a (mostly) intact big-league team, the Pirates represented what Dominicans had in common with the people of the United States.

Media coverage of the exhibitions reached beyond the sports pages, with reports and images in *El Caribe*'s society pages that extended the camaraderie on the field more explicitly to Balaguer and the United States.[27] A reception at the residence of US ambassador John H. Crimmins and his wife, Margaret, included the United States in the festivities, though with little commentary beyond the usual social reporting of who was present.[28] In covering the reception hosted by Balaguer later the same afternoon, the society pages interpreted the president's support for Dominican baseball and provided a subtle reminder of US support for his government. Photos of Balaguer embracing national baseball hero Julián Javier and shaking hands with longtime Winter League standout Danilo Rivas, who, as fans knew, had combined with the young Pedro Borbón to blank the Pirates in the Dominican team's only victory in the series, provided visible evidence of Balaguer's connection to Dominican baseball. Among the three photos that pictured the event, the only image with a representative from the Pirates showed Balaguer and vice president Augusto Lora posing with Pirates manager Danny Murtaugh, whose gratitude to the Dominican people and good impression of the country led Balaguer to declare the visit a success.[29] Despite the Dominican Development Foundation's work to organize the exhibition and to initiate Balaguer's involvement, Dominicans saw Balaguer, not the foundation, embracing Dominican ballplayers and lavishing the Pirates and their executives with diplomatic niceties.[30]

The extraordinary achievements of the Dominican baseball ambassadors in the United States in 1966 helped Balaguer quell tensions from the April War and US-led intervention during the first years of his presidency. The Pirates visit in 1967 solidified his message of support for Dominican baseball, while the Dominican Development Foundation's leadership in organizing the series offered a positive image of the social benefits of development, one backed by the United States through its baseball ambassadors. Balaguer's affiliation with the national pastime and its heroes created an image of calm and stability to balance reports of coercion by the "uncontrollable forces" that attacked survivors of the April War and others opposed to Balaguer.[31] His support for the Industrial Incentives Law of 1968 confirmed Balaguer's commitment to national development and his allegiance to the industrialists and US business leaders who had ousted Bosch. With his development credentials secured, Balaguer began to respond more directly to social demands ahead of his reelection campaign for 1970. Finally responding to sportswriters who had criticized the limits of professional baseball even before the April War, Balaguer embraced amateur sport to defend the social benefits of his development program to the Dominicans on whose votes he depended. A government donation of $25,000 to support the nation's hosting of the Amateur Baseball World Series in 1969 demonstrated Balaguer's concern for the Dominican population to citizens at home and across the Americas.

Making a Nation in Amateur Baseball

Securing the Dominican Winter League after the civil war, the successes of Dominican players in the United States, and the exhibition series with the Pirates confirmed the Dominican Republic's position as a "Mecca" of professional baseball and emphasized the individual opportunity made possible by development. But Dominicans wanted more. With a spike in violence occurring across the country, and as he considered running for a second term, Balaguer oversaw government projects in amateur sport to build his reputation both at home and abroad. This investment would fulfill Dominican expectations that the government build up the nation while allowing Balaguer to showcase Dominican progress to citizens across the Americas. The Industrial Incentives Law of 1968 and continuing austerity measures against workers appeased the national industrial class, foreign investors, and US officials to such a degree that Balaguer could even pursue limited relations with Cuba, which raised his regional status as a champion of sovereignty and pluralism as well as his national reputation. Although national sports director Horacio Veras ran smaller, local amateur sports projects throughout Balaguer's first term, the Amateur World Series marked a turning point as the regime publicly committed to amateur sport and inter-American relations as part of the nation-making project. The Amateur World Series provided an international stage for Balaguer to showcase the progress Dominicans had made since the civil war. Beyond physical rebuilding, the Balaguer administration and press corps emphasized the security and stability in the country along with the fraternal sporting spirit. Declarations of sports unity such as those by Veras and Juan García Saleta, the president of the Dominican Olympic Committee (Comité Olímpico Dominicano, COD) during the awards ceremony confirmed the success of the series in fulfilling Dominican hopes for stronger relations among all Latin Americans.[32]

In his requests for government support, Veras emphasized the many domestic and international benefits of hosting the 1969 Amateur World Series.[33] As Veras explained in his requests to the directors of government departments for donations of $500 for the event, the honor of hosting confirmed the country's international reputation.[34] In addition, Veras and his boss, Altagracia Bautista de Suárez, the head of Education, Arts, and Culture, stressed the promise of the series to encourage youths to participate in sports and foster "all kinds of fraternal sentiments among participants."[35] Partnerships extended to private industries as well as public offices, all of whom Veras had begun recruiting to support sports projects when he served under the Triumvirate. As Veras told *¡Ahora!* sports editor José A. González in February 1965, he would build sports installations of all types, from recreational tracks in rural communities to an Olympic complex in the capital, to "open the way for youths [to develop] healthy bodies and minds."[36] The April War ended Veras's plans to host the Amateur World Series in 1965, but four years later, he filled the desire of Dominican sports lovers and what he described as Balaguer's destiny to serve as patron to these "festivities of American Fraternity."[37]

Dominicans surely saw welcoming delegations from ten different countries for the largest international sporting event in their country as a national achievement, but excitement in the press centered on Cuba and the long-awaited return of their sporting relationship. Cuba was one of the Dominican Republic's oldest and closest sporting allies, since immigrants from there and Puerto Rico helped establish baseball as the Dominican national pastime.[38] Throughout August 1969, *El Caribe* carried updates about the status of Cuban visas, endorsements of the renewed sporting fraternity, and curiosity about the Cubans themselves. One columnist poked fun at all the attention directed at the Cubans and mused, "We will see that despite Fidel, [. . .] they are definitely not so weird and terrifying as we imagine the nonexistent Martians."[39] But beneath the humor, the columnist recognized the political intrigue surrounding the Cuban players and the prospect of a US-Cuba confrontation. After the Cubans arrived and spectators saw the apolitical ballplayers for themselves, other sportswriters suggested that sports exchanges with the Cubans should continue and intimated that Cuban officials would discuss a plan for doing so with Balaguer at an upcoming reception.[40] The headline over two stories about the series finale suggested that Veras had agreed at least in principle to these exchanges and awaited only a formal invitation.[41] Whether the sportswriter's reference to "concrete realities" in backing sports exchanges referred to warming relations among Latin American countries and Cuba as the 1970s approached or to the government plan to expand amateur sport, Dominicans began to imagine a return to the sporting fraternity that had characterized their relations with Cuba before the Castro Revolution.

The warming of the sports relationship with Cuba paralleled increasing pluralism and solidarity in Latin American politics and rising anti-US sentiment, partially in response to US interference in Latin American countries. Reports on the Cuba-US final in the Amateur World Series cited broadcasters who explained that rather than being an insult to the US players, the "Cuba, Sí! Yankees, No!" chants "reflect Latin Americans' discontent with the policies followed by the United States toward our continent."[42] In fact, many of the expressions of fraternity excluded the United States or otherwise demonstrated differences between the US delegation and those from Latin American and Caribbean countries. The contrasts began with coverage of the welcoming committees: Dominicans welcomed the Latin American and Caribbean delegations with merengues and newspaper coverage showed team officials dancing with *madrinas*, or young women assigned to the team as caretakers and supporters. *El Caribe*'s coverage of the US team instead pictured a few "university men" in smart suits and emphasized their power and their readiness to face the big guns from Cuba, Puerto Rico, Mexico, and Colombia. The band played, but there was no dancing.[43] While US officials likely hoped that rejoining the American sports fraternity was as simple as returning to the Amateur World Series for the first time since 1942, the team's presence revealed their differences while emphasizing Latin American cultural connections with Cuba. Where nations rather than economies were concerned, including in matters of sports fraternity, Dominicans and many of their regional peers recognized a stronger affinity with Cuba. Their relationship with the United States was economic and professional, like the baseball system that offered opportunities for individuals at the expense of nations. With Cuba and other Latin Americans, they could build their nations in the fraternal competition of sport.[44]

The Latin American solidarity to counter US power wasn't confined to the baseball diamond. Months before the Amateur World Series, representatives from twenty-one countries in Latin America and the Caribbean created a plan to redefine hemispheric relations in the Consensus of Viña del Mar. Although these plans were silent on Cuba, many of the countries who signed onto the plan were already reinvigorating cultural relations in 1969 and, along with Mexico, which never broke relations with Cuba, would push for Cuba's return to the Inter-American community in the early 1970s.[45] García Bongó's dedication of Cuba's victory to "all of Latin America" confirmed Cuba's place in the American fraternity. The Consensus of Viña del Mar and hopes that the tournament "would strengthen even more the relations among Latin American countries" suggested that the "prize obtained by Cuba" was defeating the United States.[46]

The return of a US delegation to the Amateur World Series after more than twenty years paralleled shifts in US foreign policy in the Americas from leadership to partnership after the inauguration of Richard M. Nixon.[47] The United States pledged a "mature partnership" with Latin American nations, by which they meant they would allow Latin American nations to choose their own paths to development and even acknowledged that some would choose state-centered paths. Despite this promised pluralism, however, Nixon and other officials explicitly excluded Cuba, maintaining without irony that Castro's support for antigovernment movements in other countries violated the principle of nonintervention. In effect, US promises of pluralism meant that the Nixon administration would tolerate authoritarianism and other violations of civil liberties if it established the stability and order necessary for capitalist development; noncapitalist models were not tolerated. Rather than promote collaboration with Latin American leaders seeking their own paths to a place in the sun, then, this proposed pluralism freed US leaders from contradictions such as sending ballplayers to the Dominican Republic even after severing diplomatic relations with the de facto government, as had happened with the 1963–1964 winter season.

In the Dominican Republic, at least, the renewed fraternity with Cuba and regional solidarity depended on violent security measures and austere economic policies. Only after proving to the United States that he was committed to order and development could Balaguer elevate himself as a champion of regional fraternity and political pluralism. Though on a smaller scale than the dirty wars in Argentina and Guatemala, the violent repression committed during the Balaguer administration was well known, and even the conservative *El Caribe* editors criticized the lack of transparency. Terror and abuse continued throughout 1969, leading the PRD to abstain from the 1970 elections, and continued even after Balaguer's second inauguration.[48]

Press coverage surrounding the Cuban team eased tensions for some by acknowledging the presence of security forces, offered warnings for prospective protesters, and normalized repression for others. When the Cubans arrived, for example, authorities promised to ensure that "Cubans act here like the other foreign visitors, with freedom and without problems of any kind" and portrayed their measures as protecting the Cubans from anti-Castro protesters of the left and right.[49] The measures appeared to protect the Cuban delegation while rationalizing the surveillance and detainment of Dominican citizens, including the arrest of two syndicalists and holding a group of university students on the way to greet the delegation at the airport.[50] Even in the celebration of sporting fraternity, Dominicans sacrificed civil liberties in the name of order.

The Amateur World Series proved a success in legitimating the Balaguer administration in the region and his so-called Bloodless Revolution at home. The US delegation's complaints of boos and jeers were easily dismissed as Dominicans and their Latin American counterparts celebrated the American fraternity they associated with amateur sport and the prospect of future exchanges with Cuba.[51] Security had ensured that stability would prevail, even after pro-Castro chants escaped from a reception of the Cuban delegation hosted by a left-leaning student federation.[52] Balaguer demonstrated his ability to ensure order while pursuing a new relationship with Cuba. As Veras awaited the formal invitation necessary to take a baseball team to the neighboring island, Dominicans imagined future exchanges with Cuba's well-trained and educated staff and a return to past triumphs in amateur sport.[53] Signs that the administration would not only support the exchanges with Cuba but also increase investment in amateur sport legitimated Balaguer's assurances that the Bloodless Revolution would foster social as well as economic development. Running mostly unopposed, Balaguer easily secured the 1970 elections and began to consolidate his regime. The national project to host the Central American and Caribbean Games in 1974 would consolidate the Bloodless Revolution and institutionalize Balaguer's Third Way in sport.

Sport and Balaguer's Third Way

Many Dominicans learned of the "extraordinary national responsibility" of hosting the Central American and Caribbean Games in the December 1970 edition of the newsmagazine *¡Ahora!*[54] Patriotic colors—red, white, and blue—lined the cover with the words "XII Juegos Centroamericanos y del Caribe" cut from the color blocks. Drawings of men pitching, wrestling, running, and playing basketball peeked through the color, demonstrating national unity in sport. Unity remained the most prominent theme as Dominicans turned to the editorial just inside the cover, which described the Central American and Caribbean Games as a long-awaited partnership between the government and the country's many sports organizations. The partnership expanded to include Dominican citizens, with sports editor Pedro Caba headlining his report "XII Central American and Caribbean Games: Extraordinary National Responsibility."[55] Preparing for the games would require millions of dollars in investment in infrastructure and training, but given Balaguer's demand for a balanced budget, Caba expected the investment to pay off in the future. More significantly, official support for the games signaled sports administrators' compliance with their duty to provide sport and physical education as an "essential part of the process of human formation."[56] Sportswriters who had criticized government spending on professional baseball at the cost of developing amateur sport finally saw officials prioritizing nation-building through amateur sport. Investment in sport and culture would unify Dominicans, Caba believed, and create a "sporting mystique that will constitute permanent progress" for the entire nation.[57] Dominican citizens joined sports leaders like Veras and Dominican Olympic Committee president García Saleta, along with sportswriters and even Balaguer himself as they worked to prepare for the games under the motto "*un compromiso de todos*," a shared duty.

While Dominican citizens and sportswriters saw the national sporting project as a possible *estímulo deportivo* for the democratic society they imagined in 1962, the Balaguer regime worked to draw Dominicans into the Bloodless Revolution. Leaders in the government debated the wisdom of hosting an event of such size and caliber, one exponentially more complex than the Amateur World Series, while the country continued to struggle with violence and dissent well into Balaguer's second term. Some even warned of communist sympathies in the Olympic Committee.[58] Rather than distract from efforts to quell the opposition, however, Balaguer embraced the games as a tool to consolidate amateur sport under the Bloodless Revolution by conflating human development through sport with his plan for economic development. The exchanges between citizens who requested sports resources and government officials who provided them mirrored the paternalism of the Trujillo era and of populist regimes in Puerto Rico and Argentina in the 1940s and 1950s.[59] Cuba's cooperation in providing technical expertise and training assistance bolstered the National Institute of Sports, Physical Education, and Recreation (INDER) as a national model. The Balaguer government applied the Cuban narrative of sport as a means to develop all citizens to validate claims that economic development would raise all Dominicans. Conflating the social and human development promised by sport with the economic development represented by policies such as the Industrial Incentives Law in the project to prepare the regional sporting tournament had lasting consequences for Dominican democracy. As Dominicans worked to fulfill the *compromiso de todos,* the regime institutionalized the paternalism of the Bloodless Revolution into a Third Way government that it called a democracy. They continued to invest in the individual prosperity and hope offered by professional sport and conformed to the popular sentiment that "practicing sports makes the nation."[60]

Less than six months into Balaguer's second term, Dominicans needed unity more than ever. Despite increases in national GDP in 1971 and 1972, which led one government official to credit the Balaguer government with "one of the most profound revolutions that any country in Latin America has achieved in recent times within a constitutional order of liberty and respect for the human dignity of people," demonstrations against the president continued, as did violent suppression.[61] The violence and repression got so bad that some warned of the possible return of US-OAS peacekeeping forces.[62] More than a year and several deaths after the relative calm of the Amateur World Series, the same issue of *¡Ahora!* that hailed the potential benefits of the 1974 Games described a "wave of terror" and wondered who was responsible: the opposition or the government. While *¡Ahora!* identified responsible officers in the National Police and argued that officials at higher levels, possibly Balaguer himself, turned a blind eye to their actions or, worse, directed them, Balaguer deflected. The murders and disappearances, he explained, derived from "a state of 'collective malice'" remaining from the civil war, not official commands.[63] Uniting Dominicans under the government-led shared duty of the 1974 Games, Balaguer hoped, would counter that malice with a sporting mystique.

The national project to prepare for the Central American and Caribbean Games countered accusations that the Balaguer government too often sacrificed the interests of the popular classes to support private enterprise.[64] The government provided legislative backing and financial resources to sporting projects across the country. Already in 1968, Veras and García Saleta had written legislation that defined material and technical support for sport as an obligation of the Dominican state, with the reasoning that sport was a means to "the betterment and moral, intellectual, and physical improvement of Dominican youths" and society.[65] With the project for the 1974 Games under way, the Balaguer government complied. Along with symbolic gestures such as designating 1971 the "Year of Sport," the government created a special sports development fund. From a relatively modest initial designation of just over $15,000 in 1971, the budget more than tripled the next year and rose to almost $54,000 by 1974.[66] In addition, the government offered funds for Veras's plans to develop physical education and amateur venues.[67] The overall budget for the development of sport, including school programs for physical education, increased by more than $100,000 between 1970 and 1971. Before the "Year of Sport," more funding had always been allocated to physical education than to sport-specific development programs. That, too, changed by 1972, when the budget for sports development increased by nearly $200,000, to $521,716. In 1974, the year of the regional tournament, the program received almost $900,000 in funding. Officials like Veras and García Saleta believed that if raised in the values of sport, Dominicans would learn to live "physically balanced, efficient, and satisfactory" lives and contribute to the good of the nation.[68]

Dominicans quickly and enthusiastically joined the project to fortify national sport, adopting the narrative that sport would bring personal and national progress in their requests to President Balaguer and Sports Director Veras. The leaders of a recently formed basketball club in Higuey province emphasized their "noble purpose" to form local youths into "a class worthy of belonging to this nation" in their request for a court.[69] The letter followed a telegram sent by two legislators whose request for Balaguer's help in setting up a meeting between Veras and local authorities emphasized not only the talent of local youths but also their desire to "raise our flag high during the great international event of the XII Games of 1974."[70] With less than a year remaining before the games, young people calling themselves the "legitimate representatives" of Azua requested a new multi-sport complex for the express purpose of hosting selection tournaments to determine who would represent the nation. Beyond the 1974 Games, the writers explained, the complex would fill a regional need "to develop ourselves morally, culturally, and physically through sport," and would create a "much needed permanent closeness among the southern community, as [. . .] only sport and culture [can] unite people permanently without political, racial, or religious problems."[71]

Framing their requests in the rhetoric of sport for personal and national development signaled Dominicans' integration into the Bloodless Revolution, or at least their awareness that their requests were contingent on their conformity to this nationalist and paternalist script. The administration and local sports leaders touted the benefits of sport in deterring youths from vices such as alcohol, drugs, and politics. As Santiago's sports promoter Bullo Steffani told Balaguer in his request for funds for a local tournament, "No one knows which of the youths could come out of these tournaments for professional baseball or which could be leaders of groups."[72] Reformista Party leaders from Puerto Plata later identified the groups Steffani would not name as "seditious (*revoltosa*), ex-PRD" youths and requested two sets of baseball equipment to reward their conversion to the party.[73] Other requests were more subtle in employing a paternalist script but referenced the potential political benefits of sports patronage nonetheless. The letter from Azua, for example, expressed the need for a "permanent closeness" to remind government officials of Azuanos' assistance in capturing the guerrilla force led by former colonel and April War leader Francisco Caamaño that had landed in their state weeks before to try again to overthrow the government. Though attentive to the immediate project for the 1974 Games, requests for sports patronage appealed to Balaguer's interest in political stability and conformity to his project.

Opening ceremonies for the games and coverage in *El Caribe* leading up to them declared the national sporting project a success, a duty fulfilled (*compromiso cumplido*), and credited Balaguer's leadership. In remarks after Balaguer opened the games, engineer Bienvenido Martínez Brea, who constructed the Centro Olímpico, affirmed that "the duty has been fulfilled" not only in preparing for the event but also in spreading the sporting spirit, which had "penetrated and engulfed the entire nation, making it healthy and whole (*limpiándolo a la sana*), [with Dominicans] living as one with respect and love for inalienable human dignity."[74] Dominicans owed this success to Balaguer's wisdom in ensuring that building projects for the games were modest and functional, protecting visitors and Dominicans from "subversive" groups, and supporting the "development of the body and spirit of Dominican youth" through construction projects.[75] A full-page spread in *El Caribe* conflated this human development with the economic development symbolized by aerial photos of sports installations. With the declaration that "development is an exercise of Independence," the ad stressed the historical significance of the games being inaugurated on the anniversary of national independence. Dominicans had Balaguer to thank: "[The] XII Games are an international testament to the progress brought to the country by the Government of Dr. Joaquín Balaguer, Constitutional President of the Republic."[76]

The opening of the 1974 Games and celebrations of the "festival of youth and sport" secured Balaguer's reelection in May 1974, and consolidated sport as part of the Bloodless Revolution. The day following the opening ceremonies, *El Caribe* printed excerpts from a speech in which Senate president Adriano "Nano" Uribe Silva urged Balaguer to accept the party's nomination to run for a third term. Dismissing concerns that reelection might violate the constitution, Uribe Silva stressed that reelection was necessary to "ensure the culmination of the extraordinary work of the last seven years [. . .] by a government whose vigorous action has been positively felt in all areas of national life."[77] By targeting *campesinos* and other communities that had previously lacked government attention, the national project for the games exemplified the "profound changes in specific socioeconomic structures" that Balaguer had overseen to "propel the country's nascent development."[78] A cartoon in *El Caribe* one year after the inauguration depicted the success of the sports project to incorporate youths into the Bloodless Revolution (fig. 4.2). In the cartoon, a *campesino* youth (*juventud campesina*) represented by a barefoot boy wearing too-short pants and a straw hat is shown gazing up at a tall tree labeled "amateur sport" (*deporte aficionado*). Seeing a ladder representing "COD Resolutions" (Resoluciones

Figure 4.2. "Amateur Sport to Peasant Youth," Teddy, *El Caribe*, February 27, 1975, p. 18.

del COD) leading to the treetop, the boy exclaimed, "I believe that now, yes! I am going to be able to eat from the fruits of this tree."[79] Government backing for sport gave even the most disadvantaged Dominicans the tools for their ascent.

With reelection secured and his third consecutive inauguration passed, in December 1974 Balaguer and the Reformista-led Congress institutionalized sport in the Bloodless Revolution by passing a sports law that elevated national sport from the director under the secretary of education to a cabinet position as the secretary of Sports, Physical Education, and Recreation (SEDEFIR). Charged with overseeing the continual development of amateur sport and physical education across the country, similar to Cuba's INDER, the new secretary of sports would protect the resources needed to develop Dominicans through sport. The new department also institutionalized Balaguer's position as the patron of national sport, the one who led Dominicans to progress much as a parent or teacher might guide a child, by reporting directly to him. Sportswriters and cartoonists accepted this paternalism without

Figure 4.3. "Secretary of Sports, Lending a Hand to Dominican Children," Teddy, *El Caribe*, April 21, 1976, p. 17.

explicit criticism, as in one cartoon published in April 1976 (fig. 4.3). In the cartoon, a boy in short pants representing "Dominican children" grasped the fingers of a man in a suit labeled "Sports Plans of the Secretary of Sports." With eyes shining in gratitude, the boy gazed up at the man, whose head extended beyond the frame, and said, "It is good to know that one is not so alone."[80] The secretary of sports completed the message of Balaguer's concern for the Dominican people and his leadership in their path to peace, harmony, and development. With political violence and opposition forces quieted, though not silent, after Caamaño's coup failed in 1973, Balaguer not only answered Dominican calls for self-improvement and national progress through sport but also defined the path to progress and led them on it.

Conclusion

Incorporating sport into the Bloodless Revolution allowed Balaguer to create a Dominican path to development, or a Third Way that maneuvered between the models represented in the Americas by the United States and Cuba. He met the demands of many industrialists and US business leaders by supporting and even extending the Industrial Incentives Law of 1968 and protecting them from labor unrest. To counter the negative effects of these policies, both materially and symbolically, Balaguer invested in citizens. Sports proved a valuable investment because it allowed the administration to discipline Dominicans in both the proper sporting behavior and following the proper scripts to receive funds or installations for sport practice. Most importantly, investment in amateur sport and the national project to prepare the Central American and Caribbean Games in 1974 created an image of concern for the development of Dominican citizens along with their economy. Although Balaguer's version of constitutional government fell far short of Dominican ideals for political participation and economic opportunity, the government boosted its legitimacy by responding to public needs and fulfilling requests for sports patronage. Paternalism remained integral to Dominican politics.

Internationally, Balaguer's Third Way allowed him to gain credibility as a pluralist and as a leader intent on seeing his country through development. Although not afraid to act against leftist organizations, by his second term Balaguer defended his power rather than ideology. During the campaign for 1970, he ended the prohibition against Dominican leftist parties and was willing to embrace relations with Cuba, at least in sport. Sport provided an ideal platform for this new relationship with Cuba. Balaguer fulfilled popular demands and gained advice not only for success in the games but also for building a new national sports apparatus that favored amateur sport as a means to develop democratic citizens. Hosting large international sporting events like the Amateur World Series and Central American and Caribbean Games also projected the Dominican Republic as a leader in regional sports rather than a mere participant, raising Balaguer's reputation as a regional leader. As Latin Americans increasingly came together to balance US influence in the region through the early 1970s, Balaguer ensured that he and the Dominican Republic remained relevant. Participation in amateur sport offered a path for building Latin American unity and demonstrating the power of solidarity.

Renewed relations with Cuba and the Bloodless Revolution as a Third Way also reframed Dominican relations with the United States. The "Cuba, Sí! Yankees, No!" chants at the Amateur World Series final and tensions in the International Baseball Federations (IBAF) during the series foretold of divisions in amateur baseball along political lines defined by the United States and Cuba. Some Latin American nations participated on both sides, trying to avoid the infiltration of politics into sport; in the Dominican Republic, those lines were drawn between amateur and professional baseball.[81] The Bloodless Revolution allowed Dominicans to follow both paths simultaneously. Cuba provided a model for amateur sport and developing Dominican citizens for the good of the nation, a model institutionalized in the Dominican Republic by the secretary of sports. The United States provided not just a model but a path for individual citizens to attain the material benefits of economic development. The paths coexisted under the Bloodless Revolution with relatively little tension so long as the Balaguer administration could afford to invest in both paths. When the economic crisis of the mid-1970s hit, Balaguer found a new model.

FIVE

Sliding into Third

The Cibao Summer League and Baseball as Development

Julián Javier smiled as he stood in center field of La Vega's new stadium holding the banner for his team, the Arroceros del Nordeste (Northeastern Rice Farmers) from San Francisco de Macorís. The inauguration ceremonies for the new public stadium coincided with those for the Cibao Summer League (Liga de Verano del Cibao), founded in April 1975 by business and sport leaders from the Cibao region north of Santo Domingo to increase opportunities in professional baseball on the island, extend professional baseball to cities in the interior of the country, and establish the heart of a baseball industry in the Cibao region. In a sign of support for the league and the government's program to expand national sports, a capacity crowd of more than ten thousand cheered as president Joaquín Balaguer announced the beginning of the next phase of construction, which would add a covered volleyball-basketball court alongside the million-dollar baseball stadium. As he looked to his side at Félix Santana, the manager-player for La Vega's Indios del Valle (Valley Indians), Javier no doubt felt good about the opportunity the league offered to men like Santana, who had bounced around the minor leagues for the entirety of his fourteen-year career in US baseball. Having never played in the major leagues, Santana lacked the generous pension guaranteed those, like Javier, who had played more than ten seasons in the big leagues.[1] With his earning potential dwindling as he entered his thirties, Santana relied on the opportunity provided by the Cibao league to extend his career by developing as a coach and manager. Even after his team fell 20–1 to the Indios, Javier celebrated "a dream come happily true" for himself, his *cibaeño* (from the Cibao) business partners, and baseball fans across the region.[2]

To the south, in the capital, Felipe Alou and the directors of the Dominican Republic Summer League (Liga de Verano de Béisbol Profesional de la República Dominicana) made final preparations for the inauguration of their own tournament. When President Balaguer spoke at their inauguration the next weekend at Estadio Quisqueya, the home field of the Fieras Capitaleñas (Capital Savages), a crowd of nearly three thousand applauded his announcement that the government would begin construction for a new baseball field in San Cristóbal, the home of the visiting Mellizos del Sur (Twins of the South). Like the Cibao Summer League, the capital-based league defined its role as providing employment to players released from US baseball. Unlike the Cibao league, which pursued more experienced players from home and abroad to attract crowds, the Dominican Republic league focused on restarting the careers of young players already dismissed from US teams. Committed to signing only Dominican players, officials of the Dominican Republic Summer League saw their primary responsibility to the young men aspiring to follow the examples of compatriots like Alou and Epifanio "Epy" Obdulio Guerrero who had built careers in baseball. Guerrero joined the league in its inaugural season as the manager for the Mellizos del Sur based in San Cristóbal-Baní, a position that nicely complemented his work as a scout for the New York Yankees by offering playing experience to the prospects he trained and signed for his big-league employer.

The Cibao and Dominican Republic summer leagues represented new models for economic growth and alternatives to the unfettered capitalism practiced by major-league teams and scouts on the island. Scouts and US teams in the "free-bid market" of Caribbean scouting viewed prospective players as commodities to extract and develop abroad.[3] Boys as young as thirteen sacrificed educational opportunities for the dream of a major-league career, despite the harsh reality that many were released before they had the chance to acclimate to life abroad. The exodus of young big-league hopefuls robbed the once-vibrant amateur leagues of participants, while contractual obligations with US teams prevented their more experienced compatriots from playing in the Dominican Winter League. Latin American scouts accommodated the system to lower the hurdles such as cultural adjustment, language, and relative lack of professional coaching that slowed Dominican careers. By 1975, however, Dominicans had grown frustrated with the deleterious effects of the US model on national baseball institutions and culture. In response, business and baseball leaders built the Dominican Republic and Cibao summer leagues as new models of industry, models that favored native talent and valued the nation as a market. The leagues differed in the role they imagined for the Dominican government, the thrust of their objectives, and their levels of independence from US baseball, but both represented a Third Way between the unregulated capitalism seen in the US professional baseball model and the social emphasis of the Cuban amateur model.

The Third Way defined the relationship among economic development, social justice, and political freedom that Dominicans had equated with democratic society since they freed baseball from the Trujillo regime in the 1960s. These new, socially conscious models for development arose in an atmosphere of public debate around Balaguer's policies to support *desarrollismo*, or the idea that economic growth, rather than civil rights and democratic policies, would bring the social benefits and political freedom that Dominicans expected from democracy. Balaguer astutely seized on the Dominican Republic and Cibao summer leagues as examples of the benefits of *desarrollismo*, and specifically the policies embedded in the Industrial Incentives and Protections Law of 1968. Directors of the Cibao Summer League earned government support in the form of industrial incentives by identifying as a new, national industry based in the long-ignored Cibao, while the Dominican Republic Summer League, at least through 1978, emphasized social objectives to provide opportunity to ballplayers discarded prematurely from US baseball. Both leagues grew in the atmosphere of economic innovation and experimentation, what Dominican historian Frank Moya Pons described as a "business mentality," that emerged from the discourse around industrial incentives and the proper relationship between economic growth and opportunity in a democratic society.[4]

Promises of Opportunity and Dominican Innovations

Free-agent scouting in the Caribbean exemplified the free-market capitalist model that multinational corporations had enjoyed in many Latin

American nations since the late nineteenth century. In this model, US companies relied on cheap local labor to extract raw materials for refinement and consumption in the United States. When applied to baseball, US teams signed young Latin American ballplayers for a pittance of a signing bonus with the hope of finding a so-called diamond in the rough, a naturally gifted ballplayer who, with a bit of training, could lead the team to championships. Recognizing that the raw materials were human, major-league teams and the scouts that represented them relied on a narrative of opportunity, a promise of luxury and success, to lure Dominican baseball talent from the country. Dominican scouts, many of whom gained their positions after being released as players, served as important go-betweens in the relationship between major-league teams and the prospects. They accommodated the US model to the local realities of smaller ballplayers, meager educational opportunities, and a lack of formal youth coaching to increase their signees' chances at success and to bolster their own reputations in the "wheeler-dealer world" of free-market baseball.[5]

The US baseball model stood on a narrative of opportunity that spread from the Irish and German neighborhoods of New York and Pittsburgh in the late nineteenth and early twentieth centuries to the Caribbean by the 1960s and 1970s. In contrast to these European immigrants whose success in baseball came through their assimilation to the "up-from-the-bootstraps" myth of US progress, Dominican ballplayers and their Latin American colleagues, even Puerto Ricans who are US citizens, remained outside.[6] Given higher rates of poverty in Caribbean nations compared to the United States, the US press transformed the narrative of opportunity into one of escape that rationalized sacrifices in education and pride for the chance to play on a big-league field. A *Sports Illustrated* story on Pirates scout Howie Haak intimated this perceived desperation as Dominican hopefuls stood "rooted to the ball field," watching Haak drive away "because there is no place else for them to go and no way for them to get there."[7] Cuban Preston Gómez, then third-base coach for the Los Angeles Dodgers, put this desperation in more material terms in 1967. Low levels of education and limited career options, he explained, meant that Caribbean boys had "no chance ever of getting the luxuries and pleasures that the American boy takes for granted." With professional baseball, they too might access the fancy cars, nice clothes, and big homes that they saw stars like Juan Marichal and Roberto Clemente enjoy.[8]

The narrative of opportunity along with the perceived lack of educational and career options available to Latin American youths rationalized pulling prospects as young as thirteen out of school to sign professional contracts.[9] As one administrator in the Office of the Baseball Commissioner told *Sports Illustrated*'s Bill Brubaker in 1981, "We'd rather see kids in school, if that's the pattern in their country. But if most of them are not in school anyway and they want to play ball, then we're giving them an opportunity to earn some money."[10] Similar to the false dichotomy between unemployment and the poverty wages and dangerous conditions that Mexican workers endure in maquilas on the border, this baseball administrator and the US press suggested that even in exploiting them, US baseball was doing young players a favor.

Even local scouts, including Guerrero and Avila, employed the narrative of opportunity to rationalize their actions in the competitive world of free-agent baseball scouting. Pushed by their own competition with other scouts to secure a prospect for their major-league employers, Guerrero and Avila signed players as young as thirteen and enticed them from their homes and school with the hopes of a big-league career. Guerrero made headlines with his signing of thirteen-year-old Jimy Kelly, the namesake for the Kelly rule, which since 1984 has prohibited US teams from signing prospects younger than sixteen. Likewise, Avila employed the narrative of opportunity in response to Brubaker's question whether he was exploiting pitching prospect Rafael Montalvo by signing him at age fourteen: "Exploiting them? No, helping them. [. . .] I took this kid to Santo Domingo, put him in a boarding house, paid his rent, gave him clothes and taught him everything. [. . .] Some day soon, after he reaches the big leagues, he'll become a free agent and try to make a million dollars. That's exploitation? No way. I'm proud to say I've given this kid a chance to have a better future."[11]

Although also guilty of allowing Dominican and other Latin American youths to sacrifice education for the hope of a baseball career—though some lacked access to even that—Avila's defense of signing Montalvo revealed a significant difference between the practices by Latin America-based scouts and their colleagues based in the United States. In contrast to the few pointers Haak offered before driving away, scouts based in Latin America invested their time and even money to help major-league hopefuls overcome the unique challenges they faced compared to their US teammates.[12] Their smaller size and the necessity of learning English, both of which Alou described in 1963, were at the top of the list.[13] A feature in *People* reported that Guerrero spent time helping Dominican prospects train as infield specialists because of their smaller sizes and arranged for a surgery to remove bone chips from Tony Fernández's knees before signing the future five-time All-Star for the Toronto Blue Jays.[14] Avila's colleague on the Dodgers, Elvio Jiménez, explained that he and Avila dedicated extra time to helping a young Pedro Martínez, now a Hall of Famer, learn baseball discipline and English. Dominican scouts made these investments informally as a means to build relationships with prospects and their parents and to advance their own careers by signing promising players.[15] Local conditions required investments of time and money beyond what US-based scouts were accustomed to making, but making these investments allowed Latin American scouts to accommodate the US system for the good of their own careers and those of many of their prospects.

While Gómez suggested that their so-called hunger gave Latin American players "one big advantage over the American boys," scouts on the ground in the Dominican Republic worked to ensure that the only hunger Latin American prospects brought to US ballfields was desire. Scouts in the Dominican Republic, most prominently Guerrero and Avila, refined long-held practices for developing Dominican ballplayers to better prepare them for careers in the United States. Their investment of time and resources allowed players to overcome obstacles such as undernourishment, low levels of education, and a lack of professional training. The ownership they exercised over the baseball industry, in addition to the extended domestic labor of their wives, allowed these men to institutionalize common local practices that elevated the Dominican Republic in the global baseball industry, including the baseball academies that all major-league teams operate in the country. Their attention to prospects' success and the country's reputation in the industry also led them to participate in the creation of new baseball models, including the Dominican Republic and Cibao summer leagues.

Dominican Baseball Models

The Cibao and Dominican Republic summer leagues developed in 1975 amid deepening controversy over professional baseball in the country. The popular disgust underlying calls to develop amateur sport during Balaguer's first term escalated into what sportswriters deemed a crisis in professional baseball as fans avoided ballparks. The crisis extended throughout the Caribbean, with sportswriters reporting that all four teams in the 1975 Caribbean Series (Serie del Caribe) lost money. The Dominican contender, the Aguilas Cibaeñas, reported the greatest losses at $23,000.[16] While sportswriters offered many explanations for fans' diminished enthusiasm, all centered on the league's perceived disrespect for national players and for the history of the game in the region. Paralleling analyses of US-Latin American political and economic relations, sports leaders described a dependent relationship between Dominican and US baseball. Providing raw talent, or raw materials, to US baseball for training, or manufacture, subjugated Dominican baseball to the US organization. In this commodification of ballplayers, US teams disregarded the role of Dominican institutions, coaches, scouts, and even the players themselves in producing baseball talent. In the Winter League, this disrespect had manifested as such extensive US influence over local rosters that one Puerto Rican sportswriter lamented, "We no longer have Caribbean baseball. Now it's North American baseball in the Caribbean with native reinforcements."[17] The summer leagues confronted these issues head-on, providing opportunities for young players to continue their development and their careers after being released from US baseball, for older players to stretch their playing careers or begin new ones as coaches or trainers, and for fans to experience baseball year-round. Sportswriters from across the Caribbean looked hopefully on the Dominican Republic and Cibao summer leagues as new models for professional baseball that blended social and capitalist objectives.[18]

The most striking difference between the local summer leagues and the capitalist baseball model centered on the treatment of Dominican ballplayers. Rather than viewing them as raw materials destined for refinement in the United States, the Dominican Republic and Cibao summer leagues valued players as human capital whose skills would create national products—ballplayers, coaches, and baseball games—in a national industry. In terms of player development, the new leagues continued the work of scouts like Guerrero by providing the hundreds of Dominican players "bagged, signed, and released" by organized baseball with an opportunity to earn a salary and develop their skills.[19] The summer leagues provided these hopefuls with the playing experience that "models of success" such as Juan Marichal had gained in amateur leagues while also providing an essential salary. Some players developed their skills enough to find another opportunity in US baseball, while others continued their employment as professional ballplayers at home, as was the case for José Abreu.[20] Signed at seventeen after completing less than one year of high school, Abreu saw only twelve games over parts of two seasons in the US minor leagues. A decade later, he supported himself and his family with the meager salary he earned from the Dominican Republic Summer League. "Founded on biblical principles of protecting the hundreds of Dominican players prematurely retired from organized baseball in the United States," the summer leagues worked to provide opportunities for men like Abreu who had sacrificed education and youth for ephemeral careers in the United States.[21]

The summer leagues also helped to extend the careers of veterans who had succeeded in major-league baseball. With its backing by business leaders in the region, the Cibao Summer League was able to pay larger salaries and attract more experienced players than its counterpart based in the capital. In contrast to the Winter League, which was "throwing glorious players from this country to the street without contemplation," the Cibao Summer League offered veterans the chance to continue their playing careers even as their performance declined.[22] The Dominican Republic Summer League emphasized economic opportunities for less-developed players. The Cibao league focused on veterans, who might use the league to rehabilitate careers in the better-paying US leagues, continue their careers in a familiar environment, or gain experience as coaches, trainers, and managers. As Javier remembered, "[The Cibao Summer League] was to help a few retired players. We [the administrators] never received the benefits; the players received the benefits."[23] Jesús Alou was one such beneficiary. After being released by the New York Mets in 1976 and playing the 1977 season with the Linieros de Mao (Mao Linesmen, a reference to their place on the border) in the Cibao league, he signed a two-year contract with the Houston Astros.[24] Whether for young men like Abreu aspiring to build a career in baseball or veterans hoping to extend their productive years, the summer leagues offered Dominicans the chance to continue their baseball careers at home and, potentially, abroad.

The Dominican summer leagues worked to counter the larger structural issues behind the insults to local veterans in the US capitalist model by signing only free agents and limiting the number of foreign players allowed on each team. Seen most poignantly in the debates around the 1960–1961 natives-only tournament, which helped free baseball from the Trujillo regime, questions over the number of foreign players hired to reinforce each Winter League team dominated the sports pages in the months before the tournament. These debates alternated between diagnoses that the country lacked sufficient talent to ensure competitive balance and the need to give young players the opportunity to play. As US team owners came to recognize the value of the Winter League for developing US as well as Dominican talent, they exercised more influence over winter rosters and even lineups. The Aguilas's trade of veteran Ricardo "Rico" Carty to their rivals Licey, allegedly to make room for two young prospects for the Pittsburgh Pirates, exemplified this influence. Fans saw the trade as a betrayal to them, to the team, and to Carty himself.[25] By signing only free agents, both summer leagues eliminated this meddling, though they had different stances on hiring players from other countries to reinforce their teams. The Dominican Republic Summer League prohibited foreign players altogether, leaving all roster spots open to Dominican players—at least through the first four seasons.[26] The Cibao Summer League, on the other hand, embraced veteran players from across the Americas but limited teams to five foreign reinforcements and reserved the designated hitter (DH) position for Dominican veterans.[27]

In addition to explicitly extending opportunities for Dominican ballplayers, the leaders of the Dominican summer leagues restructured professional baseball to serve Dominicans beyond the ballpark. They explicitly embraced baseball's social functions as well as its economic ones. To extend the social mission to the community, the Santo Domingo–based Dominican Republic Summer League publicly supported the amateur leagues, which Felipe Alou had explained were decimated by the "indiscriminate signings" by major-league scouts.[28] The league embraced a 5 percent charge on all tickets to support amateur baseball and left the administration of the public ballparks to the Office of the Secretary of Sports. This contrast with the Dominican Winter League, which negotiated tax exonerations and administration of the public stadiums as part of a package of government concessions each year, boosted the Dominican Republic Summer League's public reputation. Although Cibao Summer League directors accepted government support in the form of new public stadiums and tax exonerations, they also backed their claims of social benefits with action. Teams and players donated time and equipment to charity, offered 10 percent of the proceeds from a double-header to support a youth tournament, and ran free clinics for young baseball enthusiasts.[29] The summer leagues created a new structure for professional baseball to address the concerns of Dominican fans who wondered, "In what ways does professional baseball benefit Dominicans?"[30] The leagues' social mission, along with their reliance on public stadiums and benefits, allowed Balaguer to incorporate them and the national pastime under his Bloodless Revolution, the promise of a democratic revolution such as John F. Kennedy had portrayed when he announced the Alliance for Progress in 1961.

Baseball as Development

By combining professional baseball with social objectives, the summer leagues created a new model for industrialization in the Dominican Republic. Questions about the benefits of professional baseball reflected popular disgust with perceptions that the Dominican economy supported members of the industrial classes at home and abroad rather than the Dominican people. As the oil crisis and other trade imbalances decreased the public funds available for government patronage through the 1970s, Dominicans resurrected debates about economic policy. The business mentality that arose with discussions around the 1968 Industrial Incentives Law permeated even the national pastime as Dominicans asked how the incentives benefited them. Again, the summer leagues provided an answer. Rather than replacements for the big-league, capitalist model tied to the Winter League, the summer leagues emerged as alternative, Dominican-led development models that would facilitate a baseball industry operating parallel to, and sometimes in cooperation with, the US system. Both summer leagues were capitalist in the sense that they relied on profits to sustain themselves. The leagues differed in their objectives, the role they imagined for the Dominican government, and their level of independence from US baseball. While both contributed to the birth of a baseball industry in the Dominican Republic, the Cibao Summer League's framing of baseball as an industry with social benefits rather than a social good itself won greater government support in the form of financial concessions and infrastructure. Through their balance of profits with social concerns, including a commitment to providing economic opportunity for victims of global capitalism, the summer leagues offered a Third Way of development that aligned with Dominican expectations for their national pastime, and for democracy.

Although both summer leagues became part of a national baseball industry that produced baseball players for global markets, only the Cibao Summer League explicitly aligned its objectives with the government's call for industrialization. Early in the first summer season in the Cibao, a political commentator for the Santiago-based newspaper *La Información* devoted his column to the league's "many social facets, along with its principal economic interests."[31] The description paralleled Dominican views, promoted since the 1960s, that industry and economic development should bring social benefits to the nation. In contrast to sportswriters' appeals that reminded fans of the capital-based league's "biblical principles" of serving ballplayers, the *cibaeño* columnist emphasized the Cibao league's economic structure and business orientation to portray it as an industry. Like its counterpart in the capital, the Cibao league worked on the "rehabilitation" of distinguished ballplayers who were "unjustly rejected by organized baseball." But they did so with a desire to produce talent and not merely out of generosity, as the columnist confirmed with the rhetorical question: "Who doubts that the Summer League will produce optimum athletes, in line with a budding industry?" (*una industria sui generis*). Taking the raw material rejected in the United States, the Cibao Summer League produced ballplayers, one of the nation's most prized exports and a popular commodity in local baseball markets.

Managers, coaches, trainers, and administrators served as skilled laborers who shaped players, and the league also recognized the individuals in these positions as human capital. Both leagues offered new opportunities for Dominicans to make careers in positions that had previously been limited to those who could secure employment through US teams or had professional connections with the Winter League. Felipe Alou and Julián Javier, both longtime major leaguers, worked off the field as team or league administrators in addition to their on-field management positions. While Alou leveraged this experience to become the first Dominican manager in the major leagues, Javier later worked in the administration of the Gigantes del Nordeste (Northeast Giants, later Gigantes del Cibao) from his native San Francisco de Macorís after the Winter League expanded to six teams in 1996.[32] Likewise, Félix Santana used his experience as a player-manager with the Indios del Valle to secure a coaching job with the Estrellas in the Dominican Winter League. Scouts such as Elvio Jiménez and Epy Guerrero worked in varying capacities with both summer leagues to bolster their careers and to assist the players they signed. One of these players, Tony Fernández, spent part of his seasons in the early 1980s with the Cibao league on his way to building a seventeen-season major-league career that included five All-Star Game appearances and four Gold Gloves.[33] In the process of producing a spectacle for local consumption, the summer leagues created new, skilled positions for Dominican sportsmen, who in many cases leveraged these skills into decades-long careers in the baseball industry.

While both summer leagues produced ballplayers, managers, coaches, trainers, and administrators, the Cibao Summer League distinguished itself over the Dominican Republic Summer League for its production of baseball games. The Cibao league's emphasis on veteran players and openness to foreign players meant that it could offer higher-level competition and greater spectacles for local consumption. League directors chose ballplayers, managers, and coaches to win games and draw fans. Leading up to the 1975 season, for example, the sporting press worked up buzz around the players destined for the Cibao league. They reminded fans of Cuban Zoilo Versalles's MVP season with the American League champion Minnesota Twins in 1965 when Versalles signed to play for Puerto Plata's Piratas del Atlántico (Atlantic Pirates). They hyped local stars like Santana too. A cartoon accompanying the announcement that Santana had signed with La Vega's Indios del Valle played on his reputation as a hard-nosed player with the Aguilas; in the cartoon, a representative of the Indios exclaimed to fans that he had just contracted this *jurel* (mackerel, tough-skinned person) to take on capable opponents.[34] The Cibao Summer League selected players like Versalles and Santana not simply to field full teams but to draw fans. With a focus on producing for local audiences, the Cibao league was not just about developing players, managers, and coaches, but also fielding competitive teams that appealed to the fans.

By producing exciting baseball spectacles, the Cibao Summer League generated employment in the region and established a basis to earn financial support similar to what the government offered other industries. As a columnist from *La Información* explained, ballgames opened "countless economic resources" for a large sector of the local population by creating jobs in concessions, ticket sales, maintenance, construction, and transportation.[35] Aware of Balaguer's desire to promote industrialization, the Cibao league directors explicitly invoked their business mentality in their discussions with President Balaguer and Secretary of Sports Castellanos. Not only would the Cibao Summer League provide "healthy diversion," the directors argued, but it would "ensure the sustenance of hundreds of families who for various months will have the favor of their job protected by the opportunity that you [Balaguer] give them."[36]

Framing the national pastime as the basis for a national industry proved effective for both the Cibao Summer League and Balaguer. The Cibao league received tax exonerations and breaks on electricity similar to those the Winter League had received since 1955, but its emphasis on economic development protected directors and government officials from criticism that they were diverting funds from amateur sport in the name of profit.[37] Instead, the concessions derived from the Industrial Incentives Law of 1968 and offered an example of the benefits that industries could bring to the nation. Balaguer needed only to point to the opportunities for employment surrounding the Cibao Summer League and the investment it brought to the region to defend the public expenditure on professional baseball. In contrast to the Winter League's dependence on the extractive model of US baseball, the Cibao league offered a platform for a national industry owned by Dominicans who invested in their compatriots. Even more so than the Dominican Republic Summer League, which followed its social orientation at least through 1978, the baseball industry centered in the Cibao operated according to Dominican expectations that true development meant a "more equitable distribution of economic and other opportunities."[38]

Development Schemes and Baseball Rivalries

Business and baseball leaders in the Cibao worked to make the region the center of a national baseball industry as the rise of the Aguilas Cibaeñas from underdog to powerhouse shifted the primary Winter League rivalry away from the capital teams, Licey and Escogido. The "great rivalry of Dominican baseball, which has existed ever since,"[39] between the Aguilas and Licey paralleled competition for favor in Balaguer's distribution of economic incentives. *Cibaeño* business leaders and academics were among the loudest critics of Balaguer's apparent favoritism for the same import-substitution industries that Trujillo had favored in the 1930s and 1940s. These policies had concentrated industries in the capital, they argued, and continued to give established industrialists in

Santo Domingo, in particular those belonging to the Consejo Nacional de Hombres de Empresa that had conspired to oust Bosch, undue political influence.[40] Economists at the Universidad Católica Madre y Maestra (UCMM) based in Santiago argued that the government should offer more incentives for industries that relied on nationally produced inputs such as the agricultural products from the Cibao, reflecting what Moya Pons described as a "strong and radical regionalism."[41] Beyond creating a handful of jobs, the economists argued, these industries would result in more integrated development as their benefits spread through society. Using these arguments, the directors of the Cibao Summer League won financial and infrastructure support from the government. In the process, they legitimated Balaguer's *desarrollismo*.

The Cibao Summer League exemplified an industry designed according to the reforms that *cibaeños* had proposed for the incentives law. On the surface, the Cibao league followed the import substitution model that Balaguer supported, producing baseball games and, to an extent, ballplayers for local consumption. But rather than generating low-skill, low-paying jobs, the league provided higher-paying jobs for skilled labor and training for employees. The league also addressed the high capital costs and isolated nature of other import-substitution industries by using national rather than imported raw materials. In doing so, they integrated other sectors—in this case, transportation, food services, and even amateur sports—into production.[42] Framing the league as an industry not only won incentives and investment from the government but also proved the benefits of the development model that the *cibaeños* proposed.

For the league directors and their *cibaeño* supporters, the success of the Cibao Summer League offered a measure of the region's potential and "a symbolic victory of a powerful but humiliated, crushed, discriminated, attacked region" over a "profound, capital-based hatred for everything from the Cibao."[43] Commentators in the Cibao pointed to this perceived hatred after Monchín Pichardo, Licey's president, told broadcasters that he had cheered for a team representing another country in the Caribbean Series rather than supporting the Aguilas. While others dismissed Pichardo's comments as "one or another joke among friends," essentially one side of good-natured trash talk among rivals, the story received attention from columnists from the capital and Cibao in the national paper *Listín Diario* as well as further comment in Santiago's *La Información*.[44] Tensions between the regions were high as business and government officials debated industrial incentives and the Aguilas and Licey chased down championships through the 1970s.

The business and baseball leaders who formed the Cibao Summer League were likely as motivated by their regionalism as their business sense in their efforts to claim the center of the national baseball industry for the Cibao.[45] Beyond shifting the axis of the "great rivalry" in the Winter League, the Cibao league shifted the balance of baseball power away from the capital. Buoyed by government infrastructure spending on the multimillion-dollar stadiums inaugurated in La Vega and San Francisco de Macorís in 1975, renovated in Puerto Plata in 1976, and constructed in Mao in 1978, the league elevated four cities in the Cibao to the status of "big-league cities," or those capable of supporting a professional baseball team.[46] Their requests for infrastructure were so successful that by the end of Balaguer's term in 1978, the Cibao region boasted more, and better, baseball stadiums than the capital. The rise of cities in the Cibao confirmed the benefits of the *cibaeño* model for development, raised the region's baseball profile, and offered Balaguer an exemplar of the eventual payoffs of industrial incentives.

In addition to raising the national profile of the Cibao region, the Cibao Summer League buffered Balaguer from criticism against what many perceived as overly favorable policies toward foreign investors.[47] In modeling their program on the Mexican League, which had a relationship with US organized baseball but maintained independent contracts, the Cibao league directors ensured their economic independence from US baseball.[48] By dealing primarily with free agents—men with no US contract—and limiting the number of foreign players, Cibao league managers could fill in lineup cards without a thought about pitch counts or at bats.[49] Fans and team leaders appreciated knowing that the best players on the team would take the field each night. Likewise, players knew that they would not be benched because an executive in a faraway city wanted a US rookie to practice his switch-hitting, and also that they would be free to abandon their contracts for better-paying opportunities in the United States.

The Cibao Summer League directors' socially conscious messaging and nationalism earned Balaguer's support and boosted his political capital in the process. In addition to demonstrating the benefits of his policies for *desarrollismo*, Balaguer's investment in the Cibao league undermined accusations of his favoritism for industries in Santo

Domingo over those in the Cibao or other interior regions. The Cibao Summer League received exonerations for electricity denied to the Dominican Republic Summer League in addition to the capital investment for multimillion-dollar sporting complexes and baseball stadiums with lights.[50] The disparity was motivated at least in part by the industrial bases on which the directors and supporters built the Cibao league. Yet Balaguer's motivations were likely political as well. His support for the Cibao Summer League and industrial incentives likely served as a cover for patronage to voters in the Cibao at a time when Balaguer saw the axis of political influence shifting to the second city, likely due at least in part to the public debates over industrial incentives. In 1978, *cibaeño* businessman and PRD senator Antonio Guzmán, a participant in the debates over incentives, overcame an attempt by the military to rig the election for Balaguer and won the presidency. Months later, Dominicans celebrated the first democratic transition of power in their nation's history.

Conclusion

By 1975, debates over the economic and political future of the nation led to a new understanding of what baseball could mean for Dominicans and for the Dominican Republic. Always at the heart of national pride and identity, baseball became an explicit tool not only for individual prosperity, as it had been for men like Felipe Alou and Juan Marichal, but also for national economic security. Young men lined the fields for a chance to sign a contract with a US team and start a career in their favorite sport. Other Dominicans invested to build businesses designed to help these players fulfill their dreams. No longer simple *pan y circo* (bread and circus) to distract the population from human rights abuses and limitations on their freedoms, baseball offered a means to attain the economic security, or access to a good life, that Dominicans expected democracy to bring. Investment in baseball as a national industry became a path of government action to benefit the people materially and an avenue for the people to forge careers. With its support for the Cibao Summer League, the Balaguer government seized the narrative of opportunity surrounding US baseball and turned it into a budding national industry.

Building an industry around the national pastime benefited Balaguer politically, making his developmentalist policies more palatable to

Dominicans who had seen concessions for industrialists damage the national social system and undermine national sovereignty. By operating as Dominicans imagined a capitalist democracy should, with market forces rather than personal favors determining the success of private enterprises, the summer leagues gave Dominicans hope in the Balaguer government's promise that industrialization would bring economic security. New stadiums in the Cibao region and in the south near Baní exemplified government largesse for national over foreign businesses. The opportunities for advancement offered to ballplayers along with the creation of jobs in concessions, transportation, and other services demonstrated the social benefits of national industry. Although they disagreed with some of the specifics of Balaguer's industrial policies, especially with how incentives were applied in the 1968 law, the directors of the Cibao Summer League, like their counterparts in the capital, created an industry that fulfilled Balaguer's promises and Dominicans' expectations. In the end, both summer leagues created the basis for Dominican control over the baseball industry. The leagues imagined slightly different relations with US baseball, with the Cibao league asserting more independence. Yet by putting Dominicans in charge of scouting, development, coaching, and playing, both leagues ensured that professional baseball was part of the national patrimony. No longer perceived as an obstacle to amateur sport, professional baseball again became a place to make the nation.

The rise of the Cibao in professional baseball paralleled the political rise of *cibaeño* candidates. Likely boosted by the regional leadership in discussions around industrial incentives, and probably because Dominicans grew tired of Balaguer's false promises to return to civilian life, PRD candidate and Santiago businessman Antonio Guzmán won the 1978 presidential elections. Although members of the military seized ballot boxes in an attempt to keep Balaguer in power, Dominicans witnessed the first democratic transition of power in their nation's history. After using sport to hold Balaguer accountable to their demands during his authoritarian *doce años,* Dominicans would continue to employ sport as they worked toward the society they had imagined in the 1960s, now under a more democratic framework.

SIX

Making the Majors

The Baseball Industry and Dominican Democracy

On Saturday, July 28, 2012, the Epy Guerrero Complex teemed with excitement as boys ages fourteen to twenty mingled with scouts at the inauguration of a new baseball league for Dominican prospects. Epy Guerrero greeted former players, parents, and scouts as he roamed the fields, happy to serve as the host for this next iteration of Dominican baseball. Scouts, players, parents, Guerrero's family, Winter League officials, and even workers from Major League Baseball's Santo Domingo office gathered at Epy's complex to celebrate the new National Prospect League (NPL) and to honor Guerrero's half century of dedication to the development of young ballplayers in the Dominican Republic. As Guerrero spoke in the pregame ceremony, he emphasized the importance of investing in youths to secure the future of the nation and his hope that efforts like the NPL would help protect Dominican ballplayers from the dubious business practices that had left many prospects with no future. Independent scouts as well as those affiliated with major-league teams cheered as Guerrero threw the first pitch toward his son Patrick, who held a bat at home plate. On the mound, in the dugout, and in the bleachers stood men who had made their careers in baseball, ready to give the first chance to the young men hoping to follow in their footsteps.

The young men on the field were only the latest beneficiaries of an innovation by Dominican scouts and baseball officials to improve ballplayers' chances and increase their own success in the global baseball industry. In fact, Dominicans like Guerrero and his predecessors and colleagues enticed both the US major leagues and the Dominican government to invest in the Dominican hub of the global baseball industry. Using their community and personal connections, scouts, sportswriters, promoters, and businessmen created the institutions synonymous with the player-development industry centered in the Dominican Republic. As seen with the Cibao Summer League, baseball and business partnerships won government support for these endeavors. Over time, scouts on the ground also persuaded their US employers to invest in the Dominican Republic, most visibly in the team academies, Dominican Summer League, and Major League Baseball (MLB) office that are today synonymous with the Dominican baseball industry. Yet MLB investments are only part of the story. As exemplified by the NPL, scouts and others who participate in the Dominican baseball industry and the communities surrounding it continue to create new institutions outside of MLB's purview. The NPL directors hosted by Guerrero were not employed by an MLB team; rather, they were independent trainers, those sometimes maligned as *buscones*. Independent trainers fill a variety of roles—coach, trainer, agent, surrogate father, teacher—for youths ages twelve to twenty who want to sign professional baseball contracts. They operate in the informal economy, largely outside the reach of MLB or Dominican government regulation, and provide an essential service to youths who want to make baseball their profession.

This chapter details how innovations in baseball attracted investment first from the Dominican government and then from Major League Baseball to help create the national pastime as a national industry after the country's first democratic transition of power in 1978. Despite worsening economic conditions amid the debt crisis and pressures for austerity, the PRD governments of Antonio Guzmán (1978–1982) and Salvador Jorge Blanco (1982–1986) worked to elevate the country's budding political democracy to an economic democracy that met popular expectations that industrialization should benefit all of society. Professional baseball was one target for innovations, and it became an early site of confrontation as Jorge Blanco worked against wealthy team owners to expand the Dominican Winter League to six teams. Expansion required Jorge Blanco to redefine professional baseball as a public good and the annual tournament as a private-public partnership. While preserving earlier narratives of sport as a means for individual and social development, this new definition also emphasized the employment opportunities in professional baseball, not only for players, coaches, trainers, and umpires on the field but also for the food vendors, maintenance workers, and ticket sellers who worked at the stadiums.

Government support for innovations such as early versions of the MLB team academies and the Dominican Summer League, both of which helped prepare Dominican youths for careers in professional baseball, followed the same rationale. Yet economic restrictions imposed by agreements with the International Monetary Fund beginning in 1984 limited government investment, and with it, regulation. After reports of abuse and exploitation by affiliated teams and workers, MLB stepped in after 2000 to take on some of the roles that the government might otherwise have performed. Rather than imposing its corporate or national interests, as some have suggested, MLB's role has often been defined by the innovations of Dominican and other Latin American scouts and officials.[1] Thus, this chapter emphasizes Dominican innovations in and contributions to the global baseball industry in part to historicize the player development hub of that system in the Dominican Republic and to provide an overview of how it operates. MLB academies, the Dominican Summer League, and independent trainers and little leagues are all essential components of MLB's orbit in the global baseball industry. All play a role, along with Dominican officials and administrators who work with MLB or affiliated teams, in driving an industry that now operates on six continents and generated a record $10.7 billion in revenue in 2019.[2]

Winter League Expansion

By expanding the Dominican Winter League from the four traditional teams—Licey, Estrellas, Escogido, and Aguilas—to six, the PRD governments directly confronted the economic elites in the country who had long benefited from government policies such as the Industrial Incentives Law of 1968. In the midst of a growing economic crisis, Dominicans who had demanded economic opportunity in the form of fair wages, full employment, and dignified conditions since the 1960s supported Law 447 to expand the league when Guzmán signed it in 1982 and Jorge Blanco worked to implement it through 1983–1984. Resistance to Law 447 mirrored that to structural change in the economy, and the league appealed to the public, courts, and US baseball in its efforts to resist. Jorge Blanco levied executive and legislative power to force expansion and even negotiated directly with organized baseball and the US baseball commissioner's office. In the process, he redefined professional baseball as a public-private partnership and a sign of the democratic government's commitment to the people. Both professional and amateur baseball, then, would develop the country's youths, bring Dominicans together in healthy recreation, create government revenue for amateur sport, and provide employment for Dominicans across the country, including the opportunity to make it to the big leagues.

Expansion began five months before the May 1982 elections, when the Senate, in which Jorge Blanco represented Santo Domingo, passed Law 447 to grant professional baseball franchises to La Romana in the east and San Cristóbal in the south. The five paragraphs rationalizing the law focused on the state's obligation to provide the means of subsistence—read employment—and recreation to its citizens. Given the increasing numbers of talented professional ballplayers in the country, the law reasoned, the Dominican Winter League's refusal to expand restricted job opportunities among Dominican players. Leaving professional baseball "under the absolute control of a private entity," then, was both inconvenient and out of touch with the country's capacity to develop players. Given the state's right to "contract, supervise, and control (*fiscalizar*)" professional sport in the country and the Office of the Secretary of Sports' position as the "only institution with the authority to grant licenses, franchises, or approvals" for the celebration of professional sporting events, Law 447 created the Azucareros del Este (Sugarmen of the East) in La Romana and the Caimanes del Sur (Alligators of the South) in San Cristóbal.[3] The law both affirmed the status of professional baseball teams as private entities and reiterated the state's ultimate authority over the annual tournaments.

Public debates over expansion dotted the sports pages through the 1982–1983 season and hit a fever pitch as preparations began for the 1983–1984 tournament. The four teams argued that Law 447 was unconstitutional and violated their autonomy and that of the league: the government had effectively forced new partners on the teams and the Dominican League. Backed by some sportswriters, including Cuquí Córdova, Dominican Winter League leaders continued to insist that expansion take place through two leagues.[4] The new teams would further divide the league's already strained economic resources and require greater support from the government during a time of diminishing public revenue, and the new teams could not be trusted to attract the fans necessary to pay their share.[5] As evidence, Estrellas owner Rafael Antún reported seeing only two hundred fans at a semifinal between the Azucareros and Caimanes. Along with Licey president Monchín Pichardo, Antún predicted the demise of winter baseball if expansion continued.[6] The Dominican League owners' insistence that the new teams prove themselves in a separate league was duplicitous, however. The Southeast League was adapted in part from the South League (Liga del Sur) cofounded by Ralph Avila in 1981 as an affiliated minor league to develop local players for the Winter League teams.[7] The players were less experienced than regular league players, which included Dominican major leaguers as well as US reinforcements. As Caimanes team official Mignolio Pujols wrote in a letter to Córdova, the Caimanes and Azucareros had the right to play under equal conditions and with proven players against the four traditional teams.[8]

As debates continued, Jorge Blanco demonstrated his commitment to remaking professional baseball for the public good. On August 5, 1983, the president presented Decree 1300, a new regulation of professional baseball to replace those in effect since the Trujillo era. The document justified state intervention in the organization of professional tournaments by explicitly defining professional baseball as part of the "public interest" given its status as the Dominican people's "principal recreation."[9] Studies and sportswriters' punditry about Law 447 and the legality of Decree 1300 pointed to the Dominican League's dependence on government financial assistance to support claims that professional baseball was a public good. As one of the country's top jurists reasoned, state support and guarantees for the annual tournaments meant that "far from being a private business, exclusive property of the clubs," professional baseball was a public service.[10] Since the league's incorporation in 1955, the teams had received direct financial gifts for the annual Winter Tournaments along with reduced rates on electricity, tax exonerations, and the use of public stadiums. Jorge Blanco based further executive action on the partnership status. On August 12 he revoked the Dominican League's incorporation, making it illegal for it to organize tournaments; the next day he granted incorporation to a new league, the National League of Professional Baseball (Liga Nacional de Base Ball Profesional, LNBP).[11] The Dominican League had refused to organize a national tournament; now it would not be allowed to.

Echoing accusations against the Bosch administration in 1963, the Dominican League and the presidents of the four teams portrayed their conflict with Jorge Blanco as a reflection of the administration's threat to private enterprise and its inability to control the ongoing strikes and protests that undermined the country's stability. In a press release on August 20, league representatives argued that Jorge Blanco's edicts and Law 447 itself "undermine the confidence that businessmen and investors ought to have in the future development of free enterprise in our country."[12] To counter claims that the public financial and infrastructural support made professional baseball more public service than private enterprise, league leaders clarified the limits of that support: the portion of money traded on par covered only approximately 30 percent of the league's costs to pay players and umpires, they had rented stadiums from the government the previous year, and they still paid over RD$70,000 for electricity in each stadium. The press release denounced the negative publicity and the regulations for professional sport as evidence of "a deliberate act" by the government to damage the league on behalf of "the transnational that has been creating a world apart in our national territory and, through Law 447, [. . .] will achieve the domination of a new activity of the Dominican people."[13]

With their reference to "the transnational" and the implications of their warnings about business and investor confidence, the Dominican League attempted to redirect public scrutiny. On the one hand, the conflict between it and the government was centered on whether baseball was defined as a private enterprise. The Dominican League continued to defend itself as a private enterprise with legitimate concerns about government intervention, while the government, the National Player's Federation (FENAPEPRO, Federación Nacional de Peloteros Profesionales), and many sportswriters defended expansion as a partial solution to the still-growing number of Dominican professional players left without jobs after short stints in the US minor leagues and the country's unemployment problem. On the other hand, the accusation that the government was conspiring with a transnational corporation, likely a reference to US conglomerate Gulf and Western, which owned the Central Romana and a number of enterprises in La Romana until 1984, was an attempt to shift public ire from their own monopoly over professional baseball to the international business.

The public accepted expansion as economic democracy, so the Dominican League's resistance to it aligned them with the national oligarchy's manipulations of strikes and protests to maintain their privileges. In their minds, only multinational corporations that sacrificed Dominican democracy for their own financial benefit were worse.[14] A letter by supporters of expansion, including leaders of the ballplayers' union, dismissed the accusations against "the transnational" while celebrating Jorge Blanco's efforts to remake professional baseball. By standing up to the league, Jorge Blanco demonstrated that "the promises he made as a presidential candidate are being achieved today from the Palacio Nacional."[15]

Rather than criticizing the government's strong-arming, the public turned against the league. For one, the league's appeal to US baseball commissioner Bowie Kuhn undermined its claims to protect Dominican baseball from outside interests.[16] Worse, Dominican League president Juan Tomás Mejía Feliú's statement that the league "only believes in the rules of [US] organized baseball and of the Confederation of the Caribbean Leagues" suggested that he placed the rules of an international business ahead of national law.[17] As an open letter to President Jorge Blanco published in *Listín Diario* argued, the league's resistance was "an attempt against the rule of law (*institucionalidad*) of the Nation" while expansion was a "social and historic necessity."[18] For the letter writers, like many fans and sportswriters, the league was acting to maintain a monopoly over professional baseball and to protect personal interests and privileges.[19] Speculations by sportswriters, fans, and players that former major-league slugger Ricardo Carty, who had played in the South League in 1982–1983, might find a position with one of the expansion teams revealed that many saw expansion as an antidote to the oft-cited problem of foreign players replacing Dominican veterans and prospects on national teams.[20] Though many Dominicans remained skeptical of expansion's benefits, the public largely supported it as a means to provide economic opportunity to Dominican ballplayers, team administrators and trainers, and stadium workers.[21]

The standoff between the Dominican League and the government ended soon after Jorge Blanco appointed longtime Aguilas executive and politician Reynaldo "Papy" Bisonó as the commissioner of professional baseball, a position created by Decree 1300 to liaise between the government and professional leagues. Bisonó was effective as a conciliatory appointment: he reached an agreement to add the four traditional teams under the newly created National League by early September and ensured that Dominicans and other players in the US major and minor leagues could participate in the league by fostering a one-year agreement with the Caribbean Confederation and US baseball commissioner's office. He next turned to details over ticket prices and government concessions, both of which affirmed professional baseball as a public service.[22] In part because they recognized the hardship imposed by a sales tax about to be implemented on manufactured goods, Bisonó and the government enforced a 1978 agreement between the league and Jesús de la Rosa, the secretary of sports at that time, to keep the price of bleacher seats at $.50.[23] For perhaps the first time since the Dominican Winter League's incorporation in 1955, the government also refused to cave in to the request for millions in cash and tax exonerations. The government provided baseball to the public but granted only about 65 percent of the dollars requested and protected funding for amateur sport and players' pensions by refusing to exonerate those taxes.[24] Although team officials complained that the concessions were insufficient to cover costs and the taxes would cut revenue, three cities in three regions celebrated inaugural ceremonies for the 1983–1984 Winter Tournament on October 20.

By framing expansion as a program to increase opportunities for Dominican players and those who worked in the national baseball industry, Jorge Blanco and PRD officials aligned professional baseball with Dominican expectations for democracy. Rather than cringe at government interference against a private enterprise, the public backed officials who stood up against private companies in defense of the public interest. Securing permission for players affiliated with organized baseball—including Dominican big-leaguers—also demonstrated the government's ability to negotiate with US-centered institutions. This win was particularly important as the PRD administration negotiated loans with commercial banks and, soon after, an austerity program with the International Monetary Fund (IMF)—although the hardship of the IMF shock program implemented in 1984 and the violence with which police quieted a protest against it that April depleted any political capital Jorge Blanco gained from expansion.[25] Austerity further restricted government support for professional (and amateur) baseball after 1984, but in standing up against the Dominican League and protecting access to professional baseball, the Jorge Blanco government aligned professional baseball with Dominican aspirations for democracy.[26] For the 1983–1984 tournament, this theory and practice aligned. After austerity, the government's ability to fulfill the obligations of providing professional baseball as a public good while maintaining a vibrant amateur system diminished. Individual Dominicans, who had been working with US teams since the 1950s and 1960s, filled in some of the gaps with their innovations to protect Dominican baseball prospects and further their own careers.

Baseball Academies, a Dominican Innovation

The baseball academies synonymous with Major League Baseball in the Dominican Republic grew from the bottom up, based on informal practices that scouts such as Epy Guerrero developed over decades, yet are sometimes likened to MLB-run sweatshops in the present.[27] This perception was an outgrowth of the unregulated "free-bid market" that Frank Deford described in his 1973 feature on Pittsburgh scout Howie Haak, which continued through the early 2000s with devasting consequences for prospects like Alexis Quiroz.[28] However, Dominican scouts founded the prototypes of the academies to help prospects not only sign with US teams but also progress through the minor-league system. Their innovation attracted additional scouts and major-league investment in the country and led to some Dominican government regulation in 1985. The system grew ad hoc, with individual MLB-affiliated teams investing according to their capabilities and objectives. After a trickle, with the Toronto Blue Jays backing Guerrero's complex in the late 1970s and the Los Angeles Dodgers building the first team academy in 1987, the academy system exploded during the 1990s as every MLB team rented or built an academy in the country.[29] Amid this boom and subsequent reports of abuse and scandal, MLB stepped in to regulate the teams, which are individual businesses, in part because of the failure or inability of the Dominican government to do so. This section offers a history of the academy system that stresses both the origins of the system with Latin American scouts like Guerrero and Avila and MLB's reluctance to step into its current role of regulation. These developments reinforce Dominicans' ownership of and active participation in the baseball industry, while revealing the complexity behind MLB's engagement in the player development industry in the Dominican Republic.

When Epy Guerrero established his complex in 1973, he fulfilled a personal dream to create a training facility and also formalized the training and support he and his Latin American colleagues had practiced with their prospects for decades. Guerrero and his colleagues knew that the "diamond-in-the-rough" players they depended on were not so much found as formed.[30] Their careers required them to invest time and often money to shape Dominican hopefuls into ballplayers. As Avila said to sportswriter Bill Brubaker, these scouts not only trained but also fed, clothed, and educated the potential signees in their charge to counter the challenges that Dominican players often faced in comparison with their US peers.[31] At the Guerrero complex in Villa Mella, a town just outside Santo Domingo, Dominican prospects as young as thirteen refined their raw physical ability through weightlifting, training, and Guerrero's instruction. They found refuge in the dormitories, ate regular meals prepared by Doña Rosario, Guerrero's wife, and attended classes for rudimentary English and, in some cases, basic literacy.[32] The training made the prospects stronger and bigger, though they were still smaller on average than their US counterparts; Guerrero directed them to infield positions where their smaller frames were less of a liability. The English classes and literacy alleviated the shock of living in the United States after they signed to play with teams there. In addition to increasing the prospects' chances of being signed and progressing through the minor-league system, Guerrero's complex, and the many versions of it operated by scouts across the region, improved the scouts' reputation among MLB teams and parents and prospects.

A decade after Guerrero formalized the practice common across the Caribbean, the Dominican government headed by Jorge Blanco stepped in to regulate baseball schools, programs, and academies. The Cibao Summer League's request for industrial incentives and the debate over expansion had clarified the economic potential of this budding industry. In 1985, Jorge Blanco signed Rule 3450 about amateur baseball schools or camps, which marked the government's recognition of a deepening partnership with US baseball teams.[33] Based on the state obligation to incentivize sports and physical education "as means [for youths] to obtain their muscular development and mental equilibrium," the ruling endorsed the schools or camps sponsored by the big-league teams but required registration with the Office of the Secretary of Sports. To register, teams needed an insurance policy of at least RD$50,000, access to sports installations (rented or owned), and a program for baseball instruction and events to prepare the athletes mentally, socially, and culturally "for their best development in Dominican society as well as in the exterior of the country."[34] The language in the ruling centered on the development and protection of youths in the camps as well as an obligation to promote baseball and other sports across the country as a means to develop the bodies and minds of Dominican youths.

Regulation of the training schools or camps further formalized the relationship between the Dominican government and major-league teams and promoted the narrative of baseball as a legitimate career prospect for Dominican hopefuls. The law centered on major-league team scouts, not only in identifying the United States as the primary destination for baseball hopefuls but also in defining scouts as individuals "accredited by a big-league organization and authorized to evaluate, recommend, and sign, on behalf of their organization, amateur ballplayers from our country." In addition to obliging academies to promote baseball as recreation, the ruling confirmed the government's view of baseball as a "decorous and well-paid career."[35] Beyond charging the secretary of sports and the national (Dominican) commissioner of professional baseball with overseeing compliance, the ruling likely changed little in how the schools or camps operated. Most programs already complied with the practices in the rule; Rule 3450 simply required the academies as well as the scouts who ran them to register with the government.

Although the Dominican government implemented the 1985 regulations and standards on academies, reports in the late 1990s and early 2000s revealed holes in its oversight and, over time, forced Major League Baseball to assume a more active role in regulating affiliated teams and employees. As part of this more active role, MLB established a satellite of the commissioner's office in Santo Domingo in 2000 that created standards for the academies and implemented a system to investigate players for drug use and identity fraud. While many, including independent trainers who spoke with anthropologist Alan Klein, have criticized the investigations and testing as violations against Dominican autonomy, the standards for academies and, more recently, requirements that teams take their obligations to educate prospects and prepare them to adjust to US culture more seriously have benefited prospects.[36] The identity investigations, such as the investigation of Miguel Sanó depicted in the documentary *Ballplayer: Pelotero*, primarily protect teams and their investments. The ad hoc nature by which the academies developed mean that even today, after teams have invested millions of dollars in complexes and MLB has spent two decades establishing standards for facilities, coaching, and education, academies sometimes lack sufficiently trained staff such as athletic trainers or doctors to administer to the growing numbers of prospects they house in their facilities. The lack of oversight by the Dominican government and failures in other areas, particularly education, have left MLB teams to take on roles others might expect governments to fill while also allowing MLB as an institution to make many of its own rules.

The Dominican Summer League

As US teams took greater interest in academies, scouts and US officials joined with Dominican baseball promoters to create the Dominican Summer League (DSL), which oversees an annual tournament among all the teams represented in the MLB academies. Baseball supporter and sportswriter Freddy Jana presided over the DSL with support from Sal Arteaga, president of the National Association of Professional Baseball Leagues (today, Minor League Baseball), along with Ralph Avila, Epy Guerrero, Jesús Alou, and others.[37] The purpose of the DSL mirrored the intentions of the Dominican Republic Summer League led by Felipe Alou in 1975: preparing young players for US baseball. Jana and his associates built on this earlier structure as well as that of the Cibao Summer League and of major-league scouts operating in Santiago to give recently signed players game-time experience and coaching without the added pressure of adjusting to life in the United States. The year before the league began in 1985, the Cibao Summer League affiliated with US baseball and officially shifted its emphasis from extending veterans' careers to preparing young professionals for US baseball. The Dominican government, which had supported the Cibao league's social and economic purpose, continued to offer support to the DSL. Although the DSL lacked the independence of the Cibao Summer League, the new league maintained Dominican control over baseball games in their country and ensured the country a place in the global baseball industry. The teams represented US-based companies, but they created jobs for Dominican coaches, managers, and umpires, and benefited Dominican players. Today, those benefits extend to all international free-agent signees.

The Dominican Summer League continued the efforts of the summer leagues initiated almost a decade before to provide opportunities for Dominican players. Guerrero and other scouts, who had also been involved in the earlier summer leagues, embraced this function because they recognized that academy training and drills honed baseball skills like fielding and throwing and gave players a chance to demonstrate them, but failed to show players' game-time instincts. In the early years, the league sometimes combined players from more than one major-league-affiliated organization to complete some of the teams. The boom in academies from the 1990s to the early 2000s led to an increase in the DSL, too, and it became the largest minor-league circuit in US baseball in 2000.[38] As of 2019, each of the thirty MLB teams fielded at least one team in the DSL, while a handful operated two or ran cooperatives to combine players with a partner MLB organization to form a second team.[39] Thus, in the 2019 season, more than 1,575 young professionals played on forty-five teams in the DSL.

The National Association's Arteaga worked with Jana on the DSL because the league also met the needs of the organizations he represented. Beyond providing local prospects with experience, the league allowed the teams to sign, train, and pay prospects without securing visas for their travel and work in the United States. Until US president George W. Bush signed the COMPETE Act into law in December 2006, the visas available for minor-league players were restricted. Academies and the DSL provided a stop-gap: players could practice and even compete under team-affiliated coaches and trainers without travel to the United States. Even with the greater flexibility of travel after 2006, their investments in the Dominican Republic so benefited the teams that they invested increasing amounts in resort-like academies. By 2019 these academies accommodated players from around the world. Even though MLB's international recruiting has expanded across six continents, Dominican players continue to make up at least half the population in most academies. Thus, the DSL has benefited Dominican players and Major League Baseball.

The Dominican government responded to the DSL with support similar to that for the academies and other private-public sporting partnerships. Though less publicity surrounded the DSL than the Winter League, DSL president Orlando Díaz noted the significance of the government's support for the league in the early years. Until the US-based teams invested in their own facilities and fields, they relied on complexes owned by the Dominican government. This type of public-private partnership aligned with beliefs that government support for baseball provided opportunities for education, employment, and even national development under the PRD governments (1978–1986) and Balaguer (1986–1996). As evidence of their support for sport as development, public entities such as the Santo Domingo City Council (Ayuntamiento del Distrito Federal) created agreements with private entities such as sport suppliers, supported sports betting centers that pay taxes directed toward amateur sports, and partnered with ownership groups to build sports installations, including a horse-racing track in Santo Domingo.[40] In a 1984 letter about the proposed Hipódromo del Caribe (El Caribe Racetrack), one investor estimated that the new track would create five thousand new jobs to double the five thousand in the Hipódromo Perla Antillana constructed in 1944. Modernizing the horse-racing industry in the country would also make it a tourist attraction, drawing fans that "treat horse-racing with the adequate ethical and moral concepts" aligned with the "stature and dignity that distinguishes this sport in the United States, England, Argentina, [and] Panama, for example."[41] Although some of these projects were completed in the next administration under Balaguer and caused controversy and political competition, they represented the government's willingness to partner with private enterprises to garner revenue for amateur sport and create jobs.[42]

The Dominican Summer League attracted US teams to invest increasing sums in the Dominican Republic and its baseball infrastructure. Founders such as Freddy Jana and Jesús Alou established the league to strengthen the position of their country and its aspiring big-leaguers in the global baseball industry. They succeeded. However, the place of the DSL in the global industry depends on its affiliation with MLB and Minor League Baseball (MiLB). As DSL president, Díaz plans and oversees the annual tournament involving increasing numbers of MLB-affiliated teams. The teams compete in a playoff to determine the annual champion, but the movement of players and the attitude of coaches affirms the tournament's emphasis on training. Like other minor leagues, the experience of playing and improving is more important than winning. On any given day, scouts, coaches, and team officials observe games from the tower while perhaps five fans, often relatives of a player or others able to pass through academy security, join inactive players in the stands. By contrast, even A-level minor-league games often include local paying fans and concessions. As the largest minor league in the US baseball industry, the DSL represents the centrality of the Dominican Republic in the global baseball industry even as it exhibits some of the limits of Dominican control.

Buscones and Dominican Innovators

Academies and the DSL are synonymous with the global baseball industry in the Dominican Republic because they are visibly affiliated with MLB and its minor-league institutions. The previous sections of this chapter showed how these institutions were incorporated into MLB's player development system and how MLB has taken on a greater role in regulating these components of its industry over time. Yet Dominican innovations and contributions to the global industry have also continued outside of MLB regulation and oversight. Before Dominican prospects enter what Alan Klein has described as the Global Commodity Chain, they and their peers spend years playing baseball in community little leagues.[43] Once they reach twelve to sixteen years of age, those who hope to sign professional contracts work with independent trainers to prepare for tryouts. Tropes in the US press, scholarship about Dominican boys' singular focus on making it to the big leagues, and the narrative of baseball as an escape from poverty obscure both the joy these youths, like their US counterparts with big-league dreams, find in their national pastime and the ways that Dominicans have accommodated MLB teams' demand for young international players. This section highlights the work of Dominicans outside of MLB to sustain Dominican baseball and the industry tied to it, with a focus on the contributions of coaches and trainers from the little leagues to the independent trainer-scout-agents sometimes called *buscones*. Those who work outside MLB continue to innovate, like the scouts before them, and create systems to protect the degree of autonomy and essential position of the Dominican Republic in the global industry as well as the interests of Dominican players. Although MLB founded the Trainer Partnership Program (TPP) to encourage compliance with MLB procedures and standards in 2018, trainers continue to operate predominantly without government or MLB oversight.

Like their peers in the United States, Dominican youths begin their formal baseball training in little leagues. "Formal" is a loose term, especially for five-year-olds, but the youths learn the fundamentals of the game as well as how to be part of a team. Leagues are often tied to the community, local foundations or organizers, and former ballplayers. With limited resources and little logistical support from the government, little leagues organize tournaments and games through personal contacts among the directors and coaches. Most leagues require a small weekly contribution of about five dollars, and some receive private support, often from former major leaguers, to help them institutionalize more regular events. For example, Ruddy Ramírez, a community organizer in Manoguayabo, a city just outside the capital, received early support from former big-leaguers Ramón Martínez and Danny Bautista as well as Pedro Martínez, whose Fundación Pedro Martínez is within walking distance from his field. The former players helped prepare the open space for a baseball diamond and dugouts. Just across town, Daniel Portorreal, who played three years in the San Francisco Giants system before his involvement in an illegal marriage led to his visa being canceled, runs Team Monota (Big Hands, a reference to Portorreal's descriptive nickname) in the Portorreal Little League. Both Ramírez and Portorreal rely on contributions from parents and state resources when available to maintain fields, pay coaches, and arrange transportation to games.

The ImpACTA Kids Foundation in Consuelo, a sugar mill community outside of San Pedro de Macorís, offers another example of the ties between little leagues and communities. The foundation oversees at least three little leagues, a number of softball teams, and a small community center that provides tutoring, classes in typing, and a place to do homework for those in need.[44] The program was founded by Manny Acta, a former major-league coach and manager whose parents still live near the fields his foundation occupies. ImpACTA Kids gives back to the Consuelo community that was devasted by the decline of the sugar industry in the 1980s, around the time San Pedro gained international renown as the "City of Shortstops" because of the impressive skills of native sons including Alfredo Griffin, Tony Fernández, and Julio César Franco.[45] Even children who cannot pay the small fee to join a team—or buy shoelaces—participate in practices and recreational events there, such as the adapted versions of MLB's Pitch, Hit, Run program that I participated in as an instructor for the CIEE Baseball in Context Summer Study Abroad program in 2012–2015 and 2017. Like Ramírez and Portorreal, the coaches and directors who show up daily instill community values in youths in addition to training them in baseball and softball fundamentals.

Little league and community programs generally serve youths ages five to sixteen before they enter the informal first stages of the baseball industry. Independent trainers, sometimes referred to as *buscones*, a reference to dogs who scare birds from bushes for hunters, provide a bridge from community-centered baseball to the industry. Although the term *buscón* initially applied to local men like Felipe Alou's college coach Horacio Martínez, a former Negro League player who alerted US team scouts and officials to potential signees through at least the 1950s and 1960s, by the twenty-first century the term had become pejorative and associated with bad actors who exploited or abused young hopefuls. Thus, those who prepare youths for tryouts with professional teams prefer to be called trainers, though they fulfill multiple roles including those of mentor, provider, chauffeur, and agent in addition to trainer and coach. Independent trainers are generally self-employed and often employ others outside the formal economy. They have only recently faced regulation by MLB and the Dominican government.

As with the academy prototype started by Epy Guerrero, independent trainers responded to a need in the system. With no interconnected little league system in the Dominican Republic, and in contrast to much of the United States, where youths develop in travel and school leagues, often at a cost to their families, Dominican youths lacked high-level personalized training and competition as they approached sixteen, the most profitable age to sign with an MLB team. While Alan Klein hailed these trainers as "new Dominicans" who challenge MLB's attempted domination of Dominican baseball, I stress the place of independent trainers in the long history of Dominican innovation in the baseball industry because they responded to the economic and social demands of a global industry operating in a country with fewer resources.[46] This historical understanding of the role of independent trainers and the Dominican player development system sheds light on Dominican innovation to help reveal limitations to MLB control.

As with all historical institutions and people, the operations of independent trainers and their objectives vary according to their resources, funding, and personal motivations. Independent training programs target boys who are further along in their development as ballplayers and provide more formal and individualized training than community little leagues. In addition to baseball instruction and higher-level competition, the programs often provide varying levels of subsistence and equipment at no immediate cost to the player but with a contract for a portion of the prospect's signing bonus. If the player does not sign with a professional team, the trainers typically get nothing in compensation or reimbursement. Based on my observations of various programs between 2012 and 2017, I divided the independent programs into three imperfect categories, according to their resources, services, and funding: (1) full-service residential programs, (2) foreign investment ventures, and (3) local programs. Recognizing the varying approaches and realities of independent trainers helps explain their actions and motivations and conveys the complexity of attempts to regulate them.

Full-service programs house, feed, and train prospects, often on schedules similar to those in the MLB team academies. Dominican Astín Jacobo, one of Klein's informants as well as a subject in the documentary *Ballplayer: Pelotero*, runs one of the best-known full-service programs.[47] MLB veteran Bartolo Colón runs another. Full-service programs look different across the country: some have manicured fields, nice dormitories, and good food; others are dark and dank. Although I did not see the dormitories at Colón's academy when I visited in 2017, the field was impressive, staff knowledgeable, and weight room good enough that Colón himself worked out there to prepare for the 2018 season with the Rangers.[48] Some programs, including the Quality Baseball Academy, have websites that showcase their facilities and services—likely to recruit prospects and attract scouts—and include links to videos of their eligible prospects.[49] Prospects enter full-service academies at various ages, but because the programs often house and feed the players, many target older prospects, such as those between fourteen and sixteen years old, who may or may not have worked with another trainer before. Youths as old as their early twenties participate in these programs, but because MLB teams place a premium on talented sixteen-year-olds, players older than that expect smaller bonuses and their trainers a lower payout. Prospects sign contracts with the programs to outline the services they will receive, such as housing and equipment, the expected time of stay, representation in negotiations, and the percentage of their signing bonus they will pay the academy. For example, a fourteen-year-old will generally promise a higher percentage of his signing bonus than a sixteen-year-old who expects to sign as soon as he is eligible. Independent trainers take 20 to 35 percent of a prospect's signing bonus and, in rare cases, more. Sometimes, the prospect will also pay a portion of his bonus to an agent, especially if he's a highly touted prospect, as was Miguel Sanó, the Minnesota Twins infielder who was featured in the *Ballplayer: Pelotero* documentary.

As with other industries in the Dominican Republic, the baseball industry has attracted its share of foreign investors. The Arias and Goodman Academy in San Pedro de Macorís is one such venture built through a partnership between local baseball scouts and trainers and a US investor. Michael Schmidt and Matthew Orr featured the Arias and Goodman Academy in articles and a video on US investors in Dominican ballplayers in 2010.[50] The conditions at the academy when I visited in summer 2012 and subsequent summers mirrored those in the 2010 video: fields trimmed and relatively high in quality, living quarters barracks-style and dark.[51] Gary Goodman, the US partner and investor with Dominican trainer Alfredo Arias, explained in the video that he wanted to raise the professionalism of the academies in the Dominican Republic in addition to earning a higher yield than in his real estate investments (12 percent). Yet his actions suggested he was focused on profit: in the 2010 article, Goodman acknowledged, "We need to upgrade the facility" given that as many as thirty players lived in small bedrooms "jammed in as if on a ship" with poor bedding. Yet in the video Goodman excused these conditions by suggesting that they were an improvement over places many prospects had lived in before.[52] This attitude reveals the implications of baseball as an escape from poverty narrative and its disregard for Dominican players' humanity and professionalism.

MLB's Trainer Partnership Program (TPP) founded in 2018 may help raise the standards of living and training—and hopefully education, another problem area in the Dominican baseball industry—for Dominican prospects. In exchange for complying with the standards of the TPP, which include regulations on academy conditions as well as submitting prospects to drug testing and earlier registration with MLB's investigations team, the trainers gain access to MLB team scouts and showcases. Even before joining the TPP, the Arias and Goodman Academy partnered with the nonprofit Dominican Republic Sports and Education Academy (DRSEA) to provide education for prospects at the academy. While the agreement would have distinguished the academy among its peers, the program was short-lived, either from a lack of resources or lack of interest.[53] The TPP raises questions about MLB interference and overreach in Dominican baseball institutions like independent academies, but the standards it establishes for academy conditions—if they are clear and enforced—may benefit prospects. The TPP could also reach prospects earlier to inform them of MLB education initiatives and career programs—although the materials available online do not mention this access as a potential benefit and MLB education programs are still decentralized across the teams.

Many trainers who now enjoy US sponsorship or some who work as coaches with the better-resourced independent academies use community connections and recognition of their baseball skills to become independent trainers. Daniel Portorreal is one such independent trainer, though the stories are as diverse as the men (and a few women) who tell them. Portorreal trains youths near his home in Manoguayabo at a large though relatively unfinished field, dividing his time between the little league and higher-level skills training for aspiring professionals. Because he recognizes his own mistakes as part of the reason for the end of his playing career, Portorreal warns his trainees about the obstacles they will face and stresses mental toughness, honesty, and good decision-making from the beginning. His prospects have enjoyed some success: his first trainee, Ulisés Joaquín, has played for a decade as a professional pitcher, moving from the Dominican Summer League in 2011 to US minor leagues through 2016, and the Mexican summer league and Dominican and Venezuelan winter leagues. A number of Portorreal's signees played in the Dominican Summer League in 2019 as well.[54] At any given time, Portorreal trains a relatively small number of youths, usually from his little league, and has a relatively humble operation. He has no housing facilities outside his own home, for example, and has less access to new equipment than some of his peers. Given his modest resources, he has also acted as a *buscón* in the more traditional sense, signing prospects to better-resourced trainers for a share of what they hope will be a higher bonus.

Trainers like Portorreal operate at the border between the baseball industry and recreational or community baseball and contribute to both. Although Portorreal has less access than better-seated trainers like Jacobo or Arias and Goodman to recent innovations such as the Trainer Partnership Program, the personal attention and community support of local trainers like Portorreal provide a boost for many. As Portorreal indicated in a 2019 interview, he travels with players to showcases and to participate in prospect leagues developed by independent trainers, such as the National Prospect League described at beginning of this chapter.[55] These leagues mirror the DSL in giving prospects game-time experience and scouts the opportunity to evaluate them in this setting. One of the longest-running prospect leagues, the Dominican Prospect League, was founded in 2010. MLB began a similar league in 2012.[56] As of 2021, independent trainers have established these leagues across the country, creating a system that mirrors the MLB team academies.

Dominicans from community-oriented little-league coaches like Ruddy Ramírez to well-resourced trainers like Astín Jacobo help baseball thrive in the Dominican Republic. They represent ongoing innovations to help youths overcome obstacles imposed by family poverty and insufficient public resources to participate in the national pastime and, in the case of a lucky few, to become professionals in the game they love. Individual Dominicans responded to the gaps in the baseball system by taking on new roles such as those of independent trainers and league directors. They also built institutions such as independent academies and, through their connections with other trainers, prospect leagues. They rightfully struggle against MLB to maintain their autonomy, as Klein emphasized. Yet they also work with MLB and its various representatives to benefit their prospects and maintain the Dominican pastime and the country's advantages in its most-loved industry.

Conclusion

The everyday actions of Dominicans and other Latin Americans on baseball fields in their home countries and in the United States created a vibrant and dynamic industry that continues to respond to some of globalization's challenges in the present. The innovations and expertise of scouts, promoters, and trainers like Epy Guerrero, Ralph Avila, Freddy Jana, and Astín Jacobo drew MLB and the teams it represents to the Dominican Republic and led to the millions of dollars in investments in the country each year. Creating institutions like the academies and the DSL helped prospects overcome some of the obstacles inherent in the differences between the United States and Dominican Republic, particularly those around education, age, income, and sports infrastructure. The independent academies continue to serve this need, though with relatively little support from MLB and the Dominican government.

The grassroots leadership in these innovations proved essential for the Dominican government as leaders worked to balance the pressure for austerity based on neoliberal ideologies of government nonintervention with their promises to invest in the people. After mobilizing the power of all three branches of government to push through expansion, in April 1984 Jorge Blanco faced protests against his agreement with the IMF to raise prices on food and medicine. While he could ensure that Dominicans could watch baseball from the bleachers for $0.50, Jorge Blanco could not resist IMF pressures to end subsidies on necessities like oil and electricity. Economic policies imposed in part from outside forces undermined the Dominican government's ability to build the economic democracy that would bring the opportunities and participation by which many Dominicans had defined true democracy since the struggle against Trujillo.

Despite the relative lack of government oversight over MLB teams and enterprises in the country, however, Dominicans continue to expect baseball to provide the justice they have long expected from democracy. Major League Baseball and individuals who work in the system, rather than the Dominican government, impose the regulations and create processes to protect prospects and other baseball workers from the inequities inherent in the system. Ironically for those who see MLB as a multinational corporation, MLB regulates itself, or the teams that fall under its purview. Contradictions in MLB actions persist, largely because of the teams' preference for signing sixteen-year-olds and the greater financial incentives they offer to these younger prospects.[57] Yet MLB has taken on the responsibility of ensuring that affiliated teams offer educational and other opportunities that prospects could not access from the government. Major League Baseball's adoption and scaling up of scouts' innovations, along with the regulation of team academies and creation of a formal investigative process for all international prospects, indicates the necessity of these kinds of adaptions for globalization, at least for cultural industries whose products overlap with public relations. For Dominican and US baseball fans, democracy still calls for justice. When the Dominican government failed to impose that justice through regulation, MLB stepped up to soften the worst of the team abuses as well as the alleged age and identity fraud against them. The lack of government oversight leaves the job of regulating Major League Baseball to Dominican citizens and engaged baseball fans.

Conclusion

On July 29, 2018, Vladimir Guerrero stepped to the podium in Cooperstown, New York, to give his Hall of Fame induction speech. Guerrero began with "Buenas tardes" (good afternoon) and continued, in Spanish, acknowledging his cohort and thanking the Montreal Expos and Los Angeles [Anaheim] Angels for their help in his major-league career. Reports on the speech commented more on the length—less than four minutes with the English translation—than the language. Although Pedro Martínez had addressed Dominican fans and family in Spanish during his speech in 2015, a full, albeit short, speech in Spanish contrasted with the long-held practice that Latin American players communicated in English throughout their careers, even as their Japanese teammates worked with translators. The media and fans' embrace of Guerrero and his Spanish-language speech evidenced the significant changes that Dominican ballplayers and baseball have brought to the global baseball industry, in part because Dominicans projected their democratic success onto the national pastime. This integration of baseball and democracy in the Dominican Republic offers important lessons about the benefits of sports history, how citizens in the Global South understood democracy and development in the Cold War, and how these understandings shifted and continue to do so.

Dominican sportswriters, fans, and politicians projected their dreams for the future and their understandings of democracy onto baseball, making the national pastime an important tool for historians today who examine those understandings and the debates about them. Sports history teaches us about more than sports. The baseball promoters who resurrected the national professional tournament in the early 1950s laid the foundation for a new institution that dictator Rafael Trujillo did not control. Debates over the rules for the annual tournament and government support revealed the limits of governmental control over baseball and the meanings people ascribed to it, even as Trujillo and, later, Joaquín Balaguer constructed new stadiums and venues. Because of the government investment in professional baseball instituted during the Trujillo regime, Dominicans saw withholding their support for the national baseball tournament, or even criticizing it, as a protest of leaders' violations of political norms. Staying home from the natives-only tournament in 1961 and tensions with players in the tournaments under the Triumvirate demonstrated Dominicans' understandings of baseball as within their control. Letters that suggested president Juan Bosch could not secure Dominican players for the 1963–1964 tournament likely made the public question his ability to fulfill his promises for a social democracy. Later, citizens took this objective upon themselves, using Balaguer's promises to check his favoritism for industries over workers and to advocate for amateur sports into the 1970s. As Dominicans continued to advocate for human along with economic development, Balaguer supported new models for professional baseball in 1975. President Salvador Jorge Blanco's framing of baseball as a private-public partnership in 1983 further entrenched Dominican understandings of baseball as a social good protected by democracy.

The global context of the Cold War shaped Dominican understandings of democracy and capitalism as well as opportunities available to Dominican citizens and ballplayers. The first Dominican big-leaguers represented the potential of baseball and all sports to raise individuals and society to the place in the sun that leaders across the Americas understood as a democratic society with a comfortable standard of living. Although the Trujillo regime took credit for ballplayers' success in the United States, the ballplayers themselves represented national potential after the dictator was brought to justice. Cuba's divergence from the democratic path expanded the opportunities available to Dominican ballplayers as US scouts turned from Cuba to the Dominican Republic for baseball talent. Dominican ballplayers like Juan Marichal proved themselves on major-league fields, causing US baseball teams and scouts to spend more time in the country. Dominican players, coaches, scouts, and government officials responded by investing more time and resources in the national pastime. The coup against Bosch in 1963 showed that US government officials and Dominican elites valued development, understood as economic growth, more than democracy, and they protected it with anticommunism. Under Balaguer, Dominicans adopted the rhetoric of development to shape baseball as a national industry that would benefit society. In other words, they redefined industry to adhere to the democratic principles of rights and opportunity they embraced in the early 1960s. The new Dominican summer leagues inaugurated in 1975 fulfilled these principles and provided the basis for a new industry in which Dominicans enjoyed a competitive advantage over their Latin American peers.

In the short term, Dominicans' conflation of baseball and democracy in their struggle against dictatorship preserved their ownership over both. Yet as more of the Dominican baseball industry integrated with US and global industries, individual Dominicans rather than society or the state benefited from this ownership. Jorge Blanco boosted his democratic credentials by redefining professional baseball as a private-public partnership even while the state increasingly relied on individual scouts and trainers to provide the services Dominicans needed to seize economic opportunities. Today, most of those individual Dominicans work for or through Major League Baseball, which has in some cases replaced the state in providing access to education, baseball training, and amateur competition.

The social democracy that Dominicans and citizens across the Americas, and likely the world, dreamed of in the 1960s has been replaced by corporate responsibility and even corporate activism. Or at least by demands for it. The common trope that baseball offers Dominicans an escape from poverty is only a more egregious example of this shift from the expectation that government protect citizens from the worst of capitalism and authoritarianism to the expectation that corporations regulate themselves and even engage in activism. Investments in secondary education by MLB teams and internship programs created by MLB responded to demands that more be done to protect the futures of the hundreds of baseball hopefuls who sacrifice their own education to sign professional contracts but fall out of the baseball system each year. Meanwhile, government and citizen emotional investment in the narrative of professional baseball's opportunities obscures alternatives. Major League Baseball's move of the 2021 All-Star Game from Atlanta to Denver over a Georgia law that restricted voting rights exemplifies how fans and consumers expect corporations to fulfill roles once expected of governments.[1]

The national pastime continues to be a reservoir of Dominican optimism. Danilo Medina, whose commercial at the Caribbean Series featured Dominican baseball heroes, won the 2012 election with his promise "To continue what is good, to correct what is bad, to do what has never been done."[2] But the ballplayers' contributions to his presidency went beyond the campaign. At a luncheon celebrating the Dominican champion delegation to the 2013 World Baseball Classic, President Medina thanked the ballplayers for "carrying a message of optimism and hope to the country" at a time when people "spoke of the possibility of revolts and problems" because of fiscal reforms that raised the price of food and other necessities.[3] The team that marched undefeated to WBC victory had wowed fans across the globe with its camaraderie, enthusiasm, and *plátano* power. According to Medina, it may also have spared his presidency by distracting Dominicans from the state's failure to secure basic goods. On the front page of the newspaper *Hoy* the next day, Medina stood surrounded by the latest crop of Dominican baseball heroes. He basked in their presence, but the ballplayers, not the president, carried Dominicans' pride, hope, and expectations as they leaned low to the ground and aimed for the stars in the signature *flecha* (arrow) pose that marked their on-field celebrations.

Notes

Introduction

1. Bell earned the American League Most Valuable Player award in 1987 after averaging .308 and recording a remarkable 134 runs batted in for the Toronto Blue Jays.

2. Organized baseball here refers to the affiliation of leagues across the Americas in the 1950s through Winter Agreements signed with the US major and minor leagues. The Dominican league's affiliation with US baseball was unofficial until the Caribbean Confederation admitted it to its membership.

3. My research question aligns with those asked in Greg Grandin, *The Last Colonial Massacre: Latin America in the Cold War* (Chicago: University of Chicago Press, 2004). On the "transnational contact zone" during the Cold War, see Gilbert M. Joseph, "What We Know Now and Should Know: Bringing Latin America More Meaningfully into Cold War Studies," in *In from the Cold: Latin America's New Encounter with the Cold War*, ed. Gilbert M. Joseph and Daniela Spenser (Durham, NC: Duke University Press, 2008), 3–46.

4. I take the idea of sport as a canvas onto which citizens project their aspirations from Louis A. Pérez Jr., "Between Baseball and Bullfighting: The Quest for Nationality in Cuba, 1868–1898," *Journal of American History* 81, no. 2 (September 1994): 493–517; Louis A. Pérez Jr., *On Becoming Cuban: Identity, Nationality, and Culture* (Chapel Hill: University of North Carolina Press, 1999); and from C. L. R. James, *Beyond a Boundary* (Durham, NC: Duke University Press, 1993). On Dominican politics, see Elizabeth S. Manley, *The Paradox of Paternalism: Women and the Politics of Authoritarianism in the Dominican Republic* (Gainesville: University Press of Florida, 2017), who models the examination of popular engagement during and against Dominican authoritarian regimes, building on scholarship on the performative and symbolic power of the Trujillo regime such as Lauren H. Derby, *The Dictator's Seduction: Politics and the Popular Imagination in the Era of Trujillo* (Durham, NC: Duke University Press, 2009); Eric Paul Roorda, *The Dictator Next Door: The Good Neighbor Policy and the Trujillo Regime in the Dominican Republic, 1930–1945* (Durham, NC: Duke University Press, 1998); and Richard Lee Turits, *Foundations of Despotism: Peasants, the Trujillo Regime, and Modernity in Dominican History* (Stanford, CA: Stanford University Press, 2004). Jonathan Hartlyn, *The Struggle for Democratic Politics in the Dominican Republic* (Chapel Hill, NC: University of North Carolina Press, 1998) offers a framework for comparing political regimes, while I

draw from Rafael Francisco de Moya Pons (Frank Moya Pons), "Industrial Incentives in the Dominican Republic, 1880–1983" (PhD diss., Columbia University, 1987) and Frank Moya Pons, *The Dominican Republic: A National History* (Princeton, NJ: Marcus Wiener Publishers, 1998) for context on Dominican political economy and, for details about class struggle during Balaguer's *doce años*, from Roberto Cassá, *Los doce años: Contrarrevolución y desarrollismo*, vol. 1 (Santo Domingo: Editora Búho, 1991). On authoritarianism in Dominican political culture, see Rosario Espinal, *Autoritarismo y democracia en la política dominicana* (Centro Ineramericano de Asesoría y Promoción Electoral, Instituto de Derechos Humanos, 1987); Ramonina Brea and Isis Duarte, *Entre la calle y la casa: Las mujeres dominicanas y la cultura política a finales del siglo II* (Santo Domingo: Editora Búho, 1999); Emelio Betances, "La cultura política autoritaria en la República Dominicana," *El Cotidiano* 152 (November-December 2008): 87–97; Valentina Peguero, *The Militarization of Culture in the Dominican Republic from the Captains General to General Trujillo* (Lincoln: University of Nebraska Press, 2004).

5. "¡Déjelos Que Ayuden, Profesor!," *La Nación*, February 24, 1963, 4.

6. On the Cold War as a negotiation among citizens of varying perspectives amid global forces shaping the options for the future, see Richard Saull, "El lugar del sur global en la conceptualización de la guerra fría: Desarrollo capitalista, revolución social y conflicto geopolítico," in *Espejos de la Guerra Fría: México, América Central y el Caribe*, ed. Daniela Spenser (México, DF: Centro de Investigaciones y Estudios Superiores en Antropología Social, 2004), 31–66; Tanya Harmer, *Allende's Chile and the Inter-American Cold War* (Chapel Hill: University of North Carolina Press, 2011), 2; Grandin, *The Last Colonial Massacre*. On the "transnational contact zone" during the Cold War, see Joseph, "What We Know Now," 4; on US-Dominican relations during the struggle for democracy, see Piero Gleijeses, *The Dominican Crisis: The 1965 Constitutionalist Revolt and American Intervention*, trans. Lawrence Lipson (Baltimore: Johns Hopkins University Press, 1978); Piero Gleijeses, *La esperanza desgarrada: La rebelión dominicana de 1965 y la invasión norteamericana* (Santo Domingo: Editoria Búho, 2012).

7. On Latin America and Cuba, see Tanya Harmer, "The 'Cuban Question' and the Cold War in Latin America, 1959–1964," *Journal of Cold War Studies* 21, no. 3 (Summer 2019): 114–151; Renata Keller, "The Latin American Missile Crisis," *Diplomatic History* 39, no. 2 (2015): 195–222; Renata Keller, *Mexico's Cold War: Cuba, the United States, and the Legacy of the Mexican Revolution* (New York: Cambridge University Press, 2015); Harmer, *Allende's Chile*; Eric Zolov, "¡Cuba Sí, Yanquis No! The Sacking of the Instituto Cultural México-Norteamericano in Morelia, Michoacan, 1961," in Joseph and Spenser, *In from the Cold*, 214–252; Daniela Spenser, "Standing Conventional Cold War History on Its Head," in Joseph and Spenser, *In from the Cold*, 381–395. Piero Gleijeses's interest in Dominican actors, including those who supported Cuba and received training from Castro, makes his work relevant as well; see Gleijeses, *The Dominican Crisis*; Gleijeses, *La esperanza desgarrada*.

8. On Dominican political economy, see Moya Pons, "Industrial Incentives in the Dominican Republic," and Moya Pons, *The Dominican Republic*.

9. On baseball and Cuban independence, see Pérez, "Between Baseball and Bullfighting"; on Cubans spreading baseball to the Dominican Republic and nationalist expressions, see Rob Ruck, *The Tropic of Baseball: Baseball in the Dominican Republic* (Westport, CT: Meckler, 1991). Like the Cuban independistas, Dominicans who imagined the nation at the ballpark pictured a raceless, or at least racially homogenous, family, yet as the growing body of scholarship on Dominican identity indicates, reality is more complicated. I engage little with these complexities. For more on Dominican racial and cultural identities, see Silvio Torres-Saillant and Ramona Hernández, *The Dominican Americans* (Westport, CT: Greenwood, 1998); Silvio Torres-Saillant, "The Tribulations of Blackness: Stages in Dominican Racial Identity," *Callaloo* 23, no. 3 (Summer 2000): 1086–1111; Teresita Martínez-Vergne, *Nation and Citizen in the Dominican Republic, 1880–1916* (Chapel Hill: University of North Carolina Press, 2005); Ginetta E. B. Candelario, *Black behind the Ears: Dominican Racial Identity from Museums to Beauty Shops* (Durham, NC: Duke University Press, 2007); April J. Mayes, *The Mulatto Republic: Class, Race, and Dominican National Identity* (Gainesville: University Press of Florida, 2014); Anne Eller, *We Dream Together: Dominican Independence, Haiti, and the Fight for Caribbean Freedom* (Durham, NC: Duke University Press, 2016); Lorgia García-Peña, *The Borders of Dominicanidad: Race, Nation, and Archives of Contradiction* (Durham, NC: Duke University Press, 2016); Dixa Ramírez, *Colonial Phantoms: Belonging and Refusal in the Dominican Americas, from the 19th Century to the Present* (New York: New York University Press, 2018); Bernardo Vega, ed., *Ensayos sobre cultura dominicana* (Santo Domingo: Museo del Hombre Dominicano, 1981). On race and baseball, see Raj Chetty, "*Más Allá del Play*: Race and the Dominican Baseball Player in *Sugar*," *Journal of West Indian Literature* 27, no. 1 (April 2019): 1–14.

10. Thomas F. Carter, *The Quality of Home Runs: The Passion, Politics, and Language of Cuban Baseball* (Durham, NC: Duke University Press, 2008); Brenda Elsey and Joshua Nadel, *Futbolera: A History of Women and Sports in Latin America* (Austin: University of Texas Press, 2019).

11. I use "Dominican family" as a symbol of the patriarchal nation upheld by Trujillo through his consumption of women and paternalism, as indicated by his honorific title Padre de la Patria Nueva, which was the dedication chosen for the first Dominican Winter League tournament in 1955. See Elizabeth Manley, "Intimate Violations: Women and the Ajusticiamiento of Dictator Rafael Trujillo, 1944–1961," *The Americas* 69, no. 1 (July 2012): 61–94; Lauren H. Derby, "The Dictator's Seduction: Gender and State Spectacle during the Trujillo Regime," in *Latin American Popular Culture: An Introduction*, ed. William H. Beezley and Linda A. Curcio-Nagy (Wilmington, DE: Scholarly Resources, Inc., 2000), 213–239.

12. Pérez, "Between Baseball and Bullfighting"; Pérez, *On Becoming Cuban*.

13. Ramón Paniagua, "Presentación," in José Mercader, *Historia de la Caricatura Dominicana*, vol. 1 (Santo Domingo: Archivo General de la Nación, 2012), 8. Also on Dominican *caricaturas*, see José Luis Sáez Ramo, "Funciones de la caricatura. Un recorrido emocional por la prensa dominicana," *Clío* 83, no. 188 (July-December 2014): 250–270; Diógenes Céspedes, "Notas sobre la caricatura periodística en RD

hoy," *Hoy digital*, November 26, 2007, https://hoy.com.do/notas-sobre-la-caricatura-periodisticaen-rd-hoy/. All cite Emilio Rodríguez Demorizi as the first to discuss the significance of *caricatura* in Dominican society. See Rodríguez Demorizi, *Caricatura y dibujo en Santo Domingo* (Santo Domingo: Editora Taller, 1977).

14. Daniel A. Gilbert demonstrates how being workers in a cultural industry allowed players to leverage their popularity to earn free agency and more favorable working conditions internationally; see Gilbert, *Expanding the Strike Zone: Baseball in the Age of Free Agency* (Amherst: University of Massachusetts Press, 2013); on cultural industries or artifacts as sites that can both resist and reflect international inequities, see Seth Fein, "Producing the Cold War in Mexico: The Public Limits of Covert Communications," in Joseph and Spenser, *In from the Cold*, 171–213; Eric Zolov, *Refried Elvis: The Rise of the Mexican Counterculture* (Berkeley: University of California Press, 1999). On the significance of emotions in sports and sport history, see Barbara Keys, "Senses and Emotions in the History of Sport," *Journal of Sport History* 40, no. 1 (Spring 2013): 21–38. All echo the conflicted view of cricket as a tool for both colonizing and resisting in James, *Beyond a Boundary*.

15. Early work by scholars on Dominican baseball examines how Dominicans became so prevalent in US baseball and the significance of baseball in the Dominican Republic. See Ruck, *The Tropic of Baseball*; Alan M. Klein, *Sugarball: The American Game, the Dominican Dream* (New Haven, CT: Yale University Press, 1991). The works that followed build on the problems caused by multinational interests identified by Ruck and Klein and warn of the danger that globalization posed to Dominicans and Dominican baseball, particularly if globalization occurred through an MLB-centered process that Klein called imperial. See Arturo J. Marcano Guevara and David P. Fidler, *Stealing Lives: The Globalization of Baseball and the Tragic Story of Alexis Quiroz* (Bloomington: Indiana University Press, 2002); Alan M. Klein, *Growing the Game: The Globalization of Major League Baseball* (New Haven, CT: Yale University Press, 2006); Rob Ruck, *Raceball: How the Major Leagues Colonized the Black and Latin Game* (Boston: Beacon, 2011). While Klein's most recent work highlights Dominican actors and acknowledges Dominican innovations such as the academy, he obscures Dominicans' persistent ownership of the *global* industry by centering MLB and ignoring the historical perspective. See Alan Klein, *Dominican Baseball: New Pride, Old Prejudice* (Philadelphia: Temple University Press, 2014).

16. Odd Arne Westad, *The Global Cold War: Third World Interventions and the Making of Our Times* (New York: Cambridge University Press, 2007), 8–38, 39–72.

17. Richard Saull, "El lugar del sur global en la conceptualización de la guerra fría: Desarrollo capitalista, revolución social y conflicto geopolítico," in *Espejos de la Guerra Fría: México, América Central y el Caribe*, ed. Daniela Spenser (México, DF: Centro de Investigaciones y Estudios Superiores en Antropología Social, 2004), 31–66; Harmer, *Allende's Chile*; Thomas C. Field Jr., Stella Krepp, and Vanni Pettinà, eds., *Latin America and the Global Cold War* (Chapel Hill: University of North Carolina Press, 2020).

18. Minutero, *El Caribe*, June 4, 1960, 2.

19. April Yoder, "Dominican Baseball and Latin American Pluralism, 1969–1974," *Oxford Research Encyclopedia of Latin American History*, September 29, 2016, https://

doi.org/10.1093/acrefore/9780199366439.013.355; Christy Thornton, "A Mexican New International Economic Order?," in *Latin America and the Global Cold War*, eds. Thomas C. Field Jr., Stella Krepp, and Vanni Pettinà (Chapel Hill: University of North Carolina Press, 2020), 301–342.

20. Dominicans use *ajusticiamiento,* which connotes "bringing to justice," to describe the assassination of Trujillo in 1961. I use the Spanish for this word throughout because the English translation (political assassination) loses the justice element and conflates the Spanish words for assassination: *ajusticiamiento* and *asesinato*.

Chapter 1: *Mens sana in corpore sano*

1. In 1955, the Dominican Winter League affiliated with US organized baseball, which included only the US minor and major leagues. Three years later, in 1958, the Dominican League joined the Caribbean Confederation, which organized the Caribbean Series each year, as a nonparticipating (in the Series) member—a further signal of the league's legitimacy, and of the reputation of Dominican baseball in the region. The leagues in the Caribbean Confederation, which included Puerto Rico, Panama, Venezuela, and Cuba, were affiliated with US organized baseball, but the confederation itself was largely autonomous from US baseball.

2. Ph, "Estadio Trujillo es Alarde de Modernismo y Comodidad; Inauguración Tendrá Lugar 7 de la Noche de Mañana En Una Ceremonia Especial," *El Caribe*, October 22, 1955, 11.

3. Lauren Derby, *The Dictator's Seduction: Politics and the Popular Imagination in the Era of Trujillo* (Durham, NC: Duke University Press, 2009).

4. Richard Lee Turits, *Foundations of Despotism: Peasants, the Trujillo Regime, and Modernity in Dominican History* (Stanford, CA: Stanford University Press, 2004), 13.

5. Valentina Peguero, *The Militarization of Culture in the Dominican Republic from the Captains General to General Trujillo* (Lincoln: University of Nebraska Press, 2004).

6. Eric Paul Roorda, *The Dictator Next Door: The Good Neighbor Policy and the Trujillo Regime in the Dominican Republic, 1930–1945* (Durham, NC: Duke University Press, 1998).

7. Derby, *The Dictator's Seduction*, 2.

8. Jonathan Blitzer with illustrations by Kelsey Dake, "Satchel Paige and the Championship for the Reelection of the General: How the Best Pitcher in the American Negro Leagues Played for the Cruelest Dictator in the Caribbean," *Atavist Magazine* 57, https://read.atavist.com/satchel-paige-and-the-championship-for-the-reelection-of-the-general.

9. Adrian Burgos Jr., *Playing America's Game: Baseball, Latinos, and the Color Line* (Berkeley: University of California Press, 2007).

10. On the organizing behind the Sports Law, see Rob Ruck, *The Tropic of Baseball: Baseball in the Dominican Republic* (New York: Meckler, 1991), 41–46.

11. On Muscular Christianity in the United States, see Clifford Putney, *Muscular Christianity: Manhood and Sports in Protestant America, 1880–1920* (Cambridge, MA: Harvard University Press, 2001); Tony Ladd and James A. Mathisen, *Muscular*

Christianity: Evangelical Protestants and the Development of American Sport (Grand Rapids, MI: Baker Books, 1999). On Muscular Christianity to "raise" populations in Latin American nations, specifically in Puerto Rico, see Antonio Sotomayor, *The Sovereign Colony: Olympic Sport, National Identity, and International Politics in Puerto Rico* (Lincoln: University of Nebraska Press, 2018), especially chap. 1, "Sport in Imperial Exchanges," 35–61. On sport and modernization in Mexico, see William H. Beezley, *Judas at the Jockey Club and Other Episodes of Porfirian Mexico* (Lincoln: University of Nebraska Press, 1987); Eric Zolov, "Showcasing the 'Land of Tomorrow': Mexico and the 1968 Olympics," *The Americas* 61, no. 2 (October 2004): 159–188. Although Beezley described late nineteenth- through early twentieth-century Mexico, the idea of sport and progress continued, as did the pursuit of "modernity," renamed development by the 1960s.

12. Rob Ruck, "The Dominican Dandy," in Ruck, *Tropic of Baseball*, 61–85; Juan Marichal with Lew Freedman, *Juan Marichal: My Journey from the Dominican Republic to Cooperstown* (Beverly, MA: Voyageur Press, 2011), especially chap. 2, "Growing Up in the Dominican Republic."

13. Ruck, *Tropic of Baseball*, chaps. 1 and 3; Orlando Inoa, "El béisbol dominicana: 70 años de historia, 1891–1961," in *El béisbol en República Dominicana: Crónica de una pasión*, Colección Cultural Verizon VII (Santo Domingo: Amigo del Hogar, 2004), 123–145.

14. On the Tragedy of Río Verde, see Cuquí Córdova, "La Tragedia de Río Verde," in *Historia del Béisbol Dominicano* (Santo Domingo: Diario Libre, 2018); on the victory in 1948, see "El Presidente Trujillo y el triunfo del equipo nacional," *La Nación*, December 13, 1948, 1.

15. "El Presidente Trujillo y el triunfo del equipo nacional," *La Nación*, December 13, 1948, 1; A. Castro Recio, "Con mi Periscopio: Una Actitud Viturable," *El Deporte al Día*, May 30, 1953, 32.

16. Inoa, "El béisbol dominicano," 138–149.

17. Inoa, "El béisbol dominicano," 138–149.

18. No. 584, DGD al Secretario de la Educación y Bellas Artes, "Proyecto de Reglamento de Base-ball Profesional," June 9, 1953, SEDEFIR 31630, 16534, Archivo General de la Nación, Santo Domingo, República Dominicana (hereafter AGN).

19. No. 1052, Director General de Deportes Lic. F Humberto Gómez O a la Secretaría de la Presidencia, November 16, 1953, SEDEFIR 31630, 16518, AGN. The National Commission included Manuel Vicente Fleiú (president), Gilberto Morillo Soto (vice president), Manfredo Moore (secretary), Leoncio Ramos, Julio A. Cuello, Osvaldo Peña Batlle, and Rodolfo Bonetti Burgos (member). Benigno del Castillo, who was president of the ad hoc committee the previous year, refused the invitation, while Rafael González, a member the previous year, was not present because he was serving in the military.

20. Memorandum, Juan I. Vicioso V., Mayor Honorario Ejército Nacional y Director General de Deportes, al Excelentísimo Señor Presidente de la República, [s.f., but referenced AS# 3406 and likely preceded April 11], SEDEFIR 31630, 16534, AGN.

21. On the advice of the director of sports, the secretary of education refused financial support to the organizers of the 1954 season, but the teams later secured support from the executive power. For the denial, see AS# 3406, Secretario de Estado de Educación y Bellas Artes Lic. Porfirio Basora R., al Señor Presidente, March 18, 1954, SEDEFIR 31630, 16583, AGN. The money was granted later on the advice to the president from the director of sports in the interest of social policy. See Memorandum, Juan I. Vicioso V., Mayor Honorario Ejército Nacional y Director General de Deportes al Excelentísimo Señor Presidente de la República, April 11, 1954, SEDEFIR 31630, 16534, AGN.

22. No. 9685, Director General del Deporte Juan Vicioso V, al Generalísimo Dr Rafael Leonidas Trujillo Molina, May 16, 1954, SEDEFIR 31630, 16534, AGN.

23. Nuestros Editoriales, "La ACD en su Vigésimo Aniversario," *El Deporte al Día*, no. 1, March 23, 1953, 3. The editorial celebrated the achievements of the ACD (Asociación de Cronistas Deportivos, or Sportswriters Association), which organized the magazine, but also honored Trujillo. The ACD claimed credit for establishing the Office of the National Director of Sports, but did so through Trujillo.

24. Memorandum, Director General de Deportes a la Presidencia, [s.f.], SEDEFIR 31630, 16534, AGN.

25. No. 1059, Director General de Deportes al Presidente de la San Rafael, C por A, Compañía de Seguros, JT Aguilar, October 4, 1954, SEDEFIR 31630, 16534, AGN.

26. Carta, Ing. Trancredo Ayubar C, Francisco Martínez Alba, Ing. Juan Sánchez Corre y Dr. José Hazim (presidents of professional baseball clubs) al Presidente Trujillo via la Secretaría de Estado de Educación y Bellas Artes Joaquín Balaguer, September 3, 1955, SEDEFIR 31630, 16567, AGN.

27. On Dominican admission to the Caribbean Confederation, which organized the Caribbean Series each year, see "Informe que la Liga Dominicana de Base-Ball Profesional, Incorporada, rinden los delegados de la Liga Dominicana, Señores Licenciados Manfredo A. Moore R. y Máximo Hernández Ortega, en relación con el resultado de sus gestiones en las reuniones celebrados por la Confederación de Base-Ball Profesional del Caribe, en la ciudad de Caracas, los días 13, 14 y 15 de agosto del año 1958," August 21, 1958, sent with Carta, Lic. Manfredo A. Moore R., Vice-Presidente de la Liga Dominican de Base-Ball Profesional, al Honorable Señor Dr. Rafael Leonidas Trujillo Molina, Benefactor de la Patria y Padre de la Patria Nueva, August 22, 1958, SEDEFIR 31630, 16567, AGN.

28. No. 1072, Director General de Deportes Andrés A. Alba Valera al Secretaría de Estado de Educación Joaquín Balaguer, June 22, 1955, SEDEFIR 31630, 16549, AGN. The document referred to three acts, two of which were included with the document (one must have been lost) that described the league's rules and organization.

29. Ph, "Con los Spikes en Alto, Un Pica en Flandes por los Viejos," *El Caribe*, September 5, 1955, 8.

30. "Pueblo Dominicano Espera la Hora de Iniciar el Clásico," *La Nación*, October 8, 1956, 8. The article offered a brief history of the development of professional baseball since 1951 and attributed these new heights in baseball—signaled by Virgil's ascent to the US major leagues and the number of quality imported players

(thirty-eight to that point)—to the Dominican League's incorporation and government support for the national pastime.

31. See, for example, Memorandum, Secretaría de Estado de Educación y Bellas Artes, Joaquín Balaguer, al Presidente de la República, September 6, 1955, SEDEFIR 31630, 16567, AGN; Carta, Lic. Jaime Vidal Velázquez, Presidente de la Liga Dominicana de Baseball Profesional, al Generalísimo Rafael Leonidas Trujillo Molina, September 20, 1956, SEDEFIR 31630, 16545, AGN. Vidal thanked Trujillo for his recommendation of the $100,000 gift to the league.

32. Ph, "Un hermoso espectáculo," *El Caribe*, October 25, 1955, 12.

33. Letter from Leo Durocher to Rafael Leonidas Trujillo Molina, April 26, 1954, SEDEFIR 31630, 16583, AGN.

34. "Ofrecen Datos de Antesalista Dominicano Virgil; Y su Abuela en C. Trujillo; Tiene Muchos Tíos, Primos," *El Caribe*, September 2, 1955, 7.

35. On the ways citizens and writers used rhetorical tricks to criticize Trujillo while performing their loyalty, see Derby, *The Dictator's Seduction*, chap. 4, "Compatriotas! El Jefe Calls," 135–172.

36. Ozzie Virgil, interview with the author, Mets Dominican Academy, Boca Chica, Dominican Republic, June 4, 2012; "El Dueño de Mayagüez da $5,500 al Antesalista Virgil Para que no Juegue Pelota; Escogido Espera Reconsidere Paso," *El Caribe*, October 29, 1955, 12.

37. Octavio, *La Nación*, September 26, 1956, 9.

38. "El Primero Big Leaguer Dominicano Retornará Hoy al País; Preparan Recibimiento al Espectacular Osvaldo Virgil," *La Nación*, October 10, 1956, 8; "Palos Azules," *La Nación*, September 29, 1956, 9; Ph, "Esta Noche," *El Caribe*, October 23, 1956, 6.

39. Cuchito Alvarez, "Habla Osvaldo Virgil: 'Me Sentía Muy Confiado y Orgulloso de Ser el Primer Jugador Dominicano En Poder Jugar en las Grandes Ligas,'" *La Nación*, October 14, 1956, 10.

40. Martínez played on Alex Pómpez's Negro League team, the New York Cubans, in the 1940s. For more on these connections, see Burgos, *Playing America's Game*, especially "Making Cuban Stars," 111–140.

41. Rafael Martorell, "El Deporte al Día," *El Caribe*, June 10, 1958, 19.

42. Rafael Martorell, "El Deporte al Día," *El Caribe*, June 10, 1958, 19.

43. Octavio, *El Caribe*, June 9, 1958, 14.

44. Rafael Martorell, "El Deporte al Día," *El Caribe*, June 10, 1958, 19.

45. Salvador Bernardino, "Baseportivas: Osvaldo Virgil, digno representante del valor dominicano en las Grandes Ligas," *El Caribe*, June 16, 1958, 19. On Detroit Tigers fans and integration, see Louis Moore, *We Will Win the Day: The Civil Rights Movement, the Black Athlete, and the Quest for Equality* (Santa Barbara, CA: Praeger, 2017), 53–56.

46. Martorell, "El Deporte al Día," *El Caribe*, June 10, 1958, 19.

47. "Progreso Deportivo," *La Nación*, June 4, 1960, 6.

48. "Enfoques: El Deporte Triunfante," *La Nación*, June 5, 1960, 6.

49. "Enfoques: El Deporte Triunfante," *La Nación*, June 5, 1960, 6.

50. "Progreso Deportivo," *La Nación*, June 4, 1960, 6.

51. "Criollos Víctimas Problema Racial en el Sureño Estado de la Florida," *La Nación*, June 6, 1960, 17.

52. "Criollos Víctimas Problema Racial en el Sureño Estado de la Florida; Vicente Enfermo Debido a Dificultades Comidas," *La Nación*, June 6, 1960, 17.

53. Manuel Neftalí Martínez, "Players Dominicanos Dicen Ser Víctimas de Perjuicio Racial en los Estados Unidos; Por Ser Negros: Rojas Alou y Antulio Martínez Tienen que Jugar aún Heridos; Añora Ausencia Discrimen en República Dominicana," *La Nación*, June 23, 1960, 1, 24. The first part of the title headlined the day's edition of the paper and directed readers to the sports section for details.

54. "Escándalo por Discriminación Racial En Dogout Indios de Cleveland; Lanzador Grant Dice Tierra de EUA No Es Libre para El," *La Nación*, September 29, 1960, 15, reprinted from *The Sporting News*, September 28, 1960. The article reported that Cleveland pitcher Jim Grant was suspended for leaving the bullpen during a game, even though he did so in response to a racial insult uttered by pitching coach Ted Wilks.

55. Martínez, *La Nación*, June 23, 1960, 24.

56. A. Domínguez de la Rosa, "Obreros de DN Repudian Discriminación de los EEUU contra los Atletas Criollos; Destacan Igualdad Imperante en RD," *La Nación*, June 26, 1960, 14. The article explained that speakers at the meeting denounced the United States and then honored the "nombre esclarecido" of Trujillo, "máximo nivelador de los valores y de las clases nacionales."

57. Minutero, *El Caribe*, June 4, 1960, 1, 2; "Democracia Social," *La Nación*, September 14, 1960, 6.

58. Letter, George Tautman, President of the National Association of Professional Basbeall Leagues, to Hipólito Herrera Billini, President of Dominican Republic League, September 2, 1960, SEDEFIR 31630, 16518, AGN.

59. "El Campeonato '16 de Mayo' Será con Peloteros Criollos: Liga Dominican se Solidariza Con la Política Nacionaliza," *La Nación*, September 9, 1960, 15; Memorandum, Secretario Dr. Aristides Alvarez Sánchez y Presidente Hipólito Herrera Billini, Liga Dominicana de Base Ball Profesional, Incorporada, al Señor Secretario de Estado de la Presidencia, September 9, 1960, SEDEFIR 31630, 16518, AGN.

60. "Cronistas Deportivos Opinan que 5 Importados Son Buenos; Hernández Llaverías Dice Pueden Venir de Otras Partes," *La Nación*, September 21, 1960, 16.

61. Ramón Alberto Ferreras, "Al Margen del Deporte," *El Caribe*, June 11, 1958, 13, established a demand for a more nationalist tournament in 1958. Billy Berroa, "Cronistas Dicen Importación Players Debe Hacerse este Año; Expresan Importados Deben Limitarse a Cinco por Team," *La Nación*, September 16, 1960, 18.

62. Rafael Francisco De Moya Pons (Frank Moya Pons), "Industrial Incentives in the Dominican Republic 1880–1983" (PhD diss., Columbia University, 1987), especially chap. 2, "Trujillo's Industrial Policy," 40–103; Turits, *Foundations of Despotism*.

63. Fidencio Garris, "Cronistas Dicen Importación Players Debe Hacerse Este Año; Expresan Importados Deben Limitarse a Cinco por Team," *La Nación*, September 16, 1960, 18.

64. Salvador Bernardino L, "Basedeportivas, Facetas del Deporte," *El Caribe*, June 3, 1960, 17.

65. Luichy Sánchez, Tertulia sobre la expansión del beisbol profesional otoño-invernal, en la ocasión de la clausura de la exposición, *¡Nos vemos en el play! Beisbol y Cultura en la República Dominicana*, Centro León, Santiago, República Dominicana, May 11, 2008, video recording. In response to a question from the audience about whether Rafael Trujillo ever interfered directly in professional baseball, Sánchez, a regular in the offices of the Aguilas Cibaeñas since childhood, when his father presided over the team, responded that the dictator and his family did not interfere with on-field play—with the notable exception of Petán Trujillo slapping Andre Rodgers of Escogido after a fight with Licey—but did influence the behind-the-scenes efforts to sign players. Although Sánchez is too young to remember the Trujillo era, he has studied baseball throughout his life and works closely with many who experienced Trujillo's regime firsthand.

66. Félix Acosta Núñez, "Rivas Poncha Doce y Gana Partido Inaugural ante 12,000 Fanáticos; Presidente de la República Hace Lanzamiento Honor," *La Nación*, October 23, 1960, 49. Balaguer replaced Héctor Trujillo as president in August 1960.

67. Acosta Núñez, "Rivas Poncha Doce y Gana Partido Inaugural Ante 12,000 Fanáticos."

Chapter 2: Politics at the Plate

1. The fans changed the "C" in Castro to a "K" as a play on the use of a "K" to signal a strikeout in baseball scoring, symbolizing their feelings that Castro had struck out for the Cuban people.

2. "Team Estrellas Cubanas Obtienen Triunfo Frente a las Dominicanas; José Vidal Dispara un Jonrón de 390 Pies," *La Nación*, November 8, 1962, 9; "Cubanos Obtiene Primer Triunfo en Serie de Beisbol; Peña Lanza esta Noche Frente a Ceferino Foy," *El Caribe*, November 8, 1962, 15. I use the phrase "brought to justice" to describe the end of Trujillo throughout to reflect Dominicans' use of the Spanish *ajusticiamiento* rather than *asesinato* to describe the event.

3. "Ornes Denuncia: Agitadores Tratarán Impedir Comicios en RD, FED y ANES; Grupos Amenazan a los Profesores," *La Nación*, October 20, 1962, 18.

4. Greg Grandin, *The Last Colonial Massacre: Latin America in the Cold War* (Chicago: University of Chicago Press, 2004).

5. Frank, *El Caribe*, December 22, 1962, 6.

6. Jean, "Magnífico Estímulo," *El Caribe*, October 5, 1962, 8.

7. "Bienvenidos," *La Nación*, October 17, 1962, 4.

8. "Estímulo Deportivo," *El Caribe*, October 4, 1962, 8. Editorials, columnists, and even political parties touted the social benefits of sport and drew explicit connections between sport and democracy. For example, see Salvador Bernardino L, "Facetas del Deporte: Importancia del Deporte en la Formación del Individuo," *El Caribe*, December 26, 1961, 9; Comité Ejecutivo Central del Partido Nacionalista Revolucionario Democrático, "Los deportes nacionales en la presente hora decisiva de la Recuperación," programa del PNRD en Radio Caribe, September 15, 1962, SEDEFIR 16588, Archivo General de la Nación, Santo Domingo, República Dominicana (hereafter AGN).

9. Special Meeting of the Inter-American Economic and Social Council, *The Charter of Punta del Este: Establishing an Alliance for Progress within the Framework of Operation Pan America*, Virtual Library of Inter-American Peace Initiatives, Organization of American States.

10. John F. Kennedy, "Address at a White House Reception for Members of Congress and for the Diplomatic Corps of the Latin American Republics," March 13, 1961, in Gerhard Peters and John T. Wooley, *The American Presidency Project*, University of California Santa Barbara, https://www.presidency.ucsb.edu/ws?pid=8531. See also "Address at a White House Reception for Members of Congress and for the Diplomatic Corps of the Latin American Republics," March 13, 1961, video, TNC-182A, Archives, JFK Library, https://www.jfklibrary.org/asset-viewer/archives/TNC/TNC-182A/TNC-182A.

11. "Centro de Coordinación Patriótica hace un llamado a favor de la República," *La Nación*, October 20, 1962, 13.

12. "Centro de Coordinación Patriótica hace un llamado a favor de la República," *La Nación*, October 20, 1962, 13. On the dangers of protests and disorder, see "La Historia Pretende Repetirse en la América Latina," *La Nación*, October 20, 1962, 4; "Un Alerta a los Padres," *La Nación*, October 20, 1962, 4; "Los Lamentables Sucesos de San Pedro de Macorís," *La Nación*, October 17, 1962, 4; "Defiendase quien pueda," *La Nación*, October 16, 1962, 3; "*Gobernador Santiago*: Preocupado por Factores Negativos de Política," *La Nación*, October 15, 1962, 1; D.O Bergés-Bordas, "Demostremos que Somos Civilizados," *El Caribe*, October 5, 1962, 8; "Ornes Denuncia: Agitadores Tratarán Impedir Comicios en RD, FED y ANES," *La Nación*, October 20, 1962, 18.

13. "Los Lamentables Sucesos de San Pedro de Macorís," *La Nación*, October 17, 1962, 4.

14. José A. González, "El Pueblo Dominicano Da Caluroso Recibimiento a Players Juan Marichal y los Hermanos Rojas Alou; Reciben Delirantes Aplausos en Recorrido por la Ciudad," *La Nación*, October 18, 1962, 11.

15. "Players en Palacio," *La Nación*, October 18, 1962, 1.

16. "Bienvenidos," *La Nación*, October 17, 1962, 4.

17. "Ceden Terrenos para Construcción de Instalaciones Deportivas," *La Nación*, October 18, 1962, 11.

18. Miche Medina, "El Line-Up del PRD," *La Nación*, October 22, 1962, 4.

19. Salvador Bernardino, "Facetas del Deporte: Bendito Sea el Deporte," *La Nación*, November 6, 1962, 10. See also "Selección Dominicana Vence al Conjunto Cubano 4 x 1; Partido se Desenvuelve Sin Alterarse el Orden," *La Nación*, November 2, 1962, 10.

20. Felipe Alou with Herm Weiskopf, *Felipe Alou . . . My Life and Baseball* (Waco, TX: Word Books, 1967), 119.

21. Alou with Weiskopf, *My Life and Baseball*, 119.

22. "La Actitud Dominicana," *La Nación*, October 26, 1962, 1. The writer explains the reasoning behind the Dominican vote in favor of the embargo against Cuba, citing the belief that sanctions against Trujillo "undoubtedly contributed to the collapse of tyranny." Support for the US actions extended to a letter circulated at

the United Nations. See "En las NU: RD Expresa Preocupación por la Crisis en América," *La Nación*, October 26, 1962, 1.

23. "Team Estrellas Cubanas Visitará el País para Jugar Serie Frente a Selección Dominicana," *La Nación*, October 24, 1962, 10; Merriman Smith, "Hoy Podría Iniciarse una Terrible Guerra Nuclear," *La Nación*, October 24, 1962, 1, 2; "RFB Señala Peligro Ofrece Cuba; Expide Comunicado Pueblo Dominicano," *La Nación*, October 24, 1962, 1; "Una amenaza continental," *La Nación*, October 24, 1962, 1.

24. "Team Estrellas Cubanas Visitará el País para Jugar Serie Frente a Selección Dominicana," *La Nación*, October 24, 1962, 10; "Orestes Miñoso Será Manager del Conjunto Estrellas Cubanas," *La Nación*, October 25, 1962, 10.

25. "Fernández Preocupado por Situación Cubana," *La Nación*, October 28, 1962, 16.

26. "En Cuba: Movilizan Players Equipos de Beisbol," *La Nación*, October 26, 1962, 18.

27. Miche Medina, "Un No Hit, No Run," *La Nación*, October 30, 1962, 4.

28. "Comunismo: ¡Qué calamidad, la única carrera que podía empujar era la de López Molina, y lo atraparon en tercera!"

29. Reginaldo Atana, "Detienen a López Molina; Policia Captura Armas; Persiguen Otros Compañeros Suyos," *La Nación*, October 29, 1962, 1, 3. The article reports that López Molina had been swimming when arrested. The front-page editorial on *La Nación* implicitly connects this luxury enjoyed by López Molina with the favoritism of the Trujillo era, "El Crimen del Engaño," *La Nación*, October 29, 1962, 1. On the plot, including the hand-drawn maps outlining it, see "Hallan Mapas de Sitios a Sabotear; Extremistas Planeaban Atentados Contra Empresas," *El Caribe*, November 3, 1962, 1, 12.

30. Salvador Bernardino, "Facetas del Deporte: Bendito Sea el Deporte," *La Nación*, November 6, 1962, 10.

31. On baseball and the Cuban Freedom Cause, see "Cuban Freedom Has Inning as Stars Play Here Sunday," *Miami Herald*, October 12, 1962; Bill Braucher, "Ah, Baseball, Cubans Love It as Always," *Miami Herald*, October 15, 1962, 3-D; Especial para *El Diario*, "Histórico Rivales Frente a Frente: Habana Empata a Dos con Almendares en Miami," *El Diario de Nueva York*, October 16, 1962, 34.

32. Misión Permanente de la República Dominican a las Naciones Unidas, quoted in "En Las NU: RD Expresa Preocupación por la Crisis en América," *La Nación*, October 26, 1962, 1. On the council's support, see no. 24935, Rafael F. Bonnelly al Secretario de Estado de Finanzas, "Exoneración de impuestos para celebración de serie de base-ball," October 27, 1962, SEDEFIR 16572, AGN, and Felipe Alou's defense that fans would have rioted if they had not played and that acting president Bonnelly told the players, "I am the president of the Dominican Republic and I say that it is all right to play." Alou with Weiskopf, *My Life and Baseball*, 119. Alou also explained that not playing would have been a victory for the communists in the country; see Felipe Alou with Arnold Hano, "Latin-American Ballplayers Need a Bill of Rights," *Sport*, November 1963, 76.

33. Herminio Portell-Villa, "Los Dominicanos y la Libertad de Cuba," *La Nación*, November 14, 1962, 4.

34. For example, "Los Extremos se Tocan," *La Nación*, October 31, 1962, 1; Reginaldo Atamay, "Máximo López Molina: Cómo un Comunista Vivía Como un Burgués," *La Nación*, October 31, 1962, 3; "El Crimen del Engaño," *La Nación*, October 29, 1962, 1; "Voces de Sensatez," *La Nación*, October 27, 1962, 1.

35. In addition to the PRD and the UCN, the two most prominent parties, the elections included the Partido de la Alianza Social Demócrata (PASD, Party of the Social Democrat Alliance), Partido Nacional (National Party, PN), Partido Revolucionario Dominicano Aútentico (PRDA, Authentic Dominican Revolutionary Party), Partido Revolucionario Social Cristiano (PRSC, Revolutionary Social Christian Party), and the Partido Vanguardia Revolucionaria Dominicana (PVRD, Party of the Dominican Revolutionary Vanguard). See Junta Central de Elecciones, "Resultado de las Elecciones Presidenciales, Congresionales y Municipales del año 1962," *Boletines*, http://resultadoselectorales.jce.gob.do/boletines/1962/nivel1962.htm. Dom Bonafede of the *Miami Herald* noted that Bosch and Fiallo were the front-runners for president, as reported in "De *Miami Herald*: Destacan Lucha Política entre Fiallo y Juan Bosch: Candidatos de Más Empuje en Contienda," *La Nación*, November 6, 1962, 16.

36. On the UCN platform, see "Dice Viriato Fiallo: La UCN es el Único Partido Capaz de Corregir los Males," *La Nación*, October 23, 1962, 18. Bosch revealed pieces of the PRD platform in the speech opening the party's convention. See Guido Féliz, "Primera Convención Nacional del PRD Fue Inaugurado Ayer," *La Nación*, October 20, 1962, 18. For an outsider's report on the candidates, see Dom Bonafede, "De *Miami Herald*: Destacan Lucha Política entre Fiallo y Juan Bosch: Candidatos de Más Empuje en Contienda," *La Nación*, November 6, 1962, 16.

37. For example, the Association of Families of the Dead and Tortured by the Past Tyrant called on Dominicans to continue to pressure the government to hold those who participated in the Trujillo regime accountable for their actions. See "Comunicado de la Asociación de Familiares de los Muertos y Tortuados por la Pasada Tiranía," *La Nación*, October 20, 1962, 12.

38. For example, see Juan Bosch, *Crisis de la democracia de América en la República Dominicana* (México: Centro de Estudios y Documentación Sociales, 1964). References taken from the fourth Dominican edition (Santo Domingo: Editora Alfa and Omega, 2005).

39. Fiallo and others attributed disorder, including that which had occurred days before in San Pedro, to extremist groups and increasingly conflated *trujillismo* and communism, or totalitarianism from the right and left, without making ideological or social distinctions. See, for example, "Ornes Denuncia: Agitadores Tratarán Impedir Comicios en RD, FED y ANES; Grupos Amenazan a los Profesores," *La Nación*, October 20, 1962, 18.

40. José A. González, "Dice Felipe Alou: 'Esta es la Serie Mundial Más Emocionante de todas," *La Nación*, October 24, 1962, 11.

41. Alou with Hano, "Latin-American Ballplayers Need a Bill of Rights," 76.

42. "Clemente Observa Juego Inaugural Serie Beisbol," *El Caribe*, November 3, 1962, 18; for speculations that Clemente, Pagán, and Cepeda might reinforce the Dominican team, see "Team Estrellas Dominicanas Es un 'Hueso Duro de Roer,'"

La Nación, October 27, 1962, 6; "La Selección Dominicana Demuestra Poder al Bate Durante las Prácticas; Jugarán Contra Conjunto de Estrellas Cubanas," *La Nación*, October 30, 1962, 8.

43. "Campaña Asistencia Social," *La Nación*, November 10, 1962, 9; quotation from "Dedicarán Obras Sociales Porcentaje de Juegos," *El Caribe*, November 9, 1962, 12. These women may have been part of the Comité Nacional de Asistencia Social that Elizabeth Manley described Gladys de los Santos working with to support women and infant health. See Elizabeth S. Manley, *The Paradox of Paternalism: Women and the Politics of Authoritarianism in the Dominican Republic* (Gainesville: University Press of Florida, 2017), 146.

44. "Dedicarán Obras Sociales Porcentaje de Juegos," *El Caribe*, November 9, 1962, 12.

45. John Bartlow Martin, Memorandum: Political Reconstruction of the Dominican Republic, January 30, 1962, 1, box 44, folder 2: Ambassador's Journal, January–December 1962, John Bartlow Martin Papers, Manuscript Division, Library of Congress, Washington, DC.

46. Robert Cantwell, "Invasion from Santo Domingo," *Sports Illustrated*, February 25, 1963, 56–57, https://www.si.com/vault/issue/42747/63.

47. Cantwell, "Invasion from Santo Domingo."

48. Cantwell, "Invasion from Santo Domingo," 56–57; Frank, *El Caribe*, December 22, 1962, 6.

49. "Resultado de las Elecciones Presidenciales, Congresionales y Municipales del Año 1962," Junta Central Electoral, 2018, http://resultadoselectorales.jce.gob.do/boletines/1962/nivel1962.htm.

50. "Profesor Bosch Dice Ser Entusiasta del Beisbol," *El Caribe*, February 23, 1962, 16; "El Presidente Electo Lanza Primera Bola en Inicio Serie Beisbol Liga Babe Ruth: Bosch Hace Remembranza de su Vida de Atleta," *La Nación*, February 23, 1962, 9.

51. "¡Déjelos Que Ayuden, Profesor!," *La Nación*, February 24, 1963, 4.

52. "Ejecutivo Lee Discurso Tras su Juramentación," *El Caribe*, February 28, 1963, 10.

53. "Ejecutivo Lee Discurso Tras su Juramentación," *El Caribe*, February 28, 1963, 10.

54. Grandin, *The Last Colonial Massacre*.

55. For example, Salvador Pittaluga N., Secretario General de la Asociación Dominicana de Periodistas y Escritores, "'Escucha, Norteamericano," *El Caribe*, February 23, 1963, 8; Freddy Gatón Arce, "A los que Están Tras las Bayahondas de la Oposición," *El Caribe*, March 15, 1963, 6; Jottin Cury, "¡Dejemos Gobernar a Bosch!," *El Caribe*, March 15, 1963, 7.

56. Moya Pons, "Industrial Incentives," 299.

57. Eliades Acosta Matos, *1963: De la guerra mediática al golpe de estado* (Santo Domingo: Ediciones Fundación Juan Bosch, 2015).

58. "Los Extremos se Tocan," *La Nación*, October 31, 1962, 1.

59. J. R. Hernández, "Téngase Miedo, Señor Presidente!," *El Caribe*, February 21, 1963, 9.

60. "Quien se crea libre de pecado, que tire la primera bola!," "La Oración," *La Nación*, March 21, 1963, 4. The cartoon was unsigned, but the style appears to be that of Miche Medina, who regularly drew for the paper, including the "Un No Hit, No Run" cartoon. The players representing the opposition in this cartoon resembled the pitcher "Libertad" in the earlier cartoon.

61. Henry Raymount, "Informan Bosch Proyecta Reducir el Sueldo a Funcionarios Públicos; Trata de Eliminar Salarios de Lujo," *El Caribe*, March 3, 1963, 1, 8.

62. Joseph Sims, "Lleras Considera Alianza Única Manera de Combatir Comunism; Califica Plan de Trascendental," *El Caribe*, March 4, 1963, 1, 8.

63. Mario Bobea Billini, "Política de Bosch es de Aflojamiento de Tensions con los Comunistas Nativos," *El Caribe*, March 13, 1963, 7.

64. On Bosch's speech, see "Bosch Dice Comunismo Es Destrucción y Muerte; Invita a FAA a Colabora en Trabajos," *El Caribe*, March 13, 1963, 1, 14; Mario Bobea Billini, "Definición Hecha por Bosch y Otros Hechos Reducen las Tensiones en el Ambiente," *El Caribe*, March 15, 1963, 7.

65. Miguel A. Hernández, "Diputado de UCN Decide Presentar Renuncia Cargo," *El Caribe*, March 6, 1963, 9; "Intranquiliza a Fiallo Situación Política RD," *El Caribe*, March 6, 1963, 9.

66. Dr. Viriato A. Fiallo, "Breve Mensaje al Pueblo Dominicano," *El Caribe*, March 12, 1963, 6.

67. Pascual Peña, "Acusan Abuso de Poder a Presidente Asamblea," *El Caribe*, March 13, 1963, 9.

68. "Signo Reconfortante," *El Caribe*, March 10, 1963, 6.

69. Frank, editorial cartoon, *El Caribe*, March 12, 1963, 6.

70. "Otra Preocupación," *El Caribe*, April 20, 1963, 6.

71. "Repugnante Arma Política," *El Caribe*, September 5, 1963, 8.

72. "Ley Confiscaciones," *El Caribe*, September 6, 1963, 10.

73. "Repugnante Arma Política," *El Caribe*, September 5, 1963, 8.

74. "Ejecutivo Expone Criterio Sobre Fomento Industrial," *El Caribe*, April 19, 1963.

75. Political Affairs & Rel. POL 1 General Policy, Background, "Secret: The Dominican Coup of September 25," October 10, 1963, Box 5, 3151: Records Relating to the Dominican Republic, 1956–1966, RG 59, National Archives and Records Administration (NARA).

76. "Teams Oriental y Licey Encuéntrense de defecto," *El Caribe*, September 6, 1963, 18.

77. Clifford Kackline, "Destacan Actividades de la Liga Dominicana Beisbol Profesional," *El Caribe*, September 7, 1963, 18; "Las Estrellas de Oriente Firman Cinco Refuerzos," *El Caribe*, September 7, 1963, 19.

78. "Presidente Bosch Pide Dejen Jugar a Nativos En Próximo Campeonato; Petición es Hecha a Ligas Mayores," *El Caribe*, September 10, 1963, 10.

79. Vice Ministro de Finanzas Dr. Luis María Guerrero G., al Director General de Deportes via el Ministro de la Presidencia, EX 9689, July 23, 1963, SEDEFIR 16567, AGN; Domingo Saint-Hilaire, hijo, "Impiden a Big Leaguers Actuar en la República," *El Caribe*, September 24, 1963, 16. Domingo Saint-Hilaire, hijo, "Reclaman Derechos

Sobre R. Hernández y O. Virgil," *El Caribe*, September 12, 1963, 17, reported that Dominican League president Julio A. Cuello asked the government to step in with the electric company and that the government had offered "ample facilities" to ensure the celebration of the national tournament. Four days later, *El Caribe* noted that the issues had been resolved with government intervention; see "Liga Beisbol Efectuará Encuentro de Estrellas," *El Caribe*, September 16, 1963, 15.

80. Domingo Saint-Hilaire, hijo, "Comisionado de Beisbol Dice Virgil y Hernández Pertenecen a Puerto Rico; Aguilas Buscan Dos Sustitutos," *El Caribe*, September 19, 1963, 18.

81. Domingo Saint-Hilaire, hijo, "Reclaman Derechos Sobre R. Hernández y O. Virgil," *El Caribe*, September 12, 1963, 17; Espacio Pagado, "Carta Abierta al Señor Presidente de la República Profesor Juan Bosch," *El Caribe*, September 12, 1963, 15.

82. Espacio Pagado, "Carta Abierta al Señor Presidente de la República Profesor Juan Bosch," *El Caribe*, September 12, 1963, 15.

83. On Dominican women's political participation, see Manley, *The Paradox of Paternalism*; April J. Mayes, "Why Dominican Feminism Moved to the Right: Class, Colour and Women's Activism in the Dominican Republic, 1880s–1940s," *Gender and History* 20, no. 2 (August 2008): 349–371; on women in the struggle against the perceived threat of communism, see also Margaret Power, *Right-Wing Women in Chile: Feminine Power and the Struggle against Allende, 1964–1973* (University Park: Penn State University Press, 2002).

84. "Desmantelan Locales Partidos de Izquierda," *El Caribe*, September 26, 1963, 18; "Policía Detiene Grupo de Estudiantes de BRUC," *El Caribe*, September 26, 1963, 13; Carlos Holguín-Veras, "Grupos de Manifestantes Lanzan Piedras a Carros," *El Caribe*, September 26, 1963, 14.

85. On the coup against Bosch, see Briefing Papers, October 10, 1963, box 5, 3151: Records Relating to the Dominican Republic, 1956–1966, RG 59, National Archives and Records Administration; Piero Gleijeses, *La Esperanza desgarrada: La rebelión dominicana de 1965 y la invasión norteamericana* (Santo Domingo: Editora Búho, 2012); Rafael Francisco De Moya Pons (Frank Moya Pons), "Industrial Incentives in the Dominican Republic, 1880–1983" (PhD diss., Columbia University, 1987); Bosch, *Crisis de la democracia de América en la República Dominicana*; Víctor Grimaldi, *Golpe y revolución: El derrocamiento de Juan Bosch y la intervención norteamericana* (Santo Domingo: Comisión Permanente de Efemeridades Patrias, 2008); Juan Bosch, "La historia secreta del golpe de 1963," in Eliades Acosta Matos, *La guerra mediática al golpe de estado* (Santo Domingo: Ediciones Fundación Juan Bosch, 2015), 619–644.

86. John F. Kennedy, "Address at a White House Reception for Members of Congress and for the Diplomatic Corps of the Latin American Republics," March 13, 1961, video, TNC-182A, Archives, JFK Library, https://www.jfklibrary.org/asset-viewer/archives/TNC/TNC-182A/TNC-182A.

Chapter 3: Criticizing Baseball, Debating Democracy

1. Miche Medina, "History Repeats with Guayubín and Chichí: Cain Killed His Brother Abel," *El Caribe*, October 24, 1963, 6. In the cartoon, the crow in the bot-

tom of the frame who delivered Medina's punchlines said, "History repeats with Guayubín and Chichí. Cain killed his brother Abel." The Licey tiger congratulated the elder Olivo, saying, "Oh, Guayubín, how tastily you cook elephant in sauce! I can't complain about your service!" Guayubín, holding cigarettes made by the sponsor for the cartoon, said, "That's not all! Here I have the best." Ph, "¿Cáin, que has hecho con tu hermano?," *El Caribe*, October 23, 1963, 6.

2. "Justifian Golpe en EU," *El Caribe*, September 30, 1963, 14; Acción Democrática Dominicana Independiente, Espacio Pagado por la Dirección de Prensa del Palacio Nacional, *El Caribe*, October 12, 1963, 11; Dirección de Prensa del Palacio Nacional, "Le Tomó el Golpe de Estado la Delantera a los Comunistas?," *El Caribe*, October 12, 1963, 2 (adapted from the *Miami Herald*, October 7, 1963); Roberto Berrellez, "Califican Reacción de Explosiva," *El Caribe*, October 15, 1963, 1, 8.

3. Miche Medina, E. León Jiménes, C. por A., "La Caricatura de Hoy," *El Caribe*, October 9, 1963, 15.

4. "Marichal Mejor Lanzador Latino en Mayores; F. Rojas Alou Finaliza Campañã con Marca 281," *El Caribe*, October 1, 1963, 13; Ph, "Marichal pinta elefantitos blanco," *El Caribe*, October 26, 1963, 18.

5. Miche Medina, "La Caricatura de Hoy," *El Caribe*, October 28, 1963, 14.

6. Pedro Justiano quoted in "Pitcher Juan Marichal Recibe Homenaje de Afición," *El Caribe*, October 31, 1963, 17.

7. "Pitcher Juan Marichal Recibe Homenaje de Afición," *El Caribe*, October 31, 1963, 17; Rafael Martorell, "Marichal y Felipe Alou Dan Liderato a Escogido," *El Caribe*, October 31, 1963, 17.

8. Pedro Justiano quoted in "Pitcher Juan Marichal Recibe Homenaje de Afición," *El Caribe*, October 31, 1963, 17.

9. Rafael Martorell, "El Deporte al Día," *El Caribe*, October 18, 1963, 19.

10. Martorell, "El Deporte al Día," *El Caribe*, October 18, 1963, 19.

11. "Presidente Bosch Pide Dejen Jugar a Nativos en Próximo Campeonato; Petición es Hecha a Ligas Mayores," *El Caribe*, September 10, 1963, 10.

12. Dirección de Prensa del Palacio Nacional, Espacio Pagado, "Juan Bosch es Comunista," *El Caribe*, October 23, 1963, 11, reprinted from Carlos Siso Maury, *Patria* (Miami), October 11, 1963.

13. Ibid. "Hicieron bien las Fuerzas Armadas de la República Dominicana al tomar la grave decisión de expulsar del Poder a un gobernante que permitía, con su impasibilidad la penetración comunista en el país."

14. Dirección de Prensa del Palacio Nacional, Espacio Pagado, "Juan Bosch es Comunista," *El Caribe*, October 23, 1963, 11.

15. On public diplomacy in the Cold War, see Nicholas Cull, *The Cold War and the United States Information Agency: American Propaganda and Public Diplomacy, 1945–1989* (New York: Cambridge University Press, 2008); Jason C. Parker, *Hearts, Minds, Voices: US Cold War Public Diplomacy and the Formation of the Third World* (New York: Oxford University Press, 2016). On the US separation of politics and diplomacy, see Emily S. Rosenberg, *Financial Missionaries to the World: The Politics and Culture of Dollar Diplomacy, 1900–1930* (Durham, NC: Duke University Press, 2003).

16. Mario Almonte, "Liga Venezolana Decidida a Celebrar los partidos de Beisbol con Criollos; Esperan Decisión de Liga Beisbol," *El Caribe*, October 6, 1963, 12.

17. Rafael Martorell, "El Deporte al Día," *El Caribe*, October 18, 1963, 19; on private organizations using sport to promote national politics, see Barbara J. Keys, *Globalizing Sport: National Rivalry and International Community in the 1930s* (Cambridge, MA: Harvard University Press, 2006), especially chaps. 3 and 4.

18. Document 361, Telegram from the Department of State to the Embassy in the Dominican Republic, Washington, October 17, 1963, *Foreign Relations of the United States, 1961–1963*, vol. 12, *American Republics*, ed. Edward C. Keefer, Harriet Dashiell Schwar, W. Taylor Fain III, and Glenn W. LaFantasie (Washington, DC: Government Printing Office, 1996), 745.

19. Stephen G. Rabe, "The Caribbean Triangle: Betancourt, Castro, and Trujillo and U.S. Foreign Policy, 1958–1963," in *Empire and Revolution: The United States and the Third World since 1945*, eds. Peter L. Hahn and Mary Ann Heiss (Columbus: Ohio State University Press, 2001), 48–70; George Ball, Document 363, Telegram from the Department of State to the Embassy in Venezuela, December 13, 1963, *Foreign Relations of the United States, 1961–1963*, vol. 12, *American Republics*, 747–48; "Venezuela—Foreign Relations," in *Venezuela: A Country Study*, ed. Richard A. Haggerty (Washington, DC: Government Printing Office, 1990), http://countrystudies.us/venezuela/50.htm.

20. LeeAnna Yarbrough Keith, "The Imperial Mind and US Intervention in the Dominican Republic, 1961–1966" (PhD diss., University of Connecticut, 1999); Thomas W. Zeiler, *Ambassadors in Pinstripes: The Spalding World Baseball Tour and the Birth of the American Empire* (Lanham, MD: Rowman and Littlefield, 2006).

21. Felipe Alou with Arnold Hano, "Latin-American Ballplayers Need a Bill of Rights," *Sport*, November 1963, 20–21, 76–79; John Bartlow Martin, *Overtaken by Events: The Dominican Crisis from the Death of Trujillo to the Civil War* (Garden City, NY: Doubleday, 1966).

22. Rafael Martorell, "Alou, Marichal, Javier y Olivo Multados por Comisionado de Beisbol; También Cubanos que Jugaron Aquí," *El Caribe*, February 5, 1963, 12.

23. "Felipe Alou Firma Contrato; Gana $25,000; Frick Exige Pago Multa para Jugar," *El Caribe*, February 10, 1963, 11.

24. Alou with Hano, "Latin-American Ballplayers Need a Bill of Rights," 76.

25. Felipe Alou with Herm Weiskopf, *My Life and Baseball* (Waco, TX: Word Books, 1966), 119.

26. Alou with Weiskopf, *My Life and Baseball*, 120.

27. Alou with Weiskopf, *My Life and Baseball*, 119; Robert Cantwell, "Invasion from Santo Domingo," *Sports Illustrated*, February 25, 1963, 57, https://www.si.com/vault/issue/42747/63.

28. Alou with Weiskopf, *My Life and Baseball*, 119. Reports about the series in the United States, often after the fact, varied on the number of games. Alou's article in *Sport* described a seven-game series while the Cantwell article rightly reported an eight-game series. Perhaps the discrepancy in Alou's 1966 autobiography resulted from forgetting the details as he recounted the situation to Weiskopf.

29. Alou with Hano, "Latin-American Ballplayers Need a Bill of Rights," 77–78.

30. Rafael Martorell, "Felipe Alou Renuncia su Retiro del Beisbol," *El Caribe*, January 1, 1963; Alou with Hano, "Latin-American Ballplayers Need a Bill of Rights," 78.

31. Alou with Hano, "Latin-American Ballplayers Need a Bill of Rights," 79.

32. Martin, *Overtaken by Events*, 205.

33. Martin, *Overtaken by Events*, 179.

34. Document 17, Airgram from the Embassy in the Dominican Republic to the Department of State, A-250, December 5, 1964, *Foreign Relations of the United States, 1964–1968*, vol. 32, *Dominican Republic; Cuba; Haiti; Guyana*, ed. Daniel Lawler, Carolyn Yee, and Edward C. Keefer (Washington, DC: Government Printing Office, 2005), https://history.state.gov/historicaldocuments/frus1964-68v32/ch1.

35. John Bartlow Martin, Memorandum: Political Reconstruction of the Dominican Republic, January 30, 1962, 5, John Bartlow Martin Papers, Library of Congress; Rosenberg, *Financial Missionaries to the World*.

36. Martin, *Overtaken by Events*, 197; Rudyard Kipling, "The White Man's Burden," *Modern History Sourcebook*, Fordham University, https://sourcebooks.fordham.edu/mod/kipling.asp; see also Patrick Brantlinger, "Kipling's 'The White Man's Burden' and Its Afterlives," *English Literature in Translation, 1880–1920* 50, no. 2 (2007): 172–191.

37. Martin, *Overtaken by Events*, 109–110, 202.

38. On this preference and its effects in the Dominican Republic, see Stephen G. Rabe, *The Killing Zone: The United States Wages Cold War in Latin America* (New York: Oxford University Press, 2012), 85–113.

39. Undersecretary of State George Ball instructed embassy officials to "state clearly and emphatically that USG will not recognize or deal with this regime as it stands. This regime and the politicians who named the cabinet represent a minority of the Dom people." Document 359, Telegram from the Department of State to the Embassy in the Dominican Republic, October 4, 1963, *Foreign Relations of the United States, 1961–1963*, vol. 12, *American Republics*, https://history.state.gov/historicaldocuments/frus1961-63v12/ch7.

40. Document 17, Airgram from the Embassy in the Dominican Republic to the Department of State, December 5, 1964, *Foreign Relations of the United States, 1964–1968*, vol. 32, *Dominican Republic; Cuba; Haiti; Guyana*.

41. See, for example, "Liga de Beisbol Impone Multa a Juan Marichal," *El Caribe*, December 20, 1963, 21. The suspension came later.

42. "Julián Javier Decidido a No Actuar con Aguilas," *El Caribe*, December 19, 1963, 17; Domingo Saint-Hilaire, hijo, "Aguilas Piden Suspensión Julián Javier; Directiva Norteña Alega Incumplimiento Contrato," *El Caribe*, December 26, 1963, 11.

43. "Liga Dominicana Beisbol Suspenden Tres Players," *El Caribe*, January 14, 1964, 13; Domingo Saint-Hilaire, hijo, "Tratan Cambiar a Javier por Jardinero M. Jiménez," *El Caribe*, January 24, 1964, 20.

44. Miche Medina, "La Caricatura de Hoy," *El Caribe*, January 10, 1964, 16.

45. "Pitcher Juan Marichal Recibe Homenaje de Afición," *El Caribe*, October 31, 1963, 17.

46. "Julián Javier Decidido No Actuar con Aguilas," *El Caribe*, December 19, 1963, 17; "El Gobierno Suspende Tres Derechos Constitucionales," *El Caribe*, December 20, 1963, 1.

47. "El Gobierno Suspende Tres Derechos Constitucionales," *El Caribe*, December 20, 1963, 1; "Triumviro Reafirma Gobierno Asumirá sus Responsabilidades," *El Caribe*, December 20, 1963, 1, 14; "Triunviro Dice Guerrillas Tratan Imponer Comunismo," *El Caribe*, December 20, 1963, 11.

48. "Busquemos una Solución," *El Caribe*, December 23, 1963, 8.

49. José F. Penson, "La Política Desplaza los Demás Pasatiempos," *El Caribe*, December 27, 1963, 16.

50. José F. Penson, "La Política Desplaza los Demás Pasatiempos," *El Caribe*, December 27, 1963, 16.

51. Ph, *El Caribe*, January 27, 1964, 17; "Licey Reacciona en Finales y Supera a las Aguilas," *El Caribe*, January 29, 1964, 15; "Licey Derrota Aguilas Empatando la Serie Final," *El Caribe*, January 31, 1964, 14.

52. Miche Medina, E. León Jiménes, C. por A., "La Caricatura de Hoy," *El Caribe*, January 31, 1964, 14.

53. Domingo Saint-Hilaire, hijo, "Protestan por Anuncio Asistencia en Encuentro," *El Caribe*, January 29, 1964, 15; "Licey Obtiene su Segundo Triunfo en Serie Final," *El Caribe*, January 30, 1964, 17; Héctor Celado, "Licey se Corona Campeón al Vencer Aguilas Cibaeñas," *El Caribe*, February 2, 1964, 1, 8.

54. Domingo Saint-Hilaire, hijo, "Players Aguilas Originan Desorden en Bar El Cerro," *El Caribe*, January 29, 1964, 15; "Licey Obtiene su Segundo Triunfo en Serie Final," *El Caribe*, January 30, 1964, 17. Although Saint-Hilaire filed his story on Tuesday, January 28, he reported that the fight had occurred on Sunday, January 26, likely after the Aguilas lost 3–0 against the Tigers in the second game.

55. "Players Licey y Aguilas Piden 50.000 Pesos para Jugar frente Venezuela," *El Caribe*, January 28, 1964, 15.

56. Domingo Saint-Hilaire, hijo, "Exigencias de Jugadores Amenazan Frustrar Serie; $16,000 Exigen Players de Aguilas para Jugar," *El Caribe*, February 5, 1964, 14.

57. Domingo Saint-Hilaire, hijo, "Plaskett Revela Disgusto con Ejecutivos Aguilas," *El Caribe*, February 5, 1964, 14; Domingo Saint-Hilaire, hijo, "Presidente de Aguilas Desmiente a E. Plaskett," *El Caribe*, February 6, 1964, 15.

58. Ph, "Con los Spikes en Alto; Nuestros Frankensteins," *El Caribe*, February 13, 1963, 12.

59. Ph, *El Caribe*, February 8, 1964, 15. See also Domingo Saint-Hilaire, hijo, "Leones de Caracas se Imponen a Aguilas; Escaso Público Presencia Juego en Estadio Cibao," *El Caribe*, February 8, 1964, 15.

60. "El Problema Nacional," *El Caribe*, February 9, 1964, 6.

61. The initial article on the clinics made no mention of US sponsorship, but a memorandum to the chief of staff from Horacio Veras, the director of sports, listed the players and indicated that they were paid by the US Department of State. See Director General de Deportes al Sr. Secretario de Estado de la Presidencia, Memorandum no. 1423, October 27, 1964, SEDEFIR 16569, AGN. The participants included Julián Javier of the St. Louis Cardinals, Cuban Mike de la Hoz and Lee

Maye of the Milwaukee Braves, Chuck Cottier and Ron Kline of the Washington Senators, Charley Lau of the Los Angeles Angels, and Dick Hall of the Baltimore Orioles. American League umpire Frank Umont directed the team, while Bob Bauman accompanied them as the sports trainer-masseuse. See "Players Mayores Darán Clínicas en País; Dominicano Julián Javier Figura entre Entrenadores," *El Caribe*, October 29, 1964, 14. After spending a week in the Dominican Republic, the group was scheduled to go on a goodwill tour through other parts of Latin America. In an interview, Javier recounted staying home after the initial incident, alleging that his daughter took ill. Interview with the author, April 17, 2012, San Francisco de Macorís, Dominican Republic.

62. "Estudiantes de un Liceo Apedrean a Deportistas," *El Caribe*, November 6, 1964, 11. On the meeting with the Triumvirate, see "Triunvirato Recibe 7 Jugadores De Pelota de las Grandes Ligas," *El Caribe*, November 5, 1964, 15, and on the ceremony at the Escogido-Aguilas game, see "Presentan Varios Players Durante Partido de Ayer," *El Caribe*, November 5, 1964, 14.

63. Domingo Saint-Hilaire, hijo, "Aseguran Julián Javier Actuará con las Aguilas," *El Caribe*, October 15, 1964, 15.

64. "Pobre Demostración de Conducta," *El Caribe*, November 6, 1964, 6.

65. Alou with Weiskopf, *My Life and Baseball*, 131–132. Alou said, "The team traveled all over South America and wherever they went they were greeted warmly—until they got to Santo Domingo. [. . .] The incident was an outbreak of anti-American feeling and the players had to leave the school grounds as fast as they could." The incident likely struck Alou more than others because he had attended the school as a youngster, and the embarrassment of the anti-US hostilities stuck with him.

66. Ph, "Angulos de la Serie Mundial II," *El Caribe*, October 13, 1964, 14.

67. Ph, "Angulos de la Serie Mundial II," *El Caribe*, October 13, 1964, 14.

68. JOH, "¡A la pelota!," *¡Ahora!*, December 19, 1964, 26.

69. For example, "Esa Cosa tan seria . . . que se llama Política," *¡Ahora!*, January 16, 1965, 11.

70. Tirso A. Váldez, hijo, "Cuadrante Deportivo," *¡Ahora!*, January 30, 1965, 56; "Cuadrante Deportivo," *¡Ahora!*, February 13, 1965, 48. Váldez was not alone. See also "Nuestras Necesidades Deportiva," *¡Ahora!*, December 12, 1964, 21.

71. Tirso A. Váldez, hijo, "Cuadrante Deportivo," *¡Ahora!*, December 19, 1964, 51.

72. Tirso A. Váldez, hijo, "Cuadrante Deportivo," *¡Ahora!*, November 14, 1964, 56.

73. Thino Pimental, "Roberto Clemente: Un Orgullo Latino," *¡Ahora!*, February 13, 1965, 47, 49; Crucigrama Deportivo, *¡Ahora!*, April 17, 1965, 59.

74. On amateur sport, see Tirso A. Váldez, hijo, "Cuadrante Deportivo," *¡Ahora!*, December 12, 1964, 25; Tirso A. Váldez, hijo, "Cuadrante Deportivo," *¡Ahora!*, December 19, 1964, 51; Tirso A. Váldez, hijo, *¡Ahora!*, January 30, 1965, 56; Tirso A. Váldez, hijo, *¡Ahora!*, February 20, 1964, 54; Tirso A. Váldez, hijo, *¡Ahora!*, April 10, 1965, 72. On incentives, see Frank Moya Pons, *Empresarios en conflicto: Políticas de industrialización y sustitución de importaciones en la República Dominicana* (Santo Domingo: Fondo para el Avace de las Ciencias Sociales, 1992), 106–119. This monograph in Spanish is a translation of Moya Pons's dissertation, "Industrial Incentives in the Dominican Republic, 1880–1983" (PhD diss., Columbia University, 1987).

75. Tirso A. Váldez, hijo, Cuadrante Deportivo, *¡Ahora!*, February 20, 1964, 54.

76. In his synthesis of Dominican history, *Cincuenta años de democracia y desarrollo dominicano 1961–2011: Logros y fracasos* (Santo Domingo: Fundación Dominicana de Estudios Económicos, 2012), Dominican scholar Eduardo J. Tejera describes the uprising against the Triumvirate as a "known secret" from January through April 1965; see also Frank Moya Pons, "La lucha por la democracia, 1961–2004," in *Historia de la República Dominicana* (Santo Domingo: Ediciones Doce Calles, Academia Dominicana de la Historia, 2010), 590–592.

77. As Piero Gleijeses calls them, "los cinco días gloriosos." In *La Esperanza desgarrada: La rebelión dominicana de 1965 y la invasión norteamericana* (Santo Domingo: Editora Búho, 2012), 2.

Chapter 4: *Así se hace Patria*

1. Alvaro Arvelo, hijo, "Notas de la Serie," *El Caribe*, August 26, 1969, 17; on the game, see the articles under the column heading "Cuba es Campeón," Alvaro Arvelo, hijo, "Efectivo Relevo" and Miguel A. Reynoso Solís, "Buena Labor PN," *El Caribe*, August 27, 1969, 1, 15.

2. Alvaro Arvelo, hijo, "Notas de la Serie," *El Caribe*, August 27, 1969, 16.

3. Miguel A. Reinoso Solís, "Buena Labor PN," *El Caribe*, August 27, 1969, 1, 15.

4. On the opening of official relations in 1998, see APTV, "Cuba/Dominican Republic: Countries Resume Diplomatic Relations," AP Archive, May 3, 1998, http://www.aparchive.com/metadata/youtube/7eb40670f845682b73bb080534655cf7.

5. On Cuban sports policy, the idea of sport for all, and the tensions with elite sport, see Paula J. Pettavino and Geralyn Pye, *Sport in Cuba: The Diamond in the Rough* (Pittsburgh: University of Pittsburgh Press, 1994); Robert Huish, Thomas F. Carter, and Simon C. Darnell, "The (Soft) Power of Sport: The Comprehensive and Contradictory Strategies of Cuba's Sport-Based Internationalism," *International Journal of Cuban Studies* 5, no. 1 (Spring 2013): 26–40.

6. Tirso A. Váldez, hijo, Cuadrante Deportivo, *¡Ahora!*, February 20, 1965, 54.

7. April Yoder, "Dominican Baseball and Latin American Pluralism, 1969–1974," *Oxford Research Encyclopedia of Latin American History*, September 29, 2016, https://oxfordre.com/latinamericanhistory/view/10.1093/acrefore/9780199366439.001.0001/acrefore-9780199366439-e-355.

8. Reem Abou-El-Fadl, *Foreign Policy as Nation Making: Turkey and Egypt in the Cold War* (New York: Cambridge University Press, 2019).

9. Felipe Alou with Peter Kerasotis, *Alou: My Baseball Journey* (Lincoln: University of Nebraska Press, 2018), 168–170.

10. Alou with Kerasotis, *Alou*, 170. US-based and Dominican historians agree with Alou's assessment; see Piero Gleijeses, *La esperanza desgarrada: La rebelión dominicana de 1965 y la invasión norteamericana* (Santo Domingo: Editora Búho, 2012); Piero Gleijeses, "Hope Denied: The US Defeat of the 1965 Revolt in the Dominican Republic," *Cold War International History Project*, working paper no. 72, November 2014, https://www.wilsoncenter.org/publication/hope-denied-the-us-defeat-the-1965-revolt-the-dominican-republic. For sources, see *Foreign Relations*

of the United States, 1964–1968, vol. 32, *Dominican Republic; Cuba; Haiti; Guyana*, eds. Daniel Lawler and Carolyn Yee (Washington, DC: Government Printing Office, 2005), Document 80, 176, https://history.state.gov/historicaldocuments/frus1964-68v32/ch1. For Dominican scholars, see Roberto Cassá, *Los doce años: Contrarrevolución y desarrollismo*, vol. 1, 2nd ed. (Santo Domingo: Editora Búho, 1991); Víctor Grimaldi, *Golpe y revolución: El derrocamiento de Juan Bosch y la intervención norteamericana* (Santo Domingo: Comisión Permanente de Efemérides Patrias, 2008).

11. Elizabeth S. Manley, *The Paradox of Paternalism: Women and the Politics of Authoritarianism in the Dominican Republic* (Gainesville: University Press of Florida, 2017), 158. See also Cassá, *Los doce años*. Jonathan Hartlyn, *The Struggle for Democratic Politics in the Dominican Republic* (Chapel Hill: University of North Carolina Press, 1998); Rosario Espinal, *Autoritarismo y democracia en la política dominicana* (San José, Costa Rica: Centro Interamericano de Asesoría y Promoción Electoral [CAPEL], 1987).

12. Suárez del Solar, "Hazaña Players Criollos Será Difícil de Igualar," *El Caribe*, October 3, 1966, 14, reported these statistics, though Baseball-Reference.com reports slightly different numbers for Felipe Alou (.327) and Ricardo Carty (.326).

13. *Time*, June 10, 1966. The cover named Marichal "The Best Right Arm in Baseball" and featured Gerald Gooch's six-step storyboard rendition of Marichal's famous high-kicking motion. The feature story, "Baseball: The Dandy Dominican," referenced Marichal's more widely known nickname, "The Dominican Dandy."

14. Almonte, *El Caribe*, October 4, 1966, 6.

15. "Buenos Embajadores," *El Caribe*, October 3, 1966, 10.

16. "Buenos Embajadores," *El Caribe*, October 3, 1966, 10.

17. "Buenos Embajadores," *El Caribe*, October 3, 1966, 10.

18. Almonte, "Triunfo Consagrador," *El Caribe*, October 4, 1966, 6.

19. This figure constitutes the 2012 equivalent of US$163,000 in 1963 (equivalent to RD$23,000) according to the Simple Purchasing Power Calculator based on the US Consumer Price Index (CPI). Although the Dominican peso was pegged to the US dollar in 1963, the CPI likely varied greatly because of different items considered in the computation of the consumer bundle. However, these figures provide a frame of reference for today's US figures. For conversions and explanation of the comparative figures, see MeasuringWorth.com; Memorándum no. 140, Director Técnico de la Oficina de Fiscalización de Obras é Inversiones del Estado, Ing. Bienvenido A. Martínez Brea, al Sr Presidente de la República, September 22, 1966, SEDEFIR, 16579, AGN. Minister of Public Works Ing. Luis Mauricio Bogaert originally estimated the costs of repairs at $52,706.94, according to Memorandum 3830, September 12, 1966, SEDEFIR, 16579, AGN. Martínez Brea, who built Estadio Quisqueya, included only the essential repairs that could be completed in time for the 1966–1967 winter season in his quote of $22,697.70.

20. Memorandum no. 1, "Sobre Campeonato Profesional 1966–1967," [s.f.], Horacio A. Veras, Director General de Deportes, al Honorable Señor Presidente de la República, SEDEFIR, 16577, AGN.

21. Carta, Dr. A. Álvarez Sánchez, Secretario de la Liga Dominicana de Baseball Profesional, Inc., al Señor Doctor Joaquín Balaguer, January 31, 1967, SEDEFIR,

16583, AGN. Veras had indicated in his undated memo that the Aguilas owed $40,000, but by January 1967 the Estrellas and Escogido distinguished themselves for carrying debts just under $19,000 each from the 1963 and 1964 seasons.

22. Memorandum, Vice Presidente Francisco Augusto Lora, a Su Excelencia, June 28, 1967, SEDEFIR 16583, AGN.

23. Fidencio Garris, "Javier 'Jugador de Dinero,'" *El Caribe*, October 17, 1967, 16.

24. Arnaldo Camilo Simó, "Alegra a Esposa de Javier Bienvenida de Fanáticos," *El Caribe*, October 17, 1967, 17.

25. Domingo Saint-Hilaire, hijo, wrote a series of articles on ticket sales: "Venden en Santiago todas Entradas Juegos Piratas," *El Caribe*, October 16, 1967, 18; "Inician Venta de Entradas Juego Piratas en Santiago," *El Caribe*, October 18, 1967, 17; "Fanáticos Región Cibaeña Darán Bienvenida Piratas," *El Caribe*, October 19, 1967, 18.

26. I have found no evidence of official US government support for the Pirates' trip, aside from the presence of embassy officials at the event, though the unclassified documents that were not available when I went to the National Archives in 2010 may now be accessible and could provide more information.

27. Derby's analysis of *El Caribe*'s "Foro Público" during the 1950s, when citizens and bureaucrats performed denunciations and panegyrics to police loyalty to Trujillo, suggests that Dominicans were attuned to the messages intended through Balaguer's performance in the society pages a decade later. See Lauren H. Derby, *The Dictator's Seduction: Politics and the Popular Imagination in the Era of Trujillo* (Durham, NC: Duke University Press, 2009), chap. 4.

28. Alvaro Arvelo, hijo, "Emabajador de EU Agasaja a Pirates de Pittsburgh," *El Caribe*, October 24, 1967, 4.

29. Uncredited photos, *El Caribe*, October 24, 1967, 6. The photos accompanied an unsigned article titled "Ejecutivo Califica Valioso Aporte de Piratas del Pittsburgh."

30. Carta, José Armenteros, Presidente, Fundación Dominicana de Desarrollo, Inc., al Dr. Joaquín Balaguer, Hon. Señor Presidente de la República, October 3, 1967, SEDEFIR, 16583, AGN.

31. On the violence and repression during Balaguer's *doce años*, see "11,000 víctimas en Doce Años de JB," *Listín Diario*, March 10, 2013, https://listindiario.com/la-republica/2013/3/9/268859/11000-victimas-en-Doce-Anos-de-JB; *Balaguer: La violencia del poder*, film directed by René Fortunato (Santo Domingo: Video Cine Palau, 2003); "Resistencia, Dictadura de Balaguer," Museo Memorial de la Resistencia Dominicana, https://www.museodelaresistencia.com/category/dictadura-de-balaguer/.

32. Rafael A. Rodríguez G., "Davalillo es el Manager del Conjunto Venezolano," *El Caribe*, August 12, 1969, 15.

33. For example, Director General de Deportes Horacio A. Veras G., Memorándum 00483, al Excelentísmo Presidente de la República Dr. Joaquín Balaguer, April 16, 1969, SEDEFIR 31630, 16545, AGN.

34. Director General de Deportes Horacio A. Veras G., no. 00679, al Señor Dr. José A. Quezada T., Secretario Administrativo de la Presidencia, April 24, 1969, SEDEFIR

31630, 16534, AGN; Director General de Deportes Horacio A. Veras, no. 00792, al Señor Director General de Turismo [Ángel Miolán], May 12, 1969, SEDEFIR 31630, 16534, AGN.

35. Secretario de Estado de Educación, Bellas Artes y Culto, Dra. Altagracia Bautista de Suárez, OM# 7943, al Secretario Administrativo de la Presidencia, May 18, 1969.

36. José A. González, "Aspiraciones Deportivas para 1965," *¡Ahora!*, February 13, 1965, 45.

37. Tirso A. Váldez, hijo, Cuadrante Deportivo, *¡Ahora!*, February 13, 1965, 48; Director General de Deportes Horacio A. Veras G., Memorándum 00483, al Excelentísmo Presidente de la República Dr. Joaquín Balaguer, April 16, 1969, SEDEFIR 31630, 16545, AGN.

38. Although Puerto Rico is a political and economic colony of the United States, its people have long identified as a distinct nation. See Antonio Sotomayor, *The Sovereign Colony: Olympic Sport, National Identity, and International Politics in Puerto Rico* (Lincoln: University of Nebraska Press, 2018).

39. Pedro Gil Iturbides, En esta Equina, "¡Qué Raros son los Cubanos!," *El Caribe*, August 14, 1969, 10.

40. Alvaro Arvelo, hijo, "Notas de la Serie," *El Caribe*, August 19, 1969, 16.

41. "Veras Favorece Club Dominicano Viaje a La Habana; Aclara Primero Necesita la Invitación Oficial," *El Caribe*, August 29, 1969, 16.

42. Quoted in Miguel A. Reinoso Solís, "Buena Labor PN," *El Caribe*, August 27, 1969, 15.

43. "Greenberg Aspira Hijo se Dedica a Batear H4; Llega Conjunto de EUA; Reúne Universitarios," *El Caribe*, August 14, 1969, 18.

44. In *The Sovereign Colony*, Sotomayor discusses Puerto Rico's Latin American identity and nationality even while being under US political control. I suggest a similar relationship in the Dominican Republic that placed Latin American cultural affinity with Cuba built through amateur baseball alongside political and economic ties with the United States seen in the professional system.

45. Comisión Especial de Cooperación Latinoamericana, Reunión Extraordinaria a Nivel Ministerial, "Consenso Latinoamericano de Viña del Mar," May 15 to 17, 1969, *Estudios Internacionales* 3, no. 11 (October-December 1969): 403–418, https://revistaei.uchile.cl/index.php/REI/article/view/18950/20080; on Cuba and Latin American pluralism, see Yoder, "Dominican Baseball and Latin American Pluralism."

46. Quoted from the manager of the Dutch Antilles on their arrival to Las Américas Airport, in Rafael A. Rodríguez G., "Davalillo es el Manager del Conjunto Venezolano," *El Caribe*, August 12, 1969, 15.

47. Henry A. Kissinger, Document 4, "Essay by Henry A. Kissinger," 1969, *Foreign Relations of the United States, 1969–1976*, vol. I, *Foundations of Foreign Policy, 1969–1972*, eds. Louis J. Smith and David H. Herschler (Washington, DC: Government Printing Office, 2003), https://history.state.gov/historicaldocuments/frus1969-76v01/d4; Nelson A. Rockefeller, "Quality of Life in the Americas," *Department of*

State Bulletin 61, no. 1589 (December 8, 1969): 493–540; Richard M. Nixon, Document 424, "Remarks at the Annual Meeting of the Inter-American Press Association," October 31, 1969, *The Public Papers of the Presidents of the United States*, University of Michigan Digital Library, https://quod.lib.umich.edu/p/ppotpus/4731731.1969.001/953?q1=Inter-American+Press+Association&view=image&size=100.

48. "Que se Esclarezca," *El Caribe*, August 20, 1969, 8; "Terrorismo: Siguen los Crímenes y Desaparaciones," *¡Ahora!*, December 21, 1970, 3; "Alto a la Violencia," *El Caribe*, August 30, 1969, 1; Cassá, *Los doce años*; Laura Faxas, *El mito roto: Sistema política y movimiento popular en la República Dominicana, 1961–1990* (México, DF: Siglo XXI Editores, SA de CV y Santo Domingo: FUNGLODE y FLACSO, 2007), 123.

49. "No Dejarán Alteren Orden Contra o Favor Delegación," *El Caribe*, August 14, 1969, 18.

50. Rafael A. Rodríguez G., "La Seguridad," accompanied a report on the Cubans' arrival under the banner "Cuba da Crédito Dirigentes de RD," *El Caribe*, August 13, 1969, 1, 16.

51. "US Nine Jeered at Santo Domingo," *New York Times*, August 26, 1969, 49.

52. "Tipifican Homenaje Gritos en Favor y Contra de Castro," *El Caribe*, August 23, 1969, 2nd ed.

53. "Veras Favorece Club Dominicano Viaje a La Habana," *El Caribe*, August 29, 1969, 16; José Joaquín Hungria Morell, "El Doble Triunfo de Dominicana," *El Caribe*, August 30, 1969, 14A.

54. *¡Ahora!*, December 21, 1970.

55. "XII Juegos Centroamericanos," *¡Ahora!*, December 21, 1970, 1; Pedro Caba, "XII Juegos Centroamericanos y del Caribe: Extraordinaria Responsabilidad Nacional," *¡Ahora!*, December 21, 1970, 73–76.

56. Caba, "XII Juegos," 74.

57. Caba, "XII Juegos," 74.

58. Horacio A. Veras G., DGD Memorándum no. 1151, al Excelentísimo Señor Presidente de la República, Dr. Joaquín Balaguer, June 25, 1970, 3, SEDEFIR 31630, 16545, AGN. A warning that García Saleta was "not patriotic" in the communication that Veras forwarded to Balaguer echoed a former sports director's accusations that García Saleta had conspired in a "Communist-type operation" in 1964. See DGD Francisco Fernández M., Memorándum al Triunvirato, April 23, 1964, SEDEFIR 31630, 16534, AGN.

59. On populist governments using sport to create a partnership with citizens, see Antonio Sotomayor, "*Un parque para cada pueblo*: Julio Enrique Monagas and the Politics of Sport and Recreation in Puerto Rico during the 1940s," *Caribbean Studies* 42, no. 2 (2014): 3–40; Raanan Rein, "*El primer deportista*: The Political Use and Abuse of Sport in Peronist Argentina," *International Journal of the History of Sport* 15, no. 2 (1998): 54–76. April Yoder, "*Un compromiso de tod@s*: Women, Olympism, and the Dominican Third Way," in *Olimpismo: The Olympic Movement in the Making of Latin America*, ed. Antonio Sotomayor and César R. Torres (Fayetteville: University of Arkansas Press, 2020), 131–147, offers more detail on Cuban assistance to Dominican athletes and officials leading up to the tournament. On Cuba's

use of sport for soft power, see Huish, Carter, and Darnell, "The (Soft) Power of Sport," 26–40.

60. On the Third Way and the international implications of Balaguer's project, see Yoder, "Dominican Baseball and Latin American Pluralism"; for the repercussions of the games for women athletes, see Yoder, "*Un compromiso de tod@s*; Contratos de Obras y Agrícolas (CONTROBRAS) e Ingenieros Civiles Asociados, Espacio Pagado, *El Caribe*, February 26, 1974, supplement 5. The sponsors' advertisement thanked Balaguer for his support for the construction of the Palacio de Deportes for the games and concluded with the slogan "Haciendo deportes, se hace patria!" (practicing sports makes the nation).

61. Víctor Goméz Bergés, quoted in "La RD Favorece Consolidación de la Libertad," *El Caribe*, November 14, 1973, 15. Citing figures from the International Committee for the Alliance for Progress, Gómez Bergés noted that the Dominican Republic's GDP increased by 7.5 percent in 1971 and 12.5 percent in 1972.

62. "Closer to Chaos," *Time*, April 13, 1970, 36. *El Caribe* revealed a concern about US intervention as early as August 1969, quoting the president of Santo Domingo's council, Rafael Vidal Martínez, who called on Dominicans to be vigilant "in order to avoid the series of acts that in other times have dragged the country toward the loss of its independence or its liberty." See "Exhorta Evitar que el País Vuelva Perder su Libertad," *El Caribe*, August 16, 1969, 2nd ed.

63. "Terrorismo: Siguen los Crímenes y Desapariciones," *¡Ahora!*, December 21, 1970, 3–4.

64. Arnaldo Bazán, "Maneras de Entender la Democracia," *La Información*, March 5, 1975, 3.

65. "Proyecto de Resolución, Creación de los Juegos Deportivos Nacionales," Director General de Deportes Horacio A. Veras, [s.f.], SEDEFIR 16545, AGN. The draft resolution in the SEDEFIR file has no date, but accompanying documents date as far back as May 21, 1968, when the DGD submitted the project to the Executive branch for approval.

66. Banco Central, *Ejecución del Presupuesto* (Santo Domingo: Banco Central, editions from 1971, 1972, 1973, 1974). The line item for Special Fund 1676, Iniciativa Práctica Deportes, appeared for the first time in the 1971 budget and steadily increased through 1976, when it more or less stabilized. The amounts cited refer to the resources collected in the fund, while another line item recorded the amounts designated for regular disbursements from the fund, probably as monthly allotments to sports federations or to clubs for equipment and coaches. Even with these numbers, the resources allotted to the organization of the 1974 Games and sports more generally lack transparency because of flexibility the regime exercised in allocating funds to different projects. Other funds, especially Fund 1469 for "Atenciones Especiales de la Presidencia," increased dramatically, with more than $1 million disbursed in 1972 and nearly $2.8 million in 1975. Balaguer appears to have exercised his own discretion in allocating these funds, as suggested by his awarding of $40,000 to the director of sports to help send a team to the 1970 Central American and Caribbean Games. See No. 6887, February 20, 1970, Presidente Balaguer al Director Nacional del Presupuesto, SEDEFIR 16534, AGN.

67. Banco Central, "Fondo General: Asignaciones por Capítulos, Programas y Objetos de Gasto," *Ejecución del Presupuesto* (Santo Domingo: Banco Central, editions for 1966–1974.)

68. A group of athletic federation presidents and young men volunteering their time to work on the Centro Olímpico wrote a message of encouragement to García Saleta; see "Un Mensaje Deportivo que Todos Debemos Leer," October 28, 1968, SEDEFIR 31630, 16545, AGN.

69. Sr. Ramón de la Rosa y demás firmantes de la Dirección del Club Juvenil de Balconcesto de Higuey, Carta al Dr. Joaquín Balaguer, Presidente de la República, September 25, 1972, SEDEFIR, 31630, 16572, AGN.

70. Senador Dr. Leopoldo Núñez Levy y Diputado Lic. Amable A. Botello, al Sr. Dr. Joaquín Balaguer, Honorable Presidente de la República, Telegrama 27-12-392, June 19, 1972, SEDEFIR 31630, 16572, AGN.

71. Gaspar L. Vichez Suero, José María D'Soto Sánchez, Dr. Felipe Ant. Moquete C, y demás, Carta al Dr. Joaquín Balaguer, Presidente Constitucional de la República Dominicana, March 20, 1973, SEDEFIR 31630, 16528, AGN.

72. Sr. Héctor "Bullo" Steffani al Dr. Quezada, Secretario Administrativo de la Presidencia, Informe deportivo, September 30, 1969, SEDEFIR 31630, 16545, AGN; José Quezada, Secretario Administrativo de la Presidencia, al DGD Héctor Veras, No. 52394, October 25, 1969, SEDEFIR 31630, 16545, AGN; Héctor Bullo Steffani al Apreciado Dr. Balaguer, Carta, November 14, 1973, SEDEFIR 31630, 16578, AGN; see also Domingo Saint-Hilaire, hijo, "Deportes Mejor Camino para Erradicar las Drogas," *La Información*, March 4, 1975, 7.

73. Secretario de Estado sin Cartera Dr. José S. Ginebra H. y Diputado Rafael Balbuena Farington, Memorándum, al Dr. Joaquín Balaguer, Honorable Presidente de la República, March 13, 1973, SEDEFIR 31630, 16516, AGN.

74. Bienvenido Martínez Brea, quoted in Tomás E. Montás, "El Deportes es Fuente de Fortaleza de la Juventud," *El Caribe*, February 28, 1974, 17.

75. On security, see Rafael Rodríguez Gómez, "La Policía Vigila Grupos Considera 'Subversivos,'" *El Caribe*, February 27, 1974, 2; "Toman Medidas Seguridad en Apertura XII Juegos," *El Caribe*, February 28, 1974, 20. Mario Alvarez, "Más de 2,000 Atletas Inician Hoy XII Juegos," *El Caribe*, February 27, 1974, 1, 8, offered more insight into the early divisions and difficulties surrounding the games as well as the compromises on government spending; Compañía Anónima Tabacalera, *El Caribe*, February 27, 1974, 3.

76. Compañía Anónima Tabacalera, *El Caribe*, February 27, 1974, 3.

77. Antonio Gil, "Uribe Silva Pide Balaguer Acepte Nueva Nominación," *El Caribe*, February 28, 1974, 14; on Uribe Silva, see César Medina, Fuera de Cámara, "Balaguer y Nano Uribe," *Listín Diario*, September 14, 2013, https://listindiario.com/puntos-de-vista/2013/09/14/292102/balaguer-y-nano-uribe—.

78. Gil, "Uribe Silva Pide," *El Caribe*, February 28, 1974, 14.

79. Teddy, *El Caribe*, February 27, 1975, 18.

80. Teddy, *El Caribe*, April 21, 1976, 17.

81. In 1973, Nicaragua, the United States, and Italy broke from IBAF to form FEMBA (Federación Mundial de Béisbol Amateur) ostensibly for administrative

reasons. FEMBA excluded Cuba, whose influence in IBAF meetings and dominance on the field likely caused many to join the new organization. See Yoder, "Dominican Baseball and Latin American Pluralism."

Chapter 5: Sliding into Third

1. In contrast to Javier, whose thirteen seasons in the big leagues qualified him for a pension, Santana had no pension to rely on after his career in the United States ended. Although Santana would still not qualify for a major-league pension today, players now qualify for the minimum pension of around $35,000 annually after just forty-three days on a big-league roster. After ten years of service, those benefits increase, and players earn up to $200,000 per year. Ozzie Virgil, interview with author, June 4, 2012, Mets Dominican Baseball Academy, Boca Chica, Dominican Republic.

2. Domingo Saint-Hilaire, hijo, "President Balaguer Inaugura Estadio LV," *La Información*, April 14, 1975, 7.

3. Frank Deford, "Liege Lord of Latin Hopes," *Sports Illustrated*, December 24, 1973, 65, https://www.si.com/vault/1973/12/24/618486/liege-lord-of-latin-hopes.

4. Rafael Francisco de Moya Pons, "Industrial Incentives in the Dominican Republic, 1880–1983" (PhD diss., Columbia University, 1987), 358.

5. Deford, "Liege Lord," 62–66, nostalgically referred to the way scouting operated in the United States before regulations and the implementation of the Amateur Draft in 1965. Deford described the Caribbean as "the last place for scouts and their teams to find unknowns, to put their ken and pride on the line in a free-bid market, to scuffle and con, even deceive one another. It is a glorious anachronism and a last hurrah for the baseball regulars who were brought up in that wheeler-dealer world" (65).

6. Felipe Alou with Arnoldo Hano, "Latin-American Ballplayers Need a Bill of Rights," *Sport*, November 1963, 77.

7. Deford, "Liege Lord," 66.

8. Frank Finch, "Dodgers Will Re-Work Rich Latin Mine," *Los Angeles Times*, June 11, 1967, B4.

9. Bill Brubaker, "Hey, Kid, Wanna Be a Star?," *Sports Illustrated*, July 13, 1981, 66, https://www.si.com/vault/issue/709377/63. See also Finch, "Dodgers Will Re-work Rich Latin Mine." For scholarly examinations, see Alan Klein, *Dominican Baseball: New Pride, Old Prejudice* (Philadelphia: Temple University Press, 2014); Rob Ruck, *Raceball: How the Major Leagues Colonized the Black and Latin Game* (Boston: Beacon, 2012); Arturo J. Marcano Guevara and David P. Fidler, *Stealing Lives: The Tragic Story of Alexis Quiroz* (Bloomington: Indiana University Press, 2002); Rob Ruck, *The Tropic of Baseball: Baseball in the Dominican Republic* (New York: Meckler, 1991); Alan M. Klein, *Sugarball: The American Game, the Dominican Dream* (New Haven, CT: Yale University Press, 1991); Samuel O. Regalado, *Viva Baseball! Latin Major Leaguers and Their Special Hunger* (Urbana: University of Illinois Press, 1998).

10. Bill Murray in Brubaker, "Hey, Kid, Wanna Be a Star?," 66.

11. Avila in Brubaker, "Hey, Kid," 75.

12. Deford, "Liege Lord," 66.

13. Alou with Hano, "Latin-American Ballplayers," 79.

14. William Plummer described some of Guerrero's tactics to sign prospects in seemingly prohibitive environments; see Plummer, "Baseball Scout Epy Guerrero Looks for Diamonds amid Hunger and Poverty," *People*, April 10, 1989, https://people.com/archive/baseball-scout-epy-guerrero-looks-for-rough-diamonds-amid-hunger-and-poverty-vol-31-no-14/.

15. Elvio Jiménez, interview with the author, Santo Domingo, June 16, 2012; Ralph Avila, interview with the author, Santo Domingo, June 28, 2012; Epy Guerrero, interview with the author, Complejo Epy Guerrero de Villa Mella, March 12, 2012, and July 28, 2012; Plummer, "Baseball Scout Epy Guerrero Looks for Diamonds Amid Hunger and Poverty"; Ruck, *The Tropic of Baseball*, especially 61–62.

16. Frank A. Estrada, "La Sexta Serie del Caribe Resulta Fracaso Económico," *El Caribe*, February 8, 1975, 16. The official exchange rate of the Dominican peso was equal to the US dollar through 1980, although a black market existed for exchange where a US dollar cost about RD$1.18 in 1975. I use the official exchange rate throughout. For a table of costs on the parallel market for 1972–1983, see Claudio Vedovato, *Politics, Foreign Trade and Economic Development: A Study of the Dominican Republic* (New York: St. Martin's, 1986), 130, which relied on figures from the Dominican Republic's Banco Central, Departamento de Estudios Económicos.

17. Don Manolo Rodríguez, "De Todo un Poco: Peloteros de Santo Domingo, Venezuela y Puerto Rico Son Ignorados por Refuerzos," *El Diario–La Prensa*, cited in Tirso A. Váldez, "Desde NY: Formulan Críticas Aumento Refuerzos," *Listín Diario*, February 15, 1975, 12.

18. Johnny Méndez, "Cronistas Favorecen Ligas Verano en RD," *Listín Diario*, February 8, 1975, 11.

19. Felipe Alou in Brubaker, "Hey Kid," 66.

20. Brubaker, "Hey, Kid," 64–66, used an uncle-nephew comparison to demonstrate the continuity in US team practices and the expectations of young players. Abreu, who said he was a good student, sacrificed a possible profession for a $2,000 signing bonus and the scouts' promises that he was a *gran prospecto* (great prospect). He was released after three weeks in spring training but found a job with another team that lasted parts of two seasons before being released for good. In 1981 he could find work only with a Dominican summer league. Brubaker described Abreu's nephew, José Rijo, who would go on to win a World Series as a pitcher with the Cincinnati Reds in 1990, leaving after his first year of high school amid promises similar to the ones Abreu had received. Brubaker then noted that the practice of signing players who gave up their education was changing, "slowly, perhaps, but finally" (p. 66).

21. Humberto Andrés Suazo, "Creen Positiva Liga de Verano," *El Caribe*, June 4, 1975, 13.

22. Elio Vega, hijo, "Correo del Fanático," *Listín Diario*, February 11, 1975, 10.

23. Julián Javier, interview with the author, San Francisco de Macorís, April 17, 2012.

24. On Alou with the Linieros, see, for example, Héctor García, "Del Orbe Liderea Liga Verano del Cibao," *El Caribe*, May 10, 1977, 24.

25. Tirso A. Váldez, "Desde NY: Formulan Críticas Aumento Refuerzos," *Listín Diario*, February 15, 1975, 12.

26. New ownership prompted a reorganization of the Dominican Republic Summer League during the 1978 season. Justo Castellanos Díaz, "Variedades," *El Caribe*, April 17, 1978, 37, proposed that the reorganization include a provision for signing players from other countries, as had been shown to work for the Cibao league.

27. Félix Acosta Núñez, "Total 75 Players Tiene Liga Cibao," *Listín Diario*, February 18, 1975, 8.

28. Alou in Brubaker, "Hey Kid," 68.

29. Leoncio Silverio Camacho, Puerto Plata, "Siguen Justa de Beisbol Pese Problemas Utiles," May 23, 1975, *La Información*, 7.

30. In Brubaker, "Hey Kid," 66, Alou described the country as being "jammed" with teenage players with fleeting careers. Elio Vega, hijo, "Correo del Fanático," *Listín Diario*, February 11, 1975, 10.

31. "Minicosas de un Latidesorden," *La Información*, May 3, 1975, 3.

32. Ozzie Virgil managed ten games for the San Diego Padres in 1984 after manager Dick Williams was suspended following three bench-clearing brawls against Atlanta, but he maintained that Alou deserves credit as the first Dominican manager in the major leagues because he became the first hired for this role when he signed with the Montreal Expos in 1992. Ozzie Virgil, interview with the author, June 4, 2012, Mets Dominican Academy, Boca Chica. On the brawl and Dick Williams's suspension, see "Williams and Torre Suspended, Fined," *New York Times*, August 17, 1984, 17, 19.

33. Fernández was named an American League All-Star in 1986, 1987, and 1988, playing shortstop behind Cal Ripken, who started each game. In 1992, Fernández played for the National League All-Stars behind Ozzie Smith, then returned to the AL roster for the 1999 game at the age of thirty-seven, again playing behind Ripken, but this time at third base. Fernández won Gold Gloves as an American League shortstop in 1986, 1987, 1988, and 1989.

34. Domingo Saint-Hilaire, hijo, La Vega, "Félix Santana Firma con Indios del Valle," *Listín Diario*, February 22, 1975, 9. The cartoon was sponsored by Reid and Pellerano, CxA., and also advertised the vehicles available for purchase there. David Morales, *Listín Diario*, February 21, 1975, 19. In it the Indian exclaimed: "I just contracted this mackerel to fight against opponents. Ok?" "¡Acabo de contratar a ete 'jurel' para chubarselo a los guapos! ¿Okey?"

35. "Minicosas de un Latidesorden," *La Información*, May 3, 1975, 3.

36. Carta del Dr. Hernando de la Mota, Presidente de la Liga de Beisbol Profesional de Verano del Cibao, Inc., et al., a Su Excelencia Dr. Joaquín Balaguer, Honorable Presidente de la República, February 17, 1975, SEDEFIR 16543, AGN.

37. Carta de la Liga de Beisbol Profesional de Verano del Cibao, Inc., a Su Excelencia Dr. Joaquín Balaguer, Honorable Presidente de la República, February 17, 1975; Oficio no. 2146, Justo Castellanos Díaz al Secretario Administrativo de

la Presidencia Quezada, Re: "Solicitud de concesión de facilidades que anualmente otorga el gobierno a la Liga Dominicana de Besibol [*sic*] Profesional," September 22, 1975, SEDEFIR 16543, AGN.

38. Abraham F. Lowenthal, "Alliance Rhetoric versus Latin American Reality," *Foreign Affairs* 48, no. 3 (April 1970): 507. A political scientist, Lowenthal described development in this way in his critique of the Alliance for Progress at the start of the 1970s. After identifying a lack of coherence in US policies with unclear definitions for "democracy" and "development" as one of the weaknesses of the Alliance for Progress in the 1960s, Lowenthal argued that US businesses would benefit more from the increase in Latin Americans' purchasing power over the long term than from the "niggardly conditions to US aid" that had accompanied financial support through the Alliance for Progress in the previous decade.

39. José Augusto Vega Imbert, interview with the author, April 17, 2012, Santiago.

40. Moya Pons traces the policies and debates around incentives from the nineteenth century to the 1980s, including the joining of economic and political influence during the Trujillato (40–103) and how capital-based industrialists leveraged their political influence against Bosch (104–145).

41. Moya Pons, "Industrial Incentives," 299; on regionalism and debates about the incentives, see especially chap. 6, "Debates on the Incentives," 253–371, and chap. 7, "Santiago versus Santo Domingo: Fighting for the Incentives," 372–441.

42. Moya Pons, "Industrial Incentives," 253–371.

43. Domingo Saint-Hilaire, hijo, "Diario Ve en el Beisbol Regionalismo Capitaleño," *Listín Diario*, February 13, 1975, 8, reprinted much of an editorial from *La Información* that accused Monchín Pichardo, the president of Licey, of cheering for a team other than the Aguilas, the national representative, in the Caribbean Series. The editorial also cited examples of broadcasters. In his column "Rectas y Curvas" for the capital-based *Listín Diario*, sports editor Félix Acosta Núñez, a native of the Cibao region, defended the comments as "one or another joke among friends" and essentially trash talk among rivals. See Félix Acosta Núñez, "De Regionalismo," *Listín Diario*, February 13, 1975, 8.

44. Félix Acosta Núñez, "De Regionalismo," *Listín Diario*, February 13, 1975, 8.

45. Moya Pons, "Industrial Incentives," 299.

46. City boosterism drove investment in professional baseball teams in the United States throughout the twentieth century, as seen in Glen Gendzel, "Competitive Boosterism: How Milwaukee Lost the Braves," *Business History Review* 69, no. 4 (Winter 1995): 530–566; Steven A. Riess, *City Games: The Evolution of American Urban Society and the Rise of Sports* (Urbana: University of Illinois Press, 1989); Neil J. Sullivan, *The Dodgers Move West* (New York: Oxford University Press, 1987); and James Edward Miller, *The Baseball Business: Pursuing Pennants and Profits in Baltimore* (Chapel Hill: University of North Carolina Press, 1990). In the Dominican Republic, professional baseball teams served as cultural markers of modernity for cities just as national airlines served countries. On these cultural markers, see Eric Paul Roorda, "The Cult of the Airplane among US Military Men and Dominicans during the US Occupation and the Trujillo Regime," in *Close Encounters of Empire: Writing the Cultural History of US-Latin American Relations*, ed. Gilbert M. Joseph,

Catherine C. Legrand, and Ricardo D. Salvatore (Durham, NC: Duke University Press, 1998), 269–310.

47. Moya Pons, "Industrial Incentives," 253–274.

48. Epy Guerrero mentioned the Mexico model multiple times in our discussions. Interview with the author, Complejo Epy Guerrero de Villa Mella, March 12, 2012, and July 28, 2012. The Mexican League's challenge to US baseball in the mid-1940s, especially with the 1946 season, when they recruited white US players in addition to integrating the usual black players, caused retaliation and near crisis in the US major leagues that reverberated through the Latin American leagues. The conflict ended with the blacklisting of players, the movement of many Latin American leagues to the winter, and the Winter Agreements that regulate player movement among the Latin American and US leagues. The Dominican Professional Baseball League (Winter League) came into this structure and followed these agreements when it was incorporated in 1955 and affiliated with the US leagues. The national tournaments in 1951–1954, before the league was incorporated, were held in the summer. See chapter 1 for details on the incorporation of the league.

49. Although the Cibao Summer League operated without an official agreement with US baseball, the directors made clear that they did not want to compete with the US organization for players. They allowed players to sign contracts with US teams without penalization. A handful of US rookies played in the Cibao Summer League during the early part of the season to prepare for their departure to US rookie leagues. However, the directors offered that opportunity only in rare circumstances. The Dominican Republic Summer League was less strict, and, as Epy Guerrero remembered, nearly failed in its inaugural year when a majority of the young players left to join their US rookie teams. Interview with the author, March 12, 2012.

50. Oficio no. 2146, Justo Castellanos Díaz al Secretario Administrativo de la Presidencia Quezada, Re: "Solicitud de concesión de facilidades que anualmente otorga el gobierno a la Liga Dominicana de Besibol [*sic*] Profesional," September 22, 1975, SEDEFIR 16543, AGN. The granting of concessions on electricity is less clear, but annotations on documents in the presidential office suggest that the Cibao Summer League had these concessions in 1975, while the Dominican Republic Summer League was forced to play day games. See Oficio no. 15298, Secretario Administrativo de la Presidencia al Administrador General de la Corporación Dominicana de Electricidad, April 30, 1975; Oficio no. 17882, Secretario Administrativo de la Presidencia al SEDEFIR, May 21, 1975; Oficio no. 1955, Administrador General de la Corporación Dominicana de Electricidad al Sr Secretario Administrativo de la Presidencia, May 12, 1975, SEDEFIR 16543, AGN.

Chapter 6: Making the Majors

1. Alan Klein compared MLB's operations in Santo Domingo and its attempt to regulate the signing process, including independent trainers, to the US occupation of the country in 1965–1966. See Klein, *Dominican Baseball: New Pride, Old Prejudice* (Philadelphia: Temple University Press, 2014), 135–151.

2. Maury Brown, "MLB Sees Record $10.7 Billion in Revenues for 2019," *Forbes*, December 21, 2019, https://www.forbes.com/sites/maurybrown/2019/12/21/mlb-sees-record-107-billion-in-revenues-for-2019/?sh=42da1b095d78.

3. Ley No. 447, que crea dos nuevas franquicias para la práctica del beisbol profesional de invierno en la República Dominicana, April 7, 1982, *Gaceta Oficial* no. 9576, April 30, 1982, 399–400. Consultoría Jurídica del Poder Ejecutivo, Consulta de Documentos, http://www.consultoria.gov.do/consulta/.

4. Cuquí Córdova, La Crónica de los Martes, "Si de Nosotros Dependiera," *Listín Diario*, August 2, 1983, 2A; Guillermo Tejeda, "Monchín Propone Dos Nuevas Ligas," *Listín Diario*, August 3, 1983, 5A.

5. Tejeda, "Monchín Propone Dos Nuevas Ligas"; Hipólito López Morrobal, *Listín Diario*, August 13, 1983, 7A.

6. Domingo Saint-Hilaire, hijo, "Antún Dice Seguirá Opuesto a Expansión," *Listín Diario*, January 29, 1983, 3A; Guillermo Tejeda, "Monchín Propone Dos Nuevas Ligas," *Listín Diario*, August 3, 1983, 5A.

7. Ralph Avila, interview with the author, June 28, 2012, Santo Domingo.

8. Mignolio Pujols in Cuquí Córdova, La Crónica de los Martes, "Los Caimanes del Sur," *Listín Diario*, August 9, 1983, 3A.

9. Decreto no. 1300 Reglamento sobre Beisbol Profesional, August 5, 1983, Consultoría Jurídica del Poder Ejecutivo, Consulta de Documentos, http://www.consultoria.gov.do/consulta/.

10. Dr. Juan Miguel Pellerano Gómez, Carta al SEDEFIR Dr. Luis A. Scheker Ortiz, July 12, 1983, SEDEFIR 31630, 16515, AGN.

11. Decreto no. 1316, August 12, 1983, *Gaceta Oficial* no. 9619.

12. Liga Dominicana de Beisbol Profesional, Comunicado, *Listín Diario*, August 20, 1983, 5A.

13. Liga Dominicana de Beisbol Profesional, Comunicado, *Listín Diario*, August 20, 1983, 5A; for the negative publicity, see Organizaciones Socio-Económicas de la Provincia de San Cristóbal, Carta Abierta al Dr. Salvador Jorge Blanco, Honorable Presidente de la República, August 4, 1983, *Listín Diario*, August 5, 1983, 3A; Guillermo Tejeda, "Jorge Blanco Analiza Beisbol," *Listín Diario*, August 6, 1983, 1A.

14. Comité Central del Partido de la Unidad Democrática (UD), Comunicado, August 7, 1983, *Listín Diario*, August 9, 1983, 11; Organizaciones Socio-Económicas de la Provincia de San Cristóbal, Carta Abierta al Dr. Salvador Jorge Blanco, Honorable Presidente de la República, August 4, 1983, *Listín Diario*, August 5, 1983, 3A; Guillermo Tejeda, "Jorge Blanco Analiza Beisbol," *Listín Diario*, August 6, 1983, 1A; R. Rodríguez Gómez, "Asegura Gobierno Va Mantener Libertades," *Listín Diario*, August 9, 1983, 3; Max Uribe, "De Nuestra Política," *Listín Diario*, August 10, 1983, 6; "La Actitud Nacional," *Listín Diario*, August 11, 1983, 6; Carta de "Dirigentes comunistas" al Dr. José Francisco Peña Gómez, "Ven PRD Gobierna para Derecha Social," *Listín Diario*, August 11, 1983, 8.

15. FENAPEPRO, Caimanes del Sur, Azucareros del Este y Comisión Organizadora del Campeonato 1983–84, "¡En hora buena, Señor Presidente!," *Listín Diario*, August 9, 1983, 3A.

16. Guillermo Tejeda, "Comisionado EU Sólo Permitirá Peloteros RD Jueguen con LIDOM," *Listín Diario*, August 6, 1983, 1A.

17. Guillermo Tejeda, "LIDOM Da Poco Crédito Documento, Federación de Peloteros Advierte," *Listín Diario*, August 4, 1983, 1A.

18. Guillermo Tejeda, "Diálogo LIDOM Sería sin SEDEFIR," *Listín Diario*, August 3, 1983, 1A; see also Guillermo Tejeda, "LIDOM Da Poco Crédito Documento, Federación de Peloteros Advierte," *Listín Diario*, August 4, 1983, 1A.

19. H. López Morrobel, *Listín Diario*, August 17, 1983, 2A.

20. H. López Morrobel, *Listín Diario*, October 29, 1981, 1A; "Bevan Rois Campeón Bate Sureste," *Listín Diario*, January 22, 1983, 9; Felix Acosta Núñez, "Campanis: Sin LIDOM no Refuerzos," *Listín Diario*, August 22, 1983, 3A.

21. H. López Morrobel, *Listín Diario*, August 17, 1983, 2A.

22. Hugo López Morrobel, *Listín Diario*, October 3, 1983, 9A.

23. "Buena Disposición," *Listín Diario*, October 12, 1983, 6; Hugo López Morrobel, "Presidente Espera Mantengan Precios Entradas Beisbol," *Listín Diario*, October 1, 1983, 8; Jesús de la Rosa, interview with the author, July 2017, Santo Domingo. Bisonó agreed with the league to raise the prices of tickets for other sections ahead of the 1984–1985 tournament. Guillermo Tejeda, "Señala Aumento Presidente Liga," *Listín Diario*, October 12, 1984, 1A.

24. "Dauhajre Pide Tacto al Adquirir Divisas," Máximo Manuel Pérez, "Albuquerque Minimimza aso Dólar," *Listín Diario*, October 8, 1983, 1, 12; Rafael Bonnelly Ricart y Eunice Lluberes, "Casa Cambio Suspenden Ventas," *Listín Diario*, October 8, 1983, 1, 10; Guillermo Tejeda, "Gobierno Otorga Facilidades Equipos," *Listín Diario*, October 15, 1984, 4A.

25. The four traditional teams have remained the same, but the two expansion teams have changed since 1982. The Caimanes struggled financially and were forced to sit out the 1986–1987 season, and then disbanded after 1988–1989. The Winter Tournament operated with five teams until 1996, when an investment group led by former big-leaguer Julián Javier established the Gigantes del Noreste (now Gigantes del Cibao) in San Francisco de Macorís. The Azucareros are now known as the Toros.

26. Guillermo Tejeda, "Jorge Blanco Asegura Habrá Beisbol," *Listín Diario*, August 7, 1983, 9.

27. For example, Ian Gordon, "Inside Major League Baseball's Dominican Sweatshop System," *Mother Jones*, March/April 2013, https://www.motherjones.com/politics/2013/03/baseball-dominican-system-yewri-guillen/.

28. Frank Deford, "Liege Lord of Latin Hopes," *Sports Illustrated*, December 24, 1973, https://vault.si.com/vault/1973/12/24/liege-lord-of-latin-hopes; Arturo J. Marcano Guevara and David P. Fidler, *Stealing Lives: The Globalization of Baseball and the Tragic Story of Alexis Quiroz* (Bloomington: Indiana University Press, 2002).

29. Letter from Peter O'Malley to Mr. Epy Guerrero, June 13, 1985, personal archives of Epy Guerrero, Complejo Epy Guerrero, Villa Mella, Dominican Republic; Ralph Avila, interview with the author, June 28, 2012, Santo Domingo, RD.

30. William Plummer, "Baseball Scout Epy Guerrero Looks for Rough Diamonds Amid Hunger and Poverty," *People*, April 10, 1989, https://people.com/archive

/baseball-scout-epy-guerrero-looks-for-rough-diamonds-amid-hunger-and-poverty-vol-31-no-14/.

31. Avila in Bill Brubaker, "Hey, Kid, Wanna Be a Star?," *Sports Illustrated*, July 13, 1981, 75, https://www.si.com/vault/issue/70937/63.

32. Plummer, "Epy Guerrero."

33. Reglamento no. 3450 sobre Escuelas o Campamentos de Beisbol de Aficionados, November 7, 1985, *Gaceta Oficial* no. 9673, November 15, 1985, 1780–1783, http://www.consultoria.gov.do/consulta/.

34. Reglamento no. 3450, Art. 1, Art. 2, 1781.

35. Reglamento no. 3450, Art 6., 1782; Art. 2(b), 1781.

36. Klein, *Dominican Baseball*, especially 135–152.

37. Orlando A. Díaz Rodríguez, Presidente de la Liga de Verano de Béisbol Profesional de la República Dominicana, interview with the author, May 29, 2012, Santo Domingo, Dominican Republic; Zoribeth Martínez Lucero, "En medio de la Pandemia la Dominican Summer League cumple 35 años," May 7, 2020, Dominican Summer League, http://dominicansummerleague.com/www/en-medio-de-la-pandemia-la-dominican-summer-league-cumple-35-anos/.

38. Dominican Summer League, ¿Quienes Somos?, http://dominicansummerleague.com/www/quines-somos/.

39. Orlando A. Díaz Rodríguez, Presidente de la Liga de Verano de Béisbol Profesional de la República Dominicana, interview with the author, May 29, 2012, Santo Domingo, Dominican Republic; Zoribeth Martínez Lucero, "En medio de la Pandemia la Dominican Summer League cumple 35 años," May 7, 2020, Dominican Summer League, http://dominicansummerleague.com/www/en-medio-de-la-pandemia-la-dominican-summer-league-cumple-35-anos/.

40. El Molino Deportivo, C. por A., carta al Sr. Rafael Abinader, Secretario de Estado de Finanzas, January 25, 1983, SEDEFIR 16515, AGN. Dr. Luis A. Scheker Ortiz, Secretario de Estado de Deportes, Educación Física y Recreación, al Ciudadano Señor Presidente de la República, Dr. Salvador Jorge Blanco, no. 01309, March 5, 1986, Programa de trabajo marzo-agosto 1986, included objectives to impose a law on sports-betting facilities during baseball season (p. 8).

41. Dr. Freddy A. Reyes Pérez, a nombre del grupo Promotor del Proyecto Hipódromo del Caribe, carta al Dr. Salvador Jorge Blanco, Presidente de la República Dominicana, August 6, 1984, y Contrato entre: El Estado Dominicano [. . .] y HIPODROMO DEL CARIBE, S.A., Sociedad de comercio organizada de conformidad con las leyes de la República Dominicana, unsigned and undated, SEDEFIR 16533, AGN.

42. The Hipódromo del Caribe was never built, but the Hipódromo V Centenario, completed in 1995, was constructed with similar purposes and was also near the Las Américas Airport. See "Sobre Nosotros, Historia," Comisión Hípica Nacional, República Dominicana, http://chn.gob.do/index.php/sobre-nosotros/historia. About possible controversies surrounding the new track, see Andres Van Der Horst, Secretario de Estado de Deportes, Educación Física y Recreación al Secretario de Estado de la Presidencia, Rafael Bello Andino, no. 2536, Denuncia contra el Presidente de la Comisión Hípica Nacional, April 6, 1987, SEDEFIR 16529, AGN.

43. Klein, *Dominican Baseball*, 17–32.

44. For more information on the ImpACTA Kids Foundation, see their website, ImpACTA Kids Foundation, 2020, https://impactakids.org/es/nosotros/.

45. For example, see Steve Wulf, "Standing Tall at Short," *Sports Illustrated*, February 9, 1987, https://vault.si.com/vault/1987/02/09/standing-tall-at-short-with-more-than-70-shortstops-in-organized-baseball-the-tiny-impoverished-dominican-republic-has-emerged-as-the-worlds-leading-exporter-of-mediocampistas.

46. Klein, *Dominican Baseball*, 91–114.

47. Ross Finkel, Trevor Martin, and Jon Paley, directors, *Ballplayer: Pelotero*, documentary, Makuhari Media, July 13, 2012.

48. I visited the Colón Academy as an instructor with the CIEE Sports and Society: Baseball in Context program in summer 2017; Academia de Béisbol y Desarollo Bartolo Colón, Altamira, Puerto Plata, República Dominicana, July 6, 2017.

49. Quality Baseball Academy, Santo Domingo, Dominican Republic, 2018, https://qualitybaseballacademy.com/.

50. Michael S. Schmidt, "New Exotic Investment: Latin Baseball Futures," *New York Times*, November 17, 2010, https://www.nytimes.com/2010/11/18/sports/baseball/18investors.html?searchResultPosition=8; Michael Orr, "The Dominican Pipeline," *New York Times*, video narrated by Michael S. Schmidt, November 18, 2010, https://www.nytimes.com/video/sports/baseball/1248069342534/the-dominican-pipeline.html?searchResultPosition=3.

51. I visited the Arias and Goodman Academy several times as an instructor with the CIEE Santo Domingo Sports and Society: Baseball in Context summer program in 2012–2015, most recently on July 10, 2015.

52. Schmidt, "New Exotic Investment"; Schmidt, "The Dominican Pipeline," 4:36–46.

53. Charles S. Farrell, "Arias and Goodman Academy Launch Education Program for Prospects," June 30, 2011, updated July 10, 2011, Baseball Reflections, http://baseballreflections.com/2011/07/10/arias-goodman-academy-launch-education-program-for-prospects/.

54. Ulises Joaquin, Baseball Reference, https://www.baseball-reference.com/register/player.fcgi?id=joaqui000uli; for more on prospects that Portorreal has signed, see "Entrevista Daniel Portorreal Bautista 'Liga Portorreal,'" Actualidad Deportiva con Michael Cuevas, Aquí y ahora con Robert del Orbe, July 17, 2019, https://www.youtube.com/watch?v=Akt7PDECyD0&feature=share; Charla de Baseball con Yohanna Núñez, Temporada 2, Show 2, "Firmó con otro nombre y se casó dos veces por negocio . . . hoy es un entrenador ejemplar," January 30, 2021, https://youtu.be/ibKdsiGzJqc.

55. "Entrevista Daniel Portorreal Bautista 'Liga Portorreal,'" Actualidad Deportiva con Michael Cuevas, Aqui y ahora con Robert del Orbe, July 17, 2019, https://www.youtube.com/watch?v=Akt7PDECyD0&feature=share.

56. Jesse Sánchez, "Dominican Prospect League Brings Hope," *MLB*, https://www.mlb.com/news/dominican-prospect-league-brings-hopes-for-aspiring-ballplayers/c-26544700; Dominican Prospect League Foundation, "About," https://www.facebook.com/Dominican-Prospect-League-Foundation-273031796082990;

Liga Amateur de los Prospectos de la MLB, El Sitio Oficial de Las Grandes Ligas de Béisbol, Santo Domingo, http://mlb.mlb.com/rd/prospect_showcase.jsp; Complejo Epy Guerrero de Villa Mella, July 28, 2012.

57. In the documentary *Ballplayer: Pelotero*, Astín Jacobo echoes what Jesús Alou lamented in Jared Goodman's documentary *Road to the Big Leagues*: prospects falsify identity documents to appear younger because the incentives for doing so are high.

Conclusion

1. "MLB Statement Regarding 2021 All-Star Game," April 2, 2021, https://www.mlb.com/press-release/press-release-mlb-statement-regarding-2021-all-star-game.

2. "Continuar lo que está bien; Corregir lo que está mal; Hacer lo que nunca se hizo."

3. Dionisio Soldevila, "Danilo: 'Triunfo del Clásico ayudó mi gobierno," *Hoy*, November 29, 2013, https://hoy.com.do/danilo-triunfo-del-clasico-ayudo-mi-gobierno/.

Bibliography

Oral History Interviews and Personal Correspondence

Acta, José Armando. Santo Domingo. March 11, 2012.

Almánzar, Carlos, Rubén Andújar, Tony Grullón, and Héctor Gómez, Club BanReservas, Santo Domingo. July 21, 2012.

Alou, Jesús Rojas. Red Sox El Toro Complex. May 10, 2012.

Alou, Moisés. Santo Domingo. February 22, 2012.

Avila, Ralph. Santo Domingo. June 28, 2012.

Carty, Ricardo "Rico." San Pedro de Macorís. June 14, 2012.

Córdova, Cuquí. Santo Domingo. January 14, 2012.

De la Rosa, Jesús. Santo Domingo. July 14, 2017.

Díaz, Orlando. Santo Domingo. May 29, 2012.

Guerrero, Epifanio "Epy" Obdulio. Complejo Epy Guerrero de Villa Mella. March 12, 2012, and July 28, 2012.

Javier, Julián. San Francisco de Macorís. April 17, 2012.

Jiménez, Elvio. Santo Domingo. June 16, 2012.

Llenas, Winston "Chilote." Oficinas de las Águilas Cibaeñas, Santiago. April 11, 2012.

Medina, Alberto. San Pedro de Macorís. June 5, 2012.

Saint-Hilaire, Domingo, hijo. Santiago. May 31, 2012.

Sánchez, Luichy, with Reynaldo "Papy" Bisonó and José Augusto Vega Imbert. Oficinas de las Águilas Cibaeñas, Santiago. May 30, 2012.

Troncoso, Tomás. Santo Domingo. July 26, 2012.

Vega Imbert, José Augusto. Santiago. April 17, 2012.

Vega Imbert, José Augusto. Personal emails, 2012–2021.

Virgil, Osvaldo "Ozzie." Mets Dominican Baseball Academy, Boca Chica. June 4, 2012.

Archival Records Consulted

Personal Papers of John Bartlow Martin, 1900–1986. Manuscript Division, Library of Congress, Washington, DC.

Records of the U.S. Information Agency, 1900–2003, and General Records of the Department of State. National Archives and Records Administration II (NARA II), College Park, MD.

Secretaría de Estado de Deportes, Educación Física y Recreación (SEDEFIR). Archivo General de la Nación, Santo Domingo, República Dominicana.

Newspapers and Magazines Consulted

Ahora (Santo Domingo)
El Caribe (Santo Domingo)
El Deporte al Día (Santo Domingo)
El Diario (New York)
La Información (Santiago)
Listín Diario (Santo Domingo)
Miami Herald (Miami)
La Nación (Santo Domingo)
Sports Illustrated (*SIVault*, http://sportsillustrated.cnn.com/vault/)
La Prensa (New York)

Books, Articles, Videos, and Websites

Abou-El-Fadl, Reem. *Foreign Policy as Nation Making: Turkey and Egypt in the Cold War*. New York: Cambridge University Press, 2019.

Acosta Matos, Eliades. *1963: De la guerra mediática al golpe de estado*. Santo Domingo: Ediciones Fundación Juan Bosch, 2015.

Alegi, Peter. *African Soccerscapes: How a Continent Changed the World's Game*. Athens: Ohio University Press, 2010.

Alegi, Peter, and Brenda Elsey. "Editors' Introduction: Historicizing the Politics and Pleasure of Sport." *Radical History Review* 2016, no. 125 (May 2016): 3–11.

Alexander, Lisa Doris. "Sports History, What's Next?" *Journal of American History* 101, no. 1 (June 2014): 173–175.

Alou, Felipe, with Arnold Hano. "Latin-American Ballplayers Need a Bill of Rights." *Sport*, November 1963, 20–21, 76–79.

Alou, Felipe, with Peter Kerasotis. *Alou: My Baseball Journey*. Lincoln: University of Nebraska Press, 2018.

Alou, Felipe, with Herm Weiskopf. *My Life and Baseball*. Waco, TX: Word Books, 1967.

Arbena, Joseph L., ed. *Sport and Society in Latin America: Diffusion, Dependency, and the Rise of Mass Culture*. New York: Greenwood, 1988.

Arbena, Joseph L., and David G. LaFrance, eds. *Sport in Latin America and the Caribbean*. Wilmington, DE: Scholarly Resources, 2002.

Baseball-Reference.com. www.baseball-reference.com.

Bass, Amy. "The Last Word on the State of Sports History." *Journal of American History* 101, no. 1 (June 2014): 195–197.

———. "State of the Field: Sports History and the 'Cultural Turn.'" *Journal of American History* 101, no. 1 (June 2014): 148–172.

Beckles, Hilary McD., and Brian Stoddart, eds. *Liberation Cricket: West Indies Cricket Culture*. Manchester, UK: Manchester University Press, 1995.

Beezley, William H. *Judas at the Jockey Club and Other Episodes of Porfirian Mexico.* Lincoln: University of Nebraska Press, 1987.

Beezley, William H., and Linda Curcio, eds. *Latin American Cultural Studies: A Reader.* Wilmington, DE: Scholarly Resources, 2000.

Bellos, Alex. *Futebol: The Brazilian Way of Life.* New York: Bloomsbury, 2002.

Betances, Emelio. "La cultura política autoritaria en la República Dominicana." *El Cotidiano* 152 (November-December 2008): 87–97.

———. *State and Society in the Dominican Republic.* Latin American Perspectives Series, No. 15. Boulder, CO: Westview, 1995.

Bjarkman, Peter C. *Baseball with a Latin Beat: A History of the Latin American Game.* Jefferson, NC: McFarland, 1994.

———. *Diamonds around the Globe: The Encyclopedia of International Baseball.* Westport, CT: Greenwood, 2005.

Blasier, Cole. *The Hovering Giant: US Responses to Revolutionary Change in Latin America, 1910–1985.* Rev. ed. Pittsburgh: University of Pittsburgh Press, 1998.

Blitzer, Jonathan, with illustrations by Kelsey Dake. "Satchel Paige and the Championship for the Reelection of the General: How the Best Pitcher in the American Negro Leagues Played for the Cruelest Dictator in the Caribbean." *The Atavist Magazine* 57. https://magazine.atavist.com/satchel-paige-and-the-championship-for-the-reelection-of-the-general/.

Bobea, Lilian. "República Dominicana. ¿Aún a la sombra del caudillismo?" *Nueva Sociedad* 189 (January-February 2004): 4–13.

Bolívar Díaz, Juan. "De la pelota a la política nace la pelótica." Tertulia de La Pelota, en ocasión de la exposición *¡Nos vemos en el play! Béisbol y cultura en la República Dominicana.* Centro León, Santiago, República Dominicana, January 17, 2007.

Borstelmann, Thomas. *The Cold War and the Color Line: American Race Relations in the Global Arena.* Cambridge, MA: Harvard University Press, 2003.

Bosch, Juan. *Crisis de la Democracia de América en la República Dominicana.* México, DF: Centro de Estudios y Documentación Sociales, 1964.

Brea, Ramonina, and Isis Duarte. *Entre la calle y la casa: Las mujeres dominicanas y la cultura política a finales del siglo XX.* Santo Domingo: Editora Búho, 1999.

Brown-John, C. Lloyd. "Economic Sanctions: The Case of the OAS and the Dominican Republic, 1960–1962." *Caribbean Studies* 15, no. 2 (July 1975): 73–105.

Burgos, Adrian, Jr. *Playing America's Game: Baseball, Latinos, and the Color Line.* Berkeley: University of California Press, 2007.

———. "Wait until Next Year: Sports History and the Quest for Respect." *Journal of American History* 101, no. 1 (June 2014): 176–180.

Butler, Judith, Ernesto Laclau, and Reinaldo Laddaga. "The Uses of Equality." *Diacritics* 27, no. 1 (Spring 1997): 2–12.

Cahn, Susan K. "Turn, Turn, Turn: There Is a Reason for Sport." *Journal of American History* 101, no. 1 (June 2014): 181–183.

Calder, Bruce J. *The Impact of Intervention: The Dominican Republic during the U.S. Occupation of 1916–1924.* Austin: University of Texas Press, 1984.

Campbell, Al. "The Birth of Neoliberalism in the United States: A Reorganization of Capitalism." In *Neoliberalism: A Critical Reader*, edited by Alfredo Saad-Filho and Deborah Johnston, 187–198. London: Pluto, 2005.

Candelario, Ginetta E. B. *Black behind the Ears: Dominican Racial Identity from Museums to Beauty Shops*. Durham, NC: Duke University Press, 2007.

Carter, Thomas F. *The Quality of Home Runs: The Passion, Politics, and Language of Cuban Baseball*. Durham, NC: Duke University Press, 2008.

Cassá, Roberto. *Los doce años: Contrarrevolución y desarrollismo*. Vol. 1, 2nd ed. Santo Domingo: Editora Buho, 1991.

Céspedes, Diógenes. "Notas sobre la caricatura periodística en RD hoy." *Hoy digital*, November 26, 2007. https://hoy.com.do/notas-sobre-la-caricatura-periodisticaen-rd-hoy/.

Chetty, Raj. "*Más Allá del Play*: Race and the Dominican Baseball Player in *Sugar*." *Journal of West Indian Literature* 27, no. 1 (April 2019): 1–14.

"Closer to Chaos." *Time*, April 13, 1970, 36.

Cobbs Hoffman, Elizabeth. *All You Need Is Love: The Peace Corps and the Spirit of the 1960s*. Cambridge, MA: Harvard University Press, 1998.

Córdova, Cuquí. "El Campeonato de 1937: 'El mejor de todos.'" In Cuquí Córdova, *Colección: Historia del Béisbol Dominicano*. Santo Domingo: published by author, 2009.

Crandall, Russell. *Gunboat Democracy: US Interventions in the Dominican Republic, Grenada, and Panama*. Lanham, MD: Rowman and Littlefield, 2006.

Crawford, Russell E. "Consensus All-American: Sport and the Promotion of the American Way of Life during the Cold War, 1946–1965." PhD diss., University of Nebraska, 2004.

Crepeau, Richard C. *Baseball: America's Diamond Mind, 1919–1941*. Orlando: University Presses of Florida, 1980.

Cull, Nicholas J. *The Cold War and the United States Information Agency: American Propaganda and Public Diplomacy, 1945–1989*. New York: Cambridge University Press, 2008.

"The Dandy Dominican." *Time*, June 10, 1966, 90–99.

Derby, Lauren H. "The Dictator's Seduction: Gender and State Spectacle during the Trujillo Regime." In *Latin American Popular Culture: An Introduction*, edited by William H. Beezley and Linda A. Curcio-Nagy, 213–239. Wilmington, DE: Scholarly Resources, 2000.

———. *The Dictator's Seduction: Politics and the Popular Imagination in the Era of Trujillo*. Durham, NC: Duke University Press, 2009.

Derby, Robin L. H., and Richard L. Turits. "Historias de terror y los terrores de la historia: La masacre haitiana de 1937 en la República Dominicana." Translated by Eugenio Rivas and Mario Alberto Torres. *Estudios sociales* 26, no. 92 (April-June 1993): 64–76.

Despradel, Fidelio. *Operación Verdad: De Heroes y Traidores*. Santo Domingo: Editora Alfa y Omega, 1990.

Dichter, Heather L. "Sport History and Diplomatic History." H-Diplo Essay no. 122, H-Diplo, H-Net, December 17, 2014. http://h-diplo.org/essays/PDF/E122.pdf.

Dichter, Heather L., and Andrew L. Johns, eds. *Diplomatic Games: Sport, Statecraft, and International Relations since 1945*. Lexington: University Press of Kentucky, 2014.

Edelman, Robert. *Serious Fun: A History of Spectator Sports in the USSR*. New York: Oxford University Press, 1993.

———. *Spartak Moscow: A History of the People's Team in the Workers' State*. Ithaca, NY: Cornell University Press, 2009.

Ediciones de Cultura. *Círculo de espera*. II Concurso de Cuentos sobre Béisbol. Santo Domingo: Editora Nacional, 2012.

Eller, Anne. *We Dream Together: Dominican Independence, Haiti, and the Fight for Caribbean Freedom*. Durham, NC: Duke University Press, 2016.

Elsey, Brenda. *Citizens and Sportsmen: Fútbol and Politics in Twentieth-Century Chile*. Austin: University of Texas Press, 2011.

———. "Cultural Ambassadorship and the Pan-American Games of the 1950s." *International Journal of the History of Sport* 33, no. 1–2 (2016): 105–126.

Elsey, Brenda, and Joshua Nadel. *Futbolera: A History of Women and Sports in Latin America*. Austin: University of Texas Press, 2019.

Espinal, Rosario. *Autoritarismo y democracia en la política dominicana*. Centro Interamericano de Asesoría y Promoción Electoral (CAPEL), Instituto de Derechos Humanos, 1987.

———. "Joaquín Balaguer: El eterno retorno de la política dominicana." *Nueva Sociedad* 118 (March-April 1992): 109–115. https://nuso.org/revista/118/presidentes-latinoamericanos-cargas-y-cargos/.

Field, Thomas C., Jr. *From Development to Dictatorship: Bolivia and the Alliance for Progress in the Kennedy Era*. Ithaca, NY: Cornell University Press, 2014.

Field, Thomas C., Jr., Stella Krepp, and Vanni Pettinà, eds. *Latin America and the Global Cold War*. Chapel Hill: University of North Carolina Press, 2020.

Finch, Frank. "Dodgers Will Re-Work Rich Latin Mine." *Los Angeles Times*, June 11, 1967, B4.

Finkel, Ross, Trevor Martin, and Jonathan Paley. *Ballplayer: Pelotero*. Documentary. Stamford, CT: Makuhari Media, 2011.

Foreign Relations of the United States, 1917–1972. Vol. VI, *Public Diplomacy, 1961–1963*. Edited by Kristin L. Ahlberg, Charles V. Hawley, and Adam M. Howard. Washington, DC: Government Publishing Office, 2017. https://history.state.gov/historicaldocuments/frus1917-72PubDipv06.

Foreign Relations of the United States, 1917–1972. Vol. VII, *Public Diplomacy, 1964–1968*. Edited by Charles V. Hawley and Adam M. Howard. Washington, DC: Government Publishing Office, 2018. https://history.state.gov/historicaldocuments/frus1917-72PubDipv07.

Foreign Relations of the United States, 1961–1963. Vol. 12, *American Republics*. Edited by Edward C. Keefer, Harriet Dashiell Schwar, and W. Taylor Fain II. Washington, DC: Government Printing Office, 1996.

Foreign Relations of the United States, 1964–1968. Vol. 32, *Dominican Republic; Cuba; Haiti; Guyana*. Edited by Daniel Lawler, Carolyn Yee, and Edward C. Keefer. Washington, DC: Government Printing Office, 2005. https://history.state.gov/historicaldocuments/frus1964-68v32/ch1.

Forment, Carlos A. "The Democratic Dribbler: Football Clubs, Neoliberal Globalization, and Buenos Aires' Municipal Election of 2003." *Public Culture* 19, no. 1 (Winter 2007): 85–116.

Fortunato, René. *La violencia del poder: Los doce años de Balaguer*. Documentary. Santo Domingo: Videocine Palau, S. A., 2003.

Fox, Elizabeth. "The Longer Term Impact of US Public Diplomacy in the Americas during WWII." In *Trials of Engagement: The Future of US Public Diplomacy*, edited by Scott Lucas and Ali Fisher, 149–159. Boston: Brill Nijhoff, 2011.

Frank, Andre Gunder. "The Development of Underdevelopment." *Monthly Review* (September 1966): 17–31.

Frieden, Jeffry A. *Global Capitalism: Its Fall and Rise in the Twentieth Century*. New York: W. W. Norton, 2007.

Friedman, Max Paul. "Retiring the Puppets, Bringing Latin America Back In: Recent Scholarship on United States-Latin American Relations." *Diplomatic History* 27, no. 5 (November 2003): 621–636.

Gaffney, Christopher Thomas. *Temples of the Earthbound Gods: Stadiums in the Cultural Landscapes of Rio de Janeiro and Buenos Aires*. Austin: University of Texas Press, 2008.

García-Peña, Lorgia. *The Borders of Dominicanidad: Race, Nation, and Archives of Contradiction*. Durham, NC: Duke University Press, 2016.

Geertz, Clifford. "Deep Play: Notes on the Balinese Cockfight." *Daedalus* 101, no. 1 (Winter 1972): 1–37.

Gendzel, Glen. "Competitive Boosterism: How Milwaukee Lost the Braves." *Business History Review* 69, no. 4 (Winter 1995): 530–566.

Gilbert, Daniel A. *Expanding the Strike Zone: Baseball in the Age of Free Agency*. Amherst: University of Massachusetts Press, 2013.

Gleijeses, Piero. *The Dominican Crisis: The 1965 Constitutionalist Revolt and American Intervention*. Translated by Lawrence Lipson. Baltimore: Johns Hopkins University Press, 1978.

———. *La esperanza desgarrada: La rebelión dominicana de 1965 y la invasión norteamericana*. Santo Domingo: Editora Búho, 2012.

González Echevarría, Roberto. *The Pride of Havana: A History of Cuban Baseball*. New York: Oxford University Press, 1999.

Goodman, Jared. *Road to the Big Leagues*. Documentary. Boston: Element Productions, 2008.

Grandin, Greg. *The Last Colonial Massacre: Latin America in the Cold War*. Chicago: University of Chicago Press, 2004.

Grimaldi, Victor. *Golpe y revolución: El derrocamiento de Juan Bosch y la intervención norteamericana*. Santo Domingo: La Comisión Permanente de Efemérides Patrias, 2008.

Grovogu, Siba. "Revolution Nonetheless: The Global South and International Relations." *Global South* 5, no. 1, Special Issue: The Global South and World Dis/Order (Spring 2011): 175–190.

Guttmann, Allen. *From Ritual to Record: The Nature of Modern Sports*. New York: Columbia University Press, 1978.

Hall, Michael R. *Sugar and Power in the Dominican Republic: Eisenhower, Kennedy, and the Trujillos.* Westport, CT: Greenwood, 2000.

Halliday, Fred, ed. *Caamaño in London: The Exile of a Latin American Revolutionary.* London: Institute for the Study of the Americas, School of Advanced Study, University of London, 2010.

Harmer, Tanya. *Allende's Chile and the Inter-American Cold War.* Chapel Hill: University of North Carolina Press, 2011.

———. "The 'Cuban Question' and the Cold War in Latin America, 1959–1964." *Journal of Cold War Studies* 21, no. 3 (Summer 2019): 114–151.

Hartlyn, Jonathan. *The Struggle for Democratic Politics in the Dominican Republic.* Chapel Hill: University of North Carolina Press, 1998.

Hermann, Hamlet. *Caracoles: La Guerrilla de Caamaño.* 3rd ed. Santo Domingo: Editora Alfa y Omega, 1980.

Hernández, Lou. *The Rise of the Latin American Baseball Leagues, 1947–1961: Cuba, the Dominican Republic, Mexico, Nicaragua, Panama, Puerto Rico, and Venezuela.* Jefferson, NC: McFarland, 2011.

Herrera Miniño, Fabio. *Una estrategia para el desarrollo dominicano.* Santiago: Universidad Católica Madre y Maestra [UCMM], 1977.

Hixson, Walter L. *Parting the Curtain: Propaganda, Culture, and the Cold War, 1945–1961.* New York: St. Martin's Press, 1997.

Hoffnung-Garskof, Jesse. *A Tale of Two Cities: Santo Domingo and New York after 1950.* Princeton, NJ: Princeton University Press, 2008.

Horn, Maja. *Masculinity after Trujillo: The Politics of Gender in Dominican Literature.* Gainesville: University Press of Florida, 2014.

Huish, Robert, Thomas F. Carter, and Simon C. Darnell. "The (Soft) Power of Sport: The Comprehensive and Contradictory Strategies of Cuba's Sport-Based Internationalism." *International Journal of Cuban Studies* 5, no. 1 (Spring 2013): 26–40.

Inoa, Orlando y Héctor J. Cruz. *El béisbol en República Dominicana: Crónica de una pasión.* Colección Cultural Verizon VII. Santo Domingo: Amigo del Hogar, 2004.

Iriye, Akira. *Global Community: The Role of International Organizations in the Making of the Contemporary World.* Berkeley: University of California Press, 2002.

Jamail, Milton H. *Full Count: Inside Cuban Baseball.* Carbondale: Southern Illinois University Press, 2000.

James, C. L. R. *Beyond a Boundary.* Durham, NC: Duke University Press, 1993. 1st ed., London: Hutchinson, 1963.

Joseph, Gilbert M. "Forging the Regional Pastime: Baseball and Class in Yucatán." In *Sport in Latin American Society: Diffusion, Dependency, and the Rise of Mass Culture,* edited by Joseph L. Arbena, 29–62. New York: Greenwood, 1988.

Joseph, Gilbert M., Catherine C. LeGrand, and Ricardo D. Salvatore, eds. *Close Encounters of Empire: Writing the Cultural History of US-Latin American Relations.* Durham, NC: Duke University Press, 1998.

Joseph, Gilbert M., and Daniela Spenser, eds. *In from the Cold: Latin America's New Encounters with the Cold War.* Durham, NC: Duke University Press, 2008.

Karush, Matthew B. "National Identity in the Sports Pages: Football and the Mass Media in 1920s Buenos Aires." *The Americas* 60, no. 1 (July 2003): 11–32.

Keith, LeeAnna Yarbrough. "The Imperial Mind and US Intervention in the Dominican Republic, 1961–1966." PhD diss., University of Connecticut, 1999.

Keller, Renata. "The Latin American Missile Crisis." *Diplomatic History* 39, no. 2 (2015): 195–222.

———. *Mexico's Cold War: Cuba, the United States, and the Legacy of the Mexican Revolution.* New York: Cambridge University Press, 2015.

Kennedy, John F. "Address at a White House Reception for Members of Congress and for the Diplomatic Corps of the Latin American Republics." March 13, 1961. Video, TNC-182A, Archives, JFK Library. https://www.jfklibrary.org/asset-viewer/archives/TNC/TNC-182A/TNC-182A.

Keys, Barbara. "The Early Cold War Olympics, 1952–1960: Political, Economic and Human Rights Dimensions." In *The Palgrave Handbook of Olympic Studies,* edited by Helen Jefferson Lenskyj and Stephen Wagg, 72–87. London: Palgrave Macmillan, 2012.

———. *Globalizing Sport: National Rivalry and International Community in the 1930s.* Cambridge, MA: Harvard University Press, 2006.

———. "Senses and Emotions in the History of Sport." *Journal of Sport History* 40, no. 1 (Spring 2013): 21–38.

Klein, Alan M. *Dominican Baseball: New Pride, Old Prejudice.* Philadelphia: Temple University Press, 2014.

———. *Growing the Game: The Globalization of Major League Baseball.* New Haven, CT: Yale University Press, 2006.

———. *Sugarball: The American Game, the Dominican Dream.* New Haven, CT: Yale University Press, 1991.

Kunz, Diane B. "A Mexican Popular Image of the United States through the Baseball Hero, Fernando Valenzuela." *Studies in Latin American Popular Culture* 4 (1985): 14–23.

Kunz, Diane B., ed. *The Diplomacy of the Crucial Decade: American Foreign Relations during the 1960s.* New York: Columbia University Press, 1994.

Kurlansky, Mark. *The Eastern Stars: How Baseball Changed the Dominican Town of San Pedro de Macorís.* New York: Riverhead Books, 2010.

Ladd, Tony, and James A. Mathisen. *Muscular Christianity: Evangelical Protestants and the Development of American Sport.* Grand Rapids, MI: Baker Books, 1999.

Lowenthal, Abraham F. "Alliance Rhetoric versus Latin American Reality." *Foreign Affairs* 48, no. 3 (April 1970): 494–508.

Mangan, J. A., ed. *The Cultural Bond: Sport, Empire, Society.* New York: Routledge, 1992.

Mangan, J. A., and LaMartine P. DaCosta, eds. *Sport in Latin American Society: Past and Present.* London: Frank Cass, 2002.

Manley, Elizabeth S. *The Paradox of Paternalism: Women and the Politics of Authoritarianism in the Dominican Republic.* Gainesville: University Press of Florida, 2017.

Mañon, Melvin. *Operación Estrella: Con Caamaño, la Resistencia y la Inteligencia Cubana.* 4th ed. Santo Domingo: Ediciones de Taller no. 269, 1990.

Marcano Guevara, Arturo J., and David P. Fidler. *Stealing Lives: The Globalization of Baseball and the Tragic Story of Alexis Quiroz*. Bloomington: Indiana University Press, 2002.

Martin, John Bartlow. *Overtaken by Events: The Dominican Crisis from the Death of Trujillo to the Civil War*. Garden City, NY: Doubleday, 1966.

Martínez-Fernández, Luis. *Torn between Empires: Economy, Society, and Patterns of Political Thought in the Hispanic Caribbean, 1840–1878*. Athens: University of Georgia Press, 1994.

Martínez-Vergne, Teresita. *Nation and Citizen in the Dominican Republic, 1880–1916*. Chapel Hill: University of North Carolina Press, 2005.

Mayes, April J. *The Mulatto Republic: Class, Race, and Dominican National Identity*. Gainesville: University Press of Florida, 2014.

———. "Why Dominican Feminism Moved to the Right: Class, Colour and Women's Activism in the Dominican Republic, 1880s-1940s." *Gender and History* 20, no. 2 (August 2008): 349–371.

McKelvey, G. Richard. *Mexican Raiders in the Major Leagues: The Pasquel Brothers vs. Organized Baseball, 1946*. Jefferson, NC: McFarland, 2006.

McPherson, Alan. "Misled by Himself: What the Johnson Tapes Reveal about the Dominican Intervention of 1965." *Latin American Research Review* 38, no. 2 (2003): 127–146.

Mercader, José. *Historia de la Caricatura Dominicana*. Vol. 1. Santo Domingo: Archivo General de la Nación, 2012.

Miller, James Edward. *The Baseball Business: Pursuing Pennants and Profits in Baltimore*. Chapel Hill: University of North Carolina Press, 1990.

Montesinos, Enrique. *Los juegos regionales más antiguos: Juegos Deportivos Centroamericanos y del Caribe*. Organización Deportiva Centroamericana y del Caribe (ODECABE/CASCO), 2013.

Moore, Louis. *We Will Win the Day: The Civil Rights Movement, the Black Athlete, and the Quest for Equality*. Santa Barbara, CA: Praeger, 2017.

Moya Pons, Frank. *The Dominican Republic: A National History*. Princeton, NJ: Marcus Wiener Publishers, 1998.

Moya Pons, Rafael Francisco De [Frank Moya Pons]. "Industrial Incentives in the Dominican Republic, 1880–1983." PhD diss., Columbia University, 1987.

Nathan, David A. "Sports History and Roberto Clemente: A Morality Tale and a Way Forward." *Journal of American History* 101, no. 1 (June 2014): 184–187.

Nye, Joseph S., Jr. "The Decline of America's Soft Power: Why Washington Should Worry." *Foreign Affairs* 83, no. 3 (May–June 2004): 16–20.

———. "Public Diplomacy and Soft Power." *Annals of the American Academy of Political and Social Science* 616, Public Diplomacy in a Changing World (March 2008): 94–109.

Organization of American States. "The Charter of Punta del Este, Establishing an Alliance for Progress within the Framework of Operation Pan America; August 17, 1961." Special Meeting of the Inter-American Economic and Social Council, Punta del Este, Uruguay. The Avalon Project: Documents in Law,

History and Diplomacy, Lillian Goldman Law Library, Yale Law School. http://avalon.law.yale.edu/20th_century/intam16.asp#1.

Paige, Jeffery M. *Coffee and Power: Revolution and the Rise of Democracy in Central America*. Cambridge, MA: Harvard University Press, 1997.

Painter, David S. *The Cold War: An International History*. New York: Routledge, 1999.

Parker, Jason C. *Hearts, Minds, Voices: US Cold War Public Diplomacy and the Formation of the Third World*. New York: Oxford University Press, 2016.

Paterson, Thomas G. *Contesting Castro: The United States and the Triumph of the Cuban Revolution*. New York: Oxford University Press, 1994.

Peguero, Valentina. *The Militarization of Culture in the Dominican Republic from the Captains General to General Trujillo*. Lincoln: University of Nebraska Press, 2004.

Pérez, Louis A., Jr. "Between Baseball and Bullfighting: The Quest for Nationality in Cuba, 1868–1898." *Journal of American History* 81, no. 2 (1994): 493–517.

———. *On Becoming Cuban: Identity, Nationality, and Culture*. Chapel Hill: University of North Carolina Press, 1999.

Perkins, Whitney T. *Constraint of Empire: The United States and Caribbean Interventions*. Westport, CT: Greenwood, 1981.

Peterson, Robert. *Only the Ball Was White: A History of Legendary Black Players and All-Black Professional Teams*. New York: Oxford University Press, 1970.

Petras, James. "The Dominican Republic: Revolution and Restoration." In *Trends and Tragedies in American Foreign Policy*, edited by Michael Parenti, 128–143. Boston: Little, Brown, 1971.

Pettavino, Paula J., and Geralyn Pye. *Sport in Cuba: The Diamond in the Rough*. Pittsburgh: University of Pittsburgh Press, 1994.

Plummer, William. "Baseball Scout Epy Guerrero Looks for Rough Diamonds Amid Hunger and Poverty." *People*, April 10, 1989, 127–134. http://www.people.com/people/archive/article/0,,20119997,00.html.

Power, Margaret. *Right-Wing Women in Chile: Feminine Power and the Struggle against Allende, 1964–1973*. University Park, PA: Penn State University Press, 2002.

Putney, Clifford. *Muscular Christianity: Manhood and Sports in Protestant America, 1880–1920*. Cambridge, MA: Harvard University Press, 2001.

Rabe, Stephen G. "The Caribbean Triangle: Betancourt, Castro, and Trujillo and U.S. Foreign Policy, 1958–1963." In *Empire and Revolution: The United States and the Third World since 1945*, edited by Peter L. Hahn and Mary Ann Heiss, 48–70. Columbus: Ohio State University Press, 2001.

———. *The Killing Zone: The United States Wages Cold War in Latin America*. New York: Oxford University Press, 2011.

———. *The Most Dangerous Area in the World: John F. Kennedy Confronts Communist Revolution in Latin America*. Chapel Hill: University of North Carolina Press, 1999.

Ramírez, Dixa. *Colonial Phantoms: Belonging and Refusal in the Dominican Americas, from the 19th Century to the Present*. New York: New York University Press, 2018.

Rankin, Monica A. *¡México, la patria! Propaganda and Production during World War II*. Lincoln: University of Nebraska Press, 2009.

Regalado, Samuel O. *Viva Baseball! Latin Major Leaguers and Their Special Hunger*. Sport and Society Series. Urbana: University of Illinois Press, 1998.

Rein, Raanan. "'*El primer deportista*': The Political Use and Abuse of Sport in Peronist Argentina." *International Journal of the History of Sport* 15, no. 2 (1998): 54–76.

Rider, Toby C. *Cold War Games: Propaganda, the Olympics, and US Foreign Policy*. Urbana: University of Illinois Press, 2016.

Riess, Steven A. *City Games: The Evolution of American Urban Society and the Rise of Sports*. Urbana: University of Illinois Press, 1989.

Roberts, Randy. "'The Two-Fisted Testing Ground of Manhood': Boxing and the Academy." *Journal of American History* 101, no. 1 (June 2014): 188–191.

Rodríguez Demorizi, Emilio. *Caricatura y dibujo en Santo Domingo*. Santo Domingo: Editora Taller, 1977.

Roorda, Eric Paul. "The Cult of the Airplane among US Military Men and Dominicans during the US Occupation and the Trujillo Regime." In *Close Encounters of Empire: Writing the Cultural History of US-Latin American Relations*, edited by Gilbert M. Joseph, Catherine C. Legrand, and Ricardo D. Salvatore, 269–310. Durham, NC: Duke University Press, 1998.

———. *The Dictator Next Door: The Good Neighbor Policy and the Trujillo Regime in the Dominican Republic, 1930–1945*. Durham, NC: Duke University Press, 1998.

Rosenberg, Emily S. *Financial Missionaries to the World: The Politics and Culture of Dollar Diplomacy, 1900–1930*. Durham, NC: Duke University Press, 2003.

Rubenstein, Anne. *Bad Language, Naked Ladies, and Other Threats to the Nation: A Political History of Comic Books in Mexico*. Durham, NC: Duke University Press, 1998.

Ruck, Rob. "The Field of Sports History at Critical Mass." *Journal of American History* 101, no. 1 (June 2014): 192–194.

———. *Raceball: How the Major Leagues Colonized the Black and Latin Game*. Boston: Beacon, 2011.

———. *The Tropic of Baseball: Baseball in the Dominican Republic*. New York: Meckler, 1991.

Ruck, Rob, and Daniel Manatt. *The Republic of Baseball: The Dominican Giants of the American Game*. Documentary. Los Angeles: Manatt Media, September 2006.

Sáez Ramo, José Luis. "Funciones de la caricatura. Un recorrido emocional por la prensa dominicana." *Clío* 83, no. 188 (July-December 2014): 250–270.

Sargeant, Daniel J. "North/South: The United States Responds to the New International Economic Order." *Humanity: An International Journal of Human Rights, Humanitarianism, and Development* 6, no. 1 (Spring 2015): 201–216.

———. *A Superpower Transformed: The Remaking of American Foreign Relations in the 1970s*. New York: Oxford University Press, 2015.

Saull, Richard. "El lugar del sur global en la conceptualización de la Guerra Fría: Desarrollo capitalista, revolución social y conflicto geopolítico." In *Espejos de la Guerra Fría: México, América Central y el Caribe*, edited by Daniela Spenser, 31–66. México, DF: Centro de Investigaciones y Estudios Superiores en Antropología Social, 2004.

Schlesinger, Arthur M., Jr. *A Thousand Days: John F. Kennedy in the White House.* Boston: Houghton Mifflin, 1965.

Scott, James C. *Domination and the Arts of Resistance: Hidden Transcripts.* New Haven, CT: Yale University Press, 1990.

———. *Weapons of the Weak: Everyday Forms of Peasant Resistance.* New Haven, CT: Yale University Press, 1985.

Servín, Elisa, Leticia Reina, and John Tutino, eds. *Cycles of Conflict, Centuries of Change: Crisis, Reform, and Revolution in Mexico.* Durham, NC: Duke University Press, 2007.

Snyder, Brad. *A Well-Paid Slave: Curt Flood's Fight for Free Agency in Professional Sports.* New York: Viking, 2006.

Sotomayor, Antonio. "*Un parque para cada pueblo*: Julio Enrique Monagas and the Politics of Sport and Recreation in Puerto Rico during the 1940s." *Caribbean Studies* 42, no. 2 (2014): 3–40.

———. *The Sovereign Colony: Olympic Sport, National Identity, and International Politics in Puerto Rico.* Lincoln: University of Nebraska Press, 2018.

Spirou, Costas, and Larry Bennett. *It's Hardly Sportin': Stadiums, Neighborhoods and the New Chicago.* DeKalb: Northern Illinois University Press, 2003.

Subsecretaria Técnica de Deportes y Oficina Nacional de Estadística. "1er Censo Nacional de Recursos Humanos en Deportes y Entidades Deportivos." Informe. Santo Domingo: Secretario de Estado de Deportes, Educación Física y Recreación [SEDEFIR], 2006.

Sullivan, Neil J. *The Dodgers Move West.* New York: Oxford University Press, 1987.

Szymanski, Stefan. *Playbooks and Checkbooks: An Introduction to the Economics of Modern Sports.* Princeton, NJ: Princeton University Press, 2009.

Taffet, Jeffrey F. *Foreign Aid as Foreign Policy: The Alliance for Progress in Latin America.* New York: Routledge, 2007.

Tejera, Eduardo J. *Cincuenta años de democracia y desarrollo dominicano 1961–2011: Logros y fracasos.* Santo Domingo: Fundación Dominicana de Estudios Económicos, 2012.

Thornton, Christy. "A Mexican New International Economic Order?" In *Latin America and the Global Cold War*, edited by Thomas C. Field Jr., Stella Krepp, and Vanni Pettinà, 301–342. Chapel Hill: University of North Carolina Press, 2020.

Torres-Saillant, Silvio. "The Tribulations of Blackness: Stages in Dominican Racial Identity." *Callaloo* 23, no. 3, Dominican Republic Literature and Culture (Summer 2000): 1086–1111.

Torres-Saillant, Silvio, and Ramona Hernández. *The Dominican Americans.* Westport, CT: Greenwood, 1998.

Toye, John, and Richard Toye. "The Origins and Interpretations of the Prebisch-Singer Thesis." *History of Political Economy* 35, no. 3 (Fall 2003): 437–467.

"Trujillo's Murder Plot." *Time*, July 18, 1960, 30.

Trumpbour, Robert C. *The New Cathedrals: Politics and Media in the History of Stadium Construction.* Syracuse, NY: Syracuse University Press, 2007.

Turits, Richard Lee. *Foundations of Despotism: Peasants, the Trujillo Regime, and Modernity in Dominican History.* Stanford, CA: Stanford University Press, 2004.

Tutino, John. *From Insurrection to Revolution in Mexico: Social Bases of Agrarian Violence, 1750–1940.* Princeton, NJ: Princeton University Press, 1986.

Tygiel, Jules. *Past Time: Baseball as History.* New York: Oxford University Press, 2000.

Váldez, Tirso A., hijo. *Notas Acerca del Beisbol Dominicano del Pasado y del Presente.* Ciudad Trujillo: Editora del Caribe, C. por A., 1958.

Vedovato, Claudio. *Politics, Foreign Trade and Economic Development: A Study of the Dominican Republic.* New York: St. Martin's, 1986.

Vega, Bernardo. *Evaluación de la política de industrialización de la República Dominicana.* Santo Domingo: [n.p.], 1973.

———. *Kennedy y los Trujillo.* Santo Domingo: Fundación Cultural Dominicana, 1991.

———. *El peligro comunista en la revolución de abril: Mito o realidad?* Santo Domingo: Fundación Cultural Dominicana, 2006.

———. *Trujillo y el control financiero norteamericano.* Santo Domingo: Fundación Cultural Dominicana, 1990.

Vega, Bernardo, ed. *Ensayos sobre cultura dominicana.* Santo Domingo: Museo del Hombre Dominicano, 1981.

Virtue, John. *South of the Color Barrier: How Jorge Pasquel and the Mexican League Pushed Baseball toward Racial Integration.* Jefferson, NC: McFarland, 2008.

Westad, Odd Arne. *The Global Cold War: Third World Interventions and the Making of Our Times.* New York: Cambridge University Press, 2007.

Wiarda, Howard J. *Dilemmas of Democracy in Latin America: Crises and Opportunity.* Lanham, MD: Rowman and Littlefield, 2005.

Yergin, Daniel, and Joseph Stanislaw. *The Commanding Heights: The Battle for the World Economy.* Rev. ed. New York: Free Press, 2002.

Yoder, April. "*Un compromiso de tod@s*: Women, Olympism, and the Dominican Third Way." In *Olimpismo: The Olympic Movement in the Making of Latin America,* edited by Antonio Sotomayor and César R. Torres, 131–147. Fayetteville: University of Arkansas Press, 2020.

———. "Dominican Baseball and Latin American Pluralism, 1969–1974." *Oxford Research Encyclopedia of Latin American History,* September 29, 2016. https://doi.org/10.1093/acrefore/9780199366439.013.355.

———. "Ownership of the Baseball Industry in the Dominican Republic." In *Sport in Latin America: Policy, Organization, Management,* edited by Gonzalo Bravo, Rosa López de D'Amico, and Charles Parrish, 148–160. New York: Routledge, 2016.

———. "Sport Policy and Political Regimes in Latin America." In *Sport in Latin America: Policy, Organization, Management,* edited by Gonzalo Bravo, Rosa López de D'Amico, and Charles Parrish, 65–76. New York: Routledge, 2016.

Yunén, Rafael Emilio, ed. *¡Nos vemos en el play! Béisbol y cultura en la República Dominicana.* Santiago de los Caballeros: Centro Leon, Centro Cultural Eduardo León Jimenes, 2008.

Zeiler, Thomas W. *Ambassadors in Pinstripes: The Spalding World Baseball Tour and the Birth of the American Empire.* Lanham, MD: Rowman and Littlefield, 2006.

———. "The Diplomatic History Bandwagon: A State of the Field." *Journal of American History* 95, no. 4 (March 2009): 1053–1073.

Index

Abou-El-Fadl, Reem, 88–89
Abreu, José, 117
Acosta Matos, Eliades, 49, 54
Acta, Manny, 142
agrarian reforms, 55–56
Aguilas Cibaeñas (team), 9, 15, 22, 32, 48, 58, 74–76, 78–80, 95, 116, 118, 121–124, 129, 133; Aguilita mascot, 75, 77
¡Ahora!, 82, 97, 101–102
Alliance for Progress, 38, 52, 55, 60, 89, 119
Alligators of the South (team). *See* San Cristóbal Caimanes del Sur (team)
Almendares (team), 42
Alou, Felipe, 8, 12, 17, 25, 27–28, 30, 36, 42, 44–45, 60–61, 70–73, 80, 83, 89, 91, 111, 114, 118, 120, 125, 138, 143; controversies regarding, 70; US career of , 8, 17, 25, 27, 60
Alou, Jesús, 11, 30, 57, 117, 138, 140; eighth Dominican big-leaguer, 57, founder of Dominican Summer League, 140; as scout, 10
Alou, Mateo "Matty," 36, 38, 91
Alou brothers, 37, 39, 46, 58, 79, 91. *See also* Alou, Felipe; Alou, Jesús; Alou, Mateo "Matty"
Alvarez, Cuchito, 26
amateur baseball, 7, 10, 12, 18, 20, 83, 88, 109, 118, 130, 136; leagues, 5, 111, 116, 118; teams, 18, 32; Rule 3450, 136
Amateur Baseball World Series (Serie Mundial de Béisbol Amateur), 10, 19–20, 87–90, 96–100, 102–103, 108, 109; of 1965, 97; of 1969, 10, 87–90, 96–100, 102; Dominican victory in 1950, 19
amateur sports, 4, 10, 12–13, 82–83, 88–90, 96, 98, 100–102, 105–106, 108–109, 115, 122–123, 126, 130, 134, 140, 150
Anglada, Julio Antonio "Toñín," 30
anticommunism, 4, 8–9, 12, 36, 42, 44, 47–48, 52, 60, 64, 69, 73, 150; anticommunist, 7, 10, 29, 36, 52, 55, 69, 81
Antún, Rafael, 131
April War, 9, 85, 94–97, 104
Argentina, 89, 100, 102, 140
Arias, Alfredo, 145–146
Arias and Goodman Academy, 145
Arroceros del Nordeste (team), 110
Arteaga, Sal, 138–139
Atlanta Braves (team), 2, 91
Augusto Lora, Francisco, 93, 95
austerity, 93, 96, 128, 134, 147
authoritarian, 54, 126; authoritarianism, 7, 31, 73, 99, 151
Autonomous University of Santo Domingo. *See* Universidad Autónoma de Santo Domingo
Aviación (team), 16, 19, 32
Avila, Ralph, 11, 114–115, 131, 135–136, 138, 147
Azuanos, 104

Baker, Gene, 74
Balaguer, Joaquín, 9–13, 16, 24–25, 33, 38, 86, 88–93, 95–98, 100–112, 115–116, 119, 121–126, 140, 150; and American fraternity, 97; and Cuba, 88, 96, 100; and *desarrollismo*/industrialization, 11, 96, 112, 121, 123, 126; *doce años*, 10, 12, 126; and Dominican baseball, 11, 92, 95, 96, 103, 150; election of, 12–13, 89, 90, 100, 105; exile, 38, 86; foreign policy of, 88; and paternalism, 13, 89–90, 102, 104, 106, 108; as patron of national sport, 106; sports law, 106
ballparks, 4–5, 33, 42, 45–47, 71, 115, 118; and democracy, 46–47
Ballplayer: Pelotero (Finkle, Martinc, and Paley), 137, 144–145
Baní, 126
Barbón, Roberto, 42; and baseball academies, 11, 115, 135, 139–140, 143–146
baseball ambassadors, 93–96; baseball diplomats, 93
baseball commissioner (USA), 31, 58, 60, 70, 129, 133–134
Baseball Hall of Fame, 2, 91, 115, 149
baseball industry, 3, 5–6, 7–8, 11, 13–14, 110, 115, 119–120, 122, 124, 128–129, 134–135, 138, 140–141, 143, 145–146, 149, 151
Batista, Fulgencio, 56
Bautista, Danny, 142
Bautista de Suárez, Altagracia, 97
Bell, Jorge (George), 1
Benefactor's Cup, 21–22
Benefactor tournament (1954), 20
Bennett, William Tapley, 72–74
Benson, Vern, 58
Betancourt, Rómulo, 29–31, 52, 68–69; Betancourt Doctrine, 68–69
big leagues, 2, 29–30, 111, 113–114, 119, 136–137, 141; big-leaguers, 9, 29, 39–40, 55, 57–58, 64, 67, 71, 74, 78–80, 83, 89, 91, 134, 142, 150
Bisonó, Reynaldo "Papy," 133–134
Black Tigers (team), 28
Bloodless Revolution. *See* Revolución sin sangre
Bobea Billini, Mario, 52–53
Bonnelly, Rafael, 71
Borbón, Pedro, 95
Bosch, Juan, 3, 8–9, 12, 36, 40, 44–45, 47–56, 58–60, 62, 67–70, 72, 81–85, 89, 96, 123, 132, 150; and communism, 8–9, 48–49, 52, 54; coup (1963), 9, 12, 50, 59, 68, 84, 150; as independent from United States, 52; "San Juan Bosch," 50; support for, among popular classes and rural Dominicans, 56
Brazil, 89
Brooklyn Dodgers (team), 25, 94
Brubaker, Bill, 114, 136
buscones, 128, 141, 143, 146
Bush, George W., 139

Caamaño, Francisco, 104, 108; failed coup, 108
Caba, Pedro, 101
Cabral, Donald Reid, 72–73, 76
Cámara de Diputados, 40, 53
Campanella, Roy, 94
campesinos, 105
Candlestick Park, 38
Cantwell, Robert, 71
capitalism, 3, 7, 11, 90, 111–112, 119, 150–151
Caribbean baseball, 116
Carter, Thomas, 4
cartoons, 5, 12, 23, 26–27, 37, 40, 43–44, 49–51, 53–54, 56–57, 62, 64–65, 74, 77, 80, 82, 91, 105, 107, 121; cartoonists, 23, 50, 77, 106
Carty, Ricardo "Rico," 2, 91, 118, 133
Castellanos, Juan Luis, 40, 121–122
Castro, Fidel, 4, 8, 29, 35, 39, 42, 44, 46, 52, 56, 68, 97–100; Cuban Revolution, 98
Cedeño, Margarita, 2

Central American and Caribbean Games, 10, 90, 101, 103, 108; of 1974, 10, 90, 101, 103–105, 108
Centro Olímpico, 105
Cepeda, Orlando, 46, 72
César Franco, Julio, 142
Chottin, George, 40
Cibao, 110–111, 112, 120, 122–125, 126; *cibaeños*, 111, 120, 122–126
City of Shortstops. *See* San Pedro de Macorís
Ciudad Trujillo. *See* Santo Domingo
Clemente, Roberto, 6, 46, 90, 113
Cleveland Indians (team), 35
coaches, 4, 5, 13, 88, 116–117, 120–121, 129, 138–142, 146–147, 150
Cold War, 7, 48, 149–150
Colombia, 31, 52, 98
Colón, Bartolo, 144
Comité Olímpico Dominicano (COD), 97, 101–102, 105
communism, 8, 10, 12, 29, 36, 39, 42–45, 48–49, 52–53, 55, 60, 69, 75, 82, 84–85; Communist Party, 59
COMPETE Act, 139
Confederación de Béisbol Profesional del Caribe, 6, 23, 133–134
constitution, Dominican, 54–56, 54, 95; of 1963, 54–56; Article 95, 54; constitutionalists, 84
Constitutional Assembly, 53–54
Consuelo, 142
Cordero, Francisco, 1–2
Córdova, Cuqui, 130
Costa Rica, 52
Council of State, 39, 42–44
coups, 5; coup of September 25, 1963, 9, 12, 59–60, 63–64, 67–69, 79, 81, 83, 85, 150; failed coup of 1973, 108
Crimmins, John H., 95
Crimmins, Margaret, 95
Cuba, 4, 8, 10, 12–13, 15, 18, 19, 31, 35, 38, 40, 42, 44, 46, 47, 52, 56, 59–60, 63–64, 68, 70–71, 80, 86, 87–90, 96–100, 102, 106, 108–109, 150; agents from government of, 80; Bay of Pigs, 4; ballplayers from, 42, 44, 70–71, 98; coaches from, 88; communism in, 68; Cuban professional league, 42; Cuban series (1962), 64; exiles from, 8, 12, 42, 46, 63; as economic model, 4, 13, 90
Cuban-Dominican Series, 41, 45–46, 48, 59–60, 70, 80; of 1962, 41, 45, 46, 48, 59, 60, 80; of 1963, 70; and cultural industries, 5, 148
Cuban Missile Crisis, 4, 12, 36, 40, 42, 48, 60
Cuban Revolution, 4, 68
Cuban Stars (team), 35, 40, 42, 44, 46, 48, 70
Cuban Winter League, 15, 45

Dark, Alvin, 72–73
Decree 1300, 131, 133
Deford, Frank, 135
De Hernández, Nora S., 46
De Javier, Inés, 93
De la Rosa, Jesús, 134
De los Santos, Emilio, 76
democracy, 1, 3–5, 7–9, 11–14, 30–31, 35–40, 43–50, 52, 54–56, 59–61, 63–64, 69–70, 73–75, 80–82, 84–85, 89–90, 94, 102, 112, 119, 125–126, 128, 132–134, 148–151; and baseball, 3, 5, 12–14, 34, 36–37, 46, 48–49, 53, 56, 59, 64, 75, 81, 86, 125, 149, 151; and capitalism, 3, 7, 126; and the Cold War, 150; and communism, 12, 36, 44, 47, 56, 64, 85; in the Dominican Republic, 3, 7–8, 12, 30–31, 35–36, 38–41, 44–45, 47–50, 52, 54–56, 58–60, 63–64, 69–70, 73, 75, 84–85, 89–90, 102, 112, 119, 125, 128, 133–134, 148–151; and economy, 5, 14, 48, 56, 59, 128, 132, 148, 149, 150; limits of, 85; social, 11, 150–151; and social justice, 7, 47- 49, 61; in the United States, 31, 45, 60, 73, 94

democratic transition (1978), 11, 13, 125–126, 128
deporte rey, 17–18, 20, 22–23, 39, 59, 74, 85
Derby, Lauren, 16–17
De Tavarez, Emilia S., 46
Detroit Tigers (team), 28, 42
development, 3–5, 8, 10–15, 18–19, 22, 25, 29, 38–39, 73, 89–90, 93, 96, 99–100, 102–109, 112, 116, 119–120, 122–129, 132, 135–136, 140–141, 143, 149–150; and capitalism, 99; and democracy, 3, 5, 11, 14, 89; in the Dominican Republic, 10, 12–13, 19, 22, 89–90, 96, 100, 105, 107–108, 112, 119, 122, 124, 125, 132, 143, 150; economic, 3, 11, 89–90, 93, 102, 105, 109, 120, 122, 123, 140, 150; and global politics, 29, 73, 99, 129, 149; human, 4, 38, 102, 105, 129, 135–136, 140; and the nation, 5, 8, 15, 18, 25, 39, 103, 104–105, 108, 140; and society, 10, 89–90, 112, 129; and sport, 3, 5, 11, 14, 96, 103, 106, 116, 126–129, 135–136, 140, 141, 143; underdevelopment, 73
Díaz, Orlando, 139–140
Diplomático (team), 20
Diplomats (team). *See* Diplomático
Dirección General de Deportes, 16, 18–19, 40
Dominican Development Foundation, 93–95
Dominican Prospect League, 147
Dominican Republic Sports and Education Academy (DRSEA), 145
Dominican Revolutionary Party, 2, 40, 44, 53. *See also* Partido Revolucionario Dominicano
Dominican Summer League (DSL), 6, 128–129, 138–141, 146–147, 151
Dominican Third Way, 4, 10, 12, 13, 90, 101, 102, 108, 109, 112, 119
Dominican Winter League, 8–11, 13, 15–17, 21–23, 25–26, 31–32, 45, 58–60, 62, 64–65, 67, 70–71, 74, 80–83, 85, 88, 90–93, 95–96, 111, 116–120, 122, 124, 127–133, 134, 139, 146; of 1955–1956, 25; of 1963–1964, 62, 88; and capitalism, 11, 119; controversies regarding, 32, 64, 74, 82; domestic players in, 25, 65; and the Dominican Republic, 8–9, 22–23, 31, 59–60, 80–81, 82–83, 88, 91–93, 96, 118, 122; expansion of, in 1983–1984, 11, 13, 120, 128–130; foreign players in, 32, 118; and other leagues, 10, 13, 71, 116, 122, 131, 139; tournaments, 90
Dominican Winter League Tournament, 8–9, 17, 29, 31, 33, 55, 57–58, 60, 62, 65, 67–69, 74–75, 78, 85, 88, 90, 92, 131, 133; of 1955–1956, 17; of 1960–1961, 17, 29, 31, 33, 69; of 1961–1962, 69; of 1963–1964, 9, 57–58, 65, 69, 74–75, 78, 85; of 1964–1965, 9; of 1966–1967, 90, 92; of 1983–1984, 133
dramaturgy of power, 17
Durocher, Leo, 25

economic development. *See* economic sanctions, 17, 29, 31–33, 62
El Caribe (newspaper), 8–9, 20, 24, 26, 28, 36–37, 47, 49, 52–60, 63–67, 74–78, 80–81, 91–95, 97–98, 100, 104–107; 1960 editorial, 8; on baseball, 47, 56, 74, 95, 97–98; on Dominican politics, 9, 52, 55–56, 58, 64, 67, 76, 80, 100, 105; UPI report in, 52
El Deporte al Día, 67
El Diario–La Prensa (newspaper), 81
elections, 3, 5, 8–10, 12–13, 36, 38–40, 42, 47–49, 53, 59, 63, 73–74, 76, 79, 81, 85–86, 89–90, 100–101, 105–106, 125–126, 130, 151; of 1962, 8, 12, 36, 42, 47, 53, 63, 85; of 1966, 85–86; of 1970, 90, 96, 100–101; of 1974, 105–106; of 1978, 13, 125–126; of 1982, 130; of 2012, 151; and April War, 9; and Balaguer, 10, 89–90, 96, 105–106; and baseball, 40, 48, 74, 81; and the Bloodless Revolution, 5, 89; and the Triumvirate, 76, 79, 85, 96

Elsey, Brenda, 4
Epy Guerrero Complex, 127, 135–136
Escogido, 20
Estadio Cibao. *See Estadio Leonidas Rhamadés*
Estadio Leonidas Rhamadés, 24, 46, 76, 79, 94
Estadio Oriental, 24, 46
Estadio Quisqueya, 1–2, 15–16, 22–25, 33, 35, 41, 46–48, 66, 76, 79, 87, 92, 111; renaming of (1961), 15
Estadio Tetelo Vargas. *See* Estadio Oriental
Estadio Trujillo. *See* Estadio Quisqueya
"Estímulo Deportivo" (editorial), 37–38
estímulo deportivo, 38, 40, 101
Estrellas Orientales (team), 15, 22, 48, 57–58, 62, 64–65, 67, 92, 120, 129, 131; elephant mascot, 64, 75

Fatherland, the, Dominican Republic as, 59, 68
Father of the New Fatherland Tournament, 25
Federación Dominicana de Béisbol, 20
Federación Nacional de Peloteros Profesionales (FENAPEPRO), 132
Fernández, Chico, 42
Fernández, Tony, 115, 121, 142
festival of youth and sport, 105
Fiallo, Viriato, 45, 53
Fieras Capitaleñas, 111
Figueres, José, 52
Final Series, 74–75, 77
foreign investment ventures, 144
Fraternity of Sportswriters of the Press and Radio, 66
Frick, Ford, 31, 58, 60, 70–71,78
Fucú, 64, 75, 77
full-service residential programs, 144
Fundación Pedro Martínez, 142

García Bongó, Jorge, 87, 99
García Carmona, Juan, 77
García Godoy, Héctor, 85–86
García Saleta, Juan, 97, 101, 103
Gigantes del Cibao (team). *See* Gigantes del Nordeste
Gigantes del Nordeste (team), 120
global baseball industry, 3, 5–7, 14, 115, 128–129, 138, 140–141, 149
globalization, 6, 14, 148
Global South, 7–8, 14, 147, 149
Gómez, Preston, 113, 115
González, Jose A., 97
González, Pedro, 78
Goodman, Gary, 145–146
Griffin, Alfredo, 142
Guatemala, 100
Guerrero, Vladimir, 149
guerrillas/guerrilleros, 69, 76
Gulf and Western Company, 132
Guzmán, Antonio, 11, 125, 126, 128, 129

Haak, Howie, 113–114, 135
Havana (Cuba), 42
Hazim Egel, Bienvenido, 39, 46
Hermanos Alou. *See* Alou brothers
Hernández, Rudy, 29–30
Herrera Billini, Hipólito, 31, 33
Higuey province, 103
Hipódromo del Caribe, 140
Hipódromo Perla Antillana, 140
horse racing, 27, 140
Houston Astros (team), 117
Hoy, 152

ImpACTA Kids Foundation, 142
Independence Day (Dominican), 47
Indios de Mayagüez, 26
Industrial Incentives Law. *See* Industrial Incentives and Protections Law of 1968
industrialization, 10, 13, 56, 119–120, 126; Industrial Incentives and Protections Law of 1968, 83, 96, 102, 108, 112, 119, 122–123, 126, 129; industrialists, 13, 21, 33, 55, 96, 108, 122, 126
International [Amateur] Baseball Federation (IBAF; FIBA), 109, 180–181n81

International Monetary Fund, 11, 129, 134, 148; and shock program, 134
International Series, 67–68, 74, 78–79

Jacobo, Astín, 144, 146–147
Jana, Freddy, 138–139, 140, 147
Javier, Julián, 9, 29–30, 45–46, 58, 70, 74–75, 78–80, 90, 93, 95, 110–111, 117, 120; as administrator, 120; and Balaguer, 95; controversies regarding, 9, 70, 74; Dominican career of, 45–46, 58, 75; international career of, 29–30, 79, 93
Jiménez, Elvio, 46, 115, 120
Jiménez, Manuel Emilio, 46
Joaquín, Ulisés, 146
Johnson administration, 69
Jorge Blanco, Salvador, 11, 128–134, 136, 148, 150–151; Decree 1300, 131; expansion of Winter League, 128–130, 133–134; protests against, 148; regulation of baseball, 136; Rule 3450, 136
Juegos Centroamericanos y del Caribe, 10, 90, 101, 103–105, 108
Justiano, Pedro, 66
Juventud Dominicana Cristiana, 35, 44

Keith, LeeAnna, 70
Kelly, Jimy, 114
Kelly, Paul, 74
Kelly rule, 114
Kennedy, John F., 38, 45, 69, 72, 119
Klein, Alan, 137, 141, 143–144, 147
Koufax, Sandy, 84
Kuhn, Bowie, 133

La Habana (team), 42
La Información (newspaper), 120–121, 124
La Nación (newspaper), 27, 37, 39–40, 43, 47–48, 50, 51
Lantigua, Enrique, 20
La Romana, 130
La Romana Azucareros del Este (team), 130–131
Latin America, 2, 3, 4, 6, 10, 11, 16, 22, 29, 57, 65, 60, 71–73, 79–81, 86–89, 97–100, 102, 109, 111, 113–115, 129, 135, 147, 149, 151; baseball in, 2; countries of, 88–89, 98–99, 109; cultural connections with Cuba of, 98; Latin Americans, 72, 80, 97–99, 109, 111, 147; players from, 60, 71–73, 80–81, 113–114, 149; unity of, 109; winter leagues in, 22
La Vega, 47, 110, 124
La Vega Indios del Valle (team), 110, 120–121
Law 447, 129–132
Leones del Escogido (team), 15, 20, 22, 26, 32–33, 48, 65–66, 74–76, 79, 92, 95, 122, 129; lion mascot, 65–66, 75
Leonidas Radhamés tournament (1953), 20
Ley Confiscaciones, 54–58
Licey, 20
Licey (team). *See* Tigres del Licey
Liga de Verano de Béisbol Profesional de la República Dominicana, 10, 13, 111–112, 115, 117, 118–122, 125–126, 128–129, 138–140, 146, 151
Liga de Verano del Cibao, 10–11, 13, 110–112, 115–126, 128–129, 136, 138; and baseball as industry, 112, 117, 119–120, 123; directors, 112, 124, 126; and Dominican government, 118, 123–125, 136; games with, 116, 121–122; players in, 116, 118, 123–124
Liga Dominicana de Base Ball Profesional, 16, 21–22
Liga Nacional de BaseBall Profesional (LNBP), 131
Linieros de Mao (team), 117
Listín Diario, 123, 133
little leagues, 129, 141–146
Lleras Camargo, Alberto, 52
López Molina, Máximo, 43–44
Los Angeles Anaheim Angels, 149

Los Angeles Dodgers, 84, 113, 135
magnífico estímulo, 36–37, 66, 78, 85

Major League Baseball (MLB), 2, 6, 7, 11, 14, 127–129, 134–148, 151; Commissioner's Office, 11, 130, 134, 137; Hall of Fame, 2, 149
major leagues, 6, 17, 25, 29, 31, 45, 57–58, 60, 74, 111, 113–115, 117–118, 121, 127, 133, 135, 137–138, 142, 149–150; teams, 5, 6, 7, 111, 113, 115, 127, 137
managers, baseball, 5, 9, 13, 28, 30, 71–72, 74, 95, 110–111, 117, 120–121, 124, 138, 142
Manley, Elizabeth, 89
Manoguayabo, 142, 146
Manzueta, Pichulí, 20
Mao (city in the Dominican Republic), 124
Mao Linesmen (team). *See* Linieros de Mao (team)
Marichal, Juan, 2, 9, 16, 19, 29–30, 36–37, 39, 46, 55, 57–58, 64–66, 70, 72, 74–76, 78–79, 83–85, 91, 113, 116, 125, 150; as the "Best Right Arm in Baseball," 91; controversies regarding, 70, 74–76, 84, 91; Dominican career of, 19, 58, 65; international career of, 29–30, 36, 84; Juan Marichal Night, 66
Marté, Rene, 33
Martin, John Bartlow, 72–73, 84–85
Martinez, Horacio, 20, 27, 143
Martínez, Pedro, 115, 142, 149
Martínez, Ramón, 142
Martínez Alba, Francisco, 20, 22
Martínez Brea, Bienvenido, 105
Martínez Smith, Antulio, 30–31
Martorell, Rafael E., 20, 67
Marxism, 4, 44, 53
Mazeroski, Bill, 95
Medina, Danilo, 2, 151–152
Medina, Miche, 24, 41, 43, 63, 65–66, 75, 77
Mejía, Hipólito, 2
Mejía Feliú, Juan Tomás, 133
Mercado de Gautier, Maricusa, 20
Mexico, 1, 31, 98–99; baseball league in, 124; workers in, 114
military, 5, 9, 16, 18, 26, 42, 54, 59, 62–63, 65, 68–69, 73, 75–76, 81, 83–85, 94, 125–126; and Article 95, 54; and elections, 125–126; and coups, 5, 9, 59, 62–63, 65, 68–69, 81, 85; infiltration by, into daily life, 16; and pro-Bosch uprising, 84; social mobility offered by, 16
Minnesota Twins (team), 121, 145
minor league, 34, 141; circuit, 139; games, 140; players, 139; system, 135–136, 138
Mirabal Reyes, Minerva, 69
modernity, 19, 22, 25
modernization, 18–20
Montalvo, Rafael, 114
Montreal Expos (team), 149
Montreal Royals (team), 94
Mota, Manuel, 78, 91
Movimiento Popular Dominicano, 43
Movimiento Revolucionario de 14 de Junio, 69
Moya Pons, Frank, 49, 60, 112, 123
Murtaugh, Danny, 95

Nadel, Joshua, 4
National Association of Professional Baseball Leagues, 31, 57–59, 138–139
National Baseball Commission, 20
national championship (Dominican Republic), 19
National Commission of Professional Baseball, 21
national industry, 5, 10–11, 13–14, 112, 116, 122, 125–126, 128, 150,
National Institute of Sports, Physical Education, and Recreation (INDER), 102, 106
National League, 6, 17, 91, 133
National Palace, 39, 47, 59, 67, 79, 84

national pastime, 3–5, 7–8, 10, 12, 17–18, 22–23, 32, 40–41, 58, 60, 63–64, 66, 74, 78, 90, 96–97, 119, 122, 125, 128, 141, 147, 149–151
National Police, 18, 59, 103
National Prospect League (NPL), 127–128, 146–147
national selection tournaments, 19
national sports director (Dominican Republic), 21, 96
National Tournament, 20–21, 23, 78, 131
national identity, Dominican, 4, 26–27, 32–33, 58–59, 70, 93, 124
natives-only Winter Tournament (1960–1961), 31–33, 117, 150
Neftalí Martínez, Manuel, 30
New Fatherland Tournament, 25
New York, 38, 113; German neighborhoods, 113; Irish neighborhoods, 113
New York Giants (team), 25–28, 32, 38, 70, 72
New York Mets (team), 117
New York Yankees (team), 38, 111
newspapers, 5, 27, 36, 49, 59, 62, 70, 79, 91, 98, 120, 152; Associated Press, 70
Neyba, 73
Nixon, Richard, 99
Northeastern Rice Farmers (team). *See* Arroceros del Nordeste
Northeast Giants (team). *See* Gigantes del Nordeste

Obdulio Guerrero, Epifanio "Epy," 11, 111, 114–116, 120, 127–128, 135–136, 138, 143, 147; Epy Guerrero Complex established by, 135; as infield specialist trainer, 115, 137; as local scout, 114, 116, 120, 135, 138–139
Office of the Secretary of Sports, Physical Education, and Recreation, 10, 13, 106, 118, 130, 136
Office of the Baseball Commissioner (US), 114, 130
Olivo, Diogenes "Guayubín," 39, 62–63, 67, 70, 74
Olivo, Federico "Chichi," 62–63
Organization of American States (OAS), 9, 29–30, 38, 62, 84, 87, 91, 102; Alliance for Progress, 38; countries in, 29–31, 38; sanctions imposed by, 29, 31, 62; US-OAS invasion, 9, 84, 91; US-OAS peacekeeping forces, 102
organized baseball, 3, 6, 15, 22, 94, 116–117, 120, 124, 130, 133–134
Ornes, Germán Emilio, 49, 54
Orr, Matthew, 145

Pagán, José, 46
Panama, 95, 140
pan-American baseball circuit, 5
Pan American Games, 19
Partido Revolucionario Dominicano (PRD), 2, 8, 40, 44–45, 49–50, 53–56, 59–60, 67–68, 100, 104, 125–126, 128–129, 134, 140; and constitution, 54; convention, 40; and coup, 59–60; and Cuba, 45; and elections, 53, 100; partisanship in, 53; AND Triumvirate, 67; and Winter League expansion, 129, 134
Pascual, Camilo, 46
paternalism, 13, 89–90, 102, 106, 108
patronage, 8, 10, 18, 104, 108, 119, 125
Peace Corps, 94
Peguero, Valentina, 16
pelótica, 2
Peña, Roberto, 78
People magazine, 115
Perry, Alonzo, 22
personalism, 8, 56
Ph (sportswriter), 80–81
Phillies (team), 30
Pichardo, Monchín, 123, 131
Pirates-Dominican All-Star game, 94
Pitch, Hit, Run program, 142
Pittsburgh Pirates (team), 29, 58, 89–90, 93–96, 113, 118
police brutality, 74
political culture, 14; dissidents, 74

Portorreal, Daniel, 142, 146
Portorreal Little League, 142
poverty, 73, 113–114, 141, 145, 147, 151
Pro-Election of General Héctor B. Trujillo Molina tournament (1952), 20
Professional Ballplayers Federation, 20
promoters, 10, 128, 138, 147, 149
propaganda, 2, 26, 31, 52
Puerto Plata, 121, 124
Puerto Plata Piratas del Atlántico (team), 121
Puerto Rican league, 6, 26, 64
Puerto Rico, 1, 15, 19, 28, 46, 97, 98, 102; Puerto Ricans, 15, 45–46, 113, 116; Winter League, 45
Pujols, Mignolio, 131

Quality Baseball Academy, 144
Quiroz, Alexis, 135

race, 28, 70–73, 80; African Americans, 28, 74; "Latin temperament," 71; segregation and discrimination, 30
Ramírez, Ruddy, 142, 147
Ramos, Pedro, 35, 46
Rangers. *See* Texas Rangers
Raymount, Henry, 51–52
Reformista Party, 104, 106
Resoluciones del COD, 105–106
Revolución sin sangre, 12, 87–90, 100–102, 104–106, 108–109, 119
revolution, 29, 44, 50, 55–56, 59–60, 71, 89, 91, 102, 119; and baseball, 55; and communism, 29; democratic, 44, 55–56, 59–60, 89, 119
Rivas, Danilo, 95
Robinson, Jackie, 94
Rodgers, André, 31, 95
Rojas Alou, Felipe. *See* Alou, Felipe
Rojas Alou, Jesús. *See* Alou, Jesus
Rojas Alou, Mateo "Matty". *See* Alou, Mateo "Matty"
Roseboro, John, 84–85, 91
Rule 3450, 136–137
Rusk, Dean, 69

Sackie, Garabato, 25
Sánchez, Buenaventura, 40
San Cristóbal, 130
San Cristóbal-Baní, 111
San Cristóbal Caimanes del Sur (team), 130–131
San Cristóbal Mellizos del Sur (team), 111
San Francisco de Macorís, 110, 120, 124
San Francisco Giants (team), 8, 17, 30, 32, 36, 72, 84, 142
Sanguillén, Manny, 95
Sanó, Miguel, 137, 145
San Pedro de Macorís, 15, 39, 93, 142, 145; City of Shortstops, 142
Santana, Félix, 110, 120, 121
Santiago, 15, 24, 58, 76, 78, 93–94, 104, 120, 123–124, 126, 138
Santo Domingo (Ciudad Trujillo), 1, 15, 35, 39, 46, 60, 76, 79, 84, 91, 93, 110, 114, 118, 122–125, 127, 130, 136–137, 140
Schmidt, Michael, 145
scouts, baseball, 5, 11, 27, 111–116, 118, 120, 126–129, 135–138, 140–141, 143–145, 147–148, 150–151
secretary of sports, 13, 44, 106–107, 109, 118, 121–122, 134, 137; archives, 44; office of the (*see* Office of the Secretary of Sports)
Semana Deportiva (Sports Week), 47, 59
senate (Dominican), 40, 105, 130
Serie del Caribe, 1–2, 23, 116, 123, 151; of 1975, 116, 123, 151; of 2012, 1
social justice, 38, 45, 47–49, 61, 112
social reforms, 39
softball teams, 142
South League, 131, 133
Southeast League, 131
sovereignty, 4, 54, 70–71, 88, 96, 125–126; and Article 95, 54; and Balaguer, 88, 96, 125–126; Cuban defense of, 4; Dominican, 70–71, 125–126
Soviet Union, 4, 7

Spanish (language), 1, 71, 73, 81, 93, 149
Sports Illustrated, 70–71, 113
Sports Law (1974), 10, 17, 19, 90, 106; of 1943, 17, 19; of 1974, 10, 90, 106
sportswriters, 17, 20, 23, 25, 28–33, 42, 46, 60, 62, 66–68, 74, 77, 79–82, 87–88, 91, 93, 96, 98, 101, 106, 115–116, 120, 128, 130–133, 136, 138, 149
stadiums, 24, 33; Yankee Stadium, New York, 38; Candlestick Park, San Francisco (California), 38
Stargell, Willie, 78, 83, 95
Steffani, Bullo, 104
St. Louis Cardinals (team), 29, 46, 58, 93
Sturla, Esther, 46
"Superior Government," 23–24

Tautman, George, 31
Tavarez Justo, Manuel, 69, 74–76; assassination of, 74–75
Texas Rangers (team), 144
Tigres del Licey (team), 9, 15, 17, 20, 22, 30, 39, 48, 57–59, 62, 65, 74–78, 118, 122–124, 129, 131; tiger mascot, 77
Toronto Blue Jays (team), 115, 135
Tragedy of Rio Verde (1948 airplane crash), 19
Trainer Partnership Program (TPP), 141, 145–146
trainers, 5, 116–117, 120–121, 128–129, 133, 137–139, 141, 143–147, 151
transnationalism, 3
Triumvirate government (Dominican Republic), 9–10, 60, 63–69, 72–76, 79, 80–85, 88, 97, 150; and paternalism, 73
trujillismo, 8, 12, 15–16, 39, 44–45, 50; anti-*trujillismo*, 44; *trujillistas*, 12, 15, 39, 45, 50
Trujillo, Héctor, 16, 20–23
Trujillo, Petán, 31
Trujillo, Ramfis, 16, 19–20, 32
Trujillo Era Tournament (1951), 20
Trujillo Molina, Rafael Leonidas, 3–4, 8–10, 12, 15–34, 38, 41, 45, 53–56, 58, 61–62, 69, 72, 86, 102, 112, 117–118, 122, 131, 148–150; *ajusticiamiento* of, 12, 157n20; and baseball, 8, 12, 15–19, 22–25, 33–34, 41, 61, 112, 148; death of, 69; and democracy, 8, 31; foreign policy of, 25, 29, 31, 122; governance by, 10, 16, 27–28, 32–33, 56; and the nation, 4, 16–19, 21, 25, 27–28, 31–32, 33–34; and the OAS, 30, 62; opposition to, 8–9, 12, 16, 33, 45, 148; paternalism of, 16, 102; Trujillato, the, 8, 15–17, 20–21, 23, 25–29, 32–33, 55–56, 58, 102, 112, 117–118, 15
Turits, Richard, 16
tutumpotes, 45, 48–50

Unión Cívico Nacional (UCN), 45, 50, 53–54
United Press International, 51, 52
United States, 3–4, 6–11, 13, 18, 22, 25–31, 33, 38, 45, 52, 57, 60, 64, 67–75, 78–81, 83–85, 88–91, 93–95, 98–100, 107–109, 113–114, 116–118, 122, 124, 134, 136, 138–141, 143, 146–147, 150; and baseball, 4, 7, 11, 25–26, 28, 60, 69, 73, 93–95, 143; and the Dominican Republic, 9, 10, 25, 31, 38, 64, 67, 69, 75, 79–81, 89–90, 94–95, 100, 107, 109, 116; Dominicans in the, 33, 45, 57, 70–71, 78, 83, 88, 90–91, 95–96, 115–117, 120, 124, 136–139, 141, 147, 150; embassy to Dominican Republic, 9; foreign policy of, 4, 29, 31, 52, 69, 70, 74, 79, 84, 91, 98–99, 113; investors from, 145; and the Organization of American States (OAS), 29, 38, 102; press, 80, 91, 113, 141; and race, 30, 94
Universidad Autónoma de Santo Domingo (UASD), 53, 63
Universidad Católica Madre y Maestra (UCMM), 123

University of Santo Domingo, 27
Uribe Silva, Adriano "Nano," 105
US baseball, 1, 3–4, 5–9, 7, 15, 18, 20, 22–23, 25–30, 32, 38, 45, 55, 58, 60, 64, 69–71, 80, 94, 110–116, 119–122, 124–128, 130, 132–134, 137–141, 143–144, 146, 148, 150; commissioner's office, 130; major leagues, 1, 3, 5, 7, 25–27, 29, 64, 120–121, 127–128, 133–134, 137, 139, 141, 143–144, 146, 148; minor leagues, 15, 110, 116, 132–134, 138, 146; Negro Leagues, 18, 20, 143; organized baseball, 32, 94, 124; professional model of, 4, 13, 112–113; teams, 6, 10, 13, 46, 83, 111, 113–114, 116, 120, 135, 138, 140

Váldez, Tirso A., 82–83, 88
Valley Indians. *See* La Vega Indios del Valle
Vanguard Nation, 19
Veale, Bob, 95
Venezuela, 1, 15, 29, 46, 52, 64, 67, 69, 78–79
Venezuelan Winter League, 9, 45, 68, 85, 146
Veras, Horacio, 87, 96–98, 100–101, 103–104
Versalles, Zoilo, 121
Vicente, Julian, 30
Villa Mella, 136
Virgil, Osvaldo "Ozzie," 1, 17, 25–30, 32
Vizcaíno, Arodis, 2

Washington Senators (team), 30
Westad, Odd Arne, 7
Winter Agreements, 6, 23
World Baseball Classic (2013), 152
World Series, 6, 8, 12, 23, 36, 38, 60, 79, 90, 93; of 1962, 8, 38, 60; of 1964, 79; of 1967, 90
World War II, 7

Yankee Stadium, 38
Year of Sport (171; Dominican Republic), 103
Year of the Benefactor (1955; Dominican Republic), 22

Zeiler, Thomas, 70